Jung in the 21st Century
Volume Two

This second volume explores Jung's understanding of synchronicity and argues that it offers an important contribution to contemporary science. Whilst the scientific world has often ignored Jung's theories as being too much like mysticism, Haule argues that what the human psyche knows beyond sensory perception is extremely valuable.

Divided into two parts, areas of discussion include:

- shaminism and mastery
- border zones of exact science
- meditation, parapsychology and psychokinesis.

Jung in the 21st Century Volume Two: Synchronicity and Science will, like the first volume, be an invaluable resource for all those in the field of analytical psychology, including students of Jung, psychoanalysts and psychotherapists with an interest in the meeting of Jung and science.

John Ryan Haule is a Jungian Analyst in private practice in Boston and a training analyst at the C. G. Jung Institute, Boston.

Jung in the 21st Century
Volume Two

Synchronicity and science

John Ryan Haule

Routledge
Taylor & Francis Group

LONDON AND NEW YORK

First published 2011
by Routledge
27 Church Road, Hove, East Sussex BN3 2FA

Simultaneously published in the USA and Canada
by Routledge
270 Madison Avenue, New York, NY 10016

Routledge is an imprint of the Taylor & Francis Group, an Informa business

© 2011 John Ryan Haule

Typeset in Times by
RefineCatch Ltd, Bungay, Suffolk
Printed and bound in Great Britain by
TJ International Ltd, Padstow,
Cornwall
Paperback cover design by Andrew Ward

This publication has been produced with paper manufactured to strict
environmental standards and with pulp derived from sustainable forests.

British Library Cataloguing in Publication Data
A catalogue record for this book is available from the British Library

Library of Congress Cataloging in Publication Data
Haule, John Ryan, 1942–
Jung in the 21st century / John Ryan Haule.
    p. cm.
Includes bibliographical references. 1. Jungian psychology. 2. Jung, C. G.
(Carl Gustav), 1875–1961. 3. Archetype (Psychology) 4. Evolutionary
psychology. 5. Coincidence. I. Title. II. Title: Jung in the twentyfirst
century.
BF173.J85H38 2010
150.19'54–dc22
                                    2010014735

ISBN: 978–0–415–57801–1 (hbk)
ISBN: 978–0–415–57802–8 (pbk)

Contents

Abbreviations   vii

1   Jung's challenge to science   1

PART I
Shamanism and the mastery of altered states   **9**

2   Jung on the mastery of altered states   11

3   The nature of shamanism   15

4   Mastery of shamanic states of consciousness   23

5   Shamanic mastery: Ayahuasqueros in the Amazon   32

6   Meditation and mastery   51

PART II
The border zones of exact science   **63**

7   The lawful irrationality of synchronicity   67

8   The promise of parapsychology   86

9   Seeing at a distance and its mastery   101

10   Psychokinesis: Mind and matter   119

11   A crisis of metaphysics   139

12   Darwin's dilemma: Evolution needs a
psychoid principle   149

13 Sketches of a universal psychoid field   171

14 Vision and reality   193

    Notes   211
    References   216
    Index   224

Abbreviations

The following works of Carl Gustav Jung are abbreviated for simplicity of reference.

CW   *The Collected Works of C. G. Jung*. Translated by R. F. C. Hull. Princeton, NJ: Princeton University Press. Volumes are identified as *CW1*, *CW2*, etc., followed by the paragraph number in which the citation occurs. Volumes *CWA*, *CWB*, *CWC* are addenda to the *Collected Works*.

FJL   *The Freud-Jung Letters: The Correspondence Between Sigmund Freud and C. G. Jung*. Edited by William McGuire. Translated by Ralph Manheim and R. F. C. Hull. Princeton, NJ: Princeton University Press, 1974.

Letters   *Letters*. Edited by Gerhard Adler with Aniela Jaffé. Translated by R. F. C. Hull. In two volumes: 1973 and 1975. Princeton, NJ: Princeton University Press.

MDR   *Memories, Dreams, Reflections*. Recorded and edited by Aniela Jaffé. Translated by Richard and Clara Winston. New York: Pantheon, 1961.

PJL   *Atom and Archetype: The Pauli/Jung Letters, 1932–1958*. Edited by C. A. Meier, with C. P. Enz and M. Fierz. Translated by David Roscoe, 2001.

Sem25   *Analytical Psychology: Notes of the Seminar Given in 1925*. Edited by William McGuire. Princeton, NJ: Princeton University Press, 1989.

Sem28   *Dream Analysis: Notes of the Seminar Given in 1928–1930*. Edited by William McGuire. Princeton, NJ: Princeton University Press, 1984.

Sem32   *The Psychology of Kundalini Yoga*. Edited by Sonu Shamdasani. Princeton, NJ: Princeton University Press, 1996.

Speaking *C. G. Jung Speaking: Interviews and Encounters*. Edited by William McGuire and R. F. C. Hull. Princeton, NJ: Princeton University Press, 1977.

Chapter 1

Jung's challenge to science

In the first volume of *Jung in the 21st Century*, we demonstrated that the theoretical framework of C. G. Jung's psychology, although formulated nearly a hundred years ago, is well supported by advances the evolutionary sciences have made in the half-century since his death. Inherited behavior patterns (archetypes), the "mirror neuron" phenomenon as well as inborn releasing mechanisms by which we recognize archetypal patterns in others or recognize compelling opportunities to enact a specific archetypal behavior ourselves can now be described and tracked physiologically with new instruments of scientific investigation. The limbic action of the complexes and psyche as the holistic process of the human organism (self)—particularly the brain—have become well known by scientists entirely unfamiliar with Jung's contributions. Furthermore, dreams as transparent messages from unconscious to conscious and dreamscape as a subjectively lived report on brain processes that generally lie outside the purview of ego have also been supported by the chemistry of neuromodulators and images produced by magnetic resonance. Neurobiologists and anthropologists have concluded that dreams help us to integrate recent waking experience with our phylogenetic heritage (the archetypes).

As long as we confine our attention to neurobiology and ethology, Analytical Psychology fits very comfortably into the world of evolutionary biology. When, however, we pursue Jung's ideas about the history of consciousness, we find them to be critical of the exclusively empirical and rational perspective of science. Historically, Jung is correct to note that our linear, rational empiricism is a late development in the history of our species. He has no argument with the achievements of science or the empiricism that has made our technical advances possible. What puts him in tension with the scientific establishment and with Western assumptions, generally, is his instance that the "irrational" experiences we typically "resent" are no less important than the rational ones we value.

It is an empirical fact that unitary brain states provide "transcendental" perspectives sometimes characterized by a *coincidentia oppositorum* that appears to be the very experience many medieval theologians described as "God." If such experiences are held in contempt today as merely superstitious or frankly pathological, Jung argues that we in the modern West have lost something of value that our ancestors a half-millennium ago took for granted. Furthermore, the capacity to cultivate and employ such altered states of consciousness (ASCs) is a universal feature of the human brain and nervous system. The fact that this capacity has not been eliminated by natural selection implies that it must not be a liability, indeed that it has very likely been essential for the survival of our species. We know rituals to generate altered states of consciousness are used by all primate species to build the emotional coherence of their troops, define their social structure and prepare to deal with future threats. Humans have used them to reduce tension between separate groups, solidify cooperation and trading networks, and explore the greater mythic cosmos that gives transcendent meaning to this one. Altered states have also served as the mental workshop that inspired our species' first ventures into agriculture, pastoralism, pottery-making and the like. The pursuit of ASCs opened the minds of our ancestors, some forty millennia ago, and set us on the great human adventure that has made modern science possible, and much more besides.

Jung had a compelling interest in altered states of consciousness, beginning in a childhood overshadowed by his mother's split personality (one side a conventional peasant, the other a daemonic prophetess) and by his pastor father's struggles with a crisis of faith that was probably responsible for his early death. Young Carl's spiritual quest began at least with his childhood vision of God defecating on the Basel Cathedral, when he first discovered that God could speak to him personally through the imagery of his own psyche and that organized religion was either ignorant of this possibility or deliberately concealing it. Jung honed such intuitions while writing *Symbols of Transformation* nearly two decades after the cathedral vision, when he discovered that all of us are living a myth, whether we know it or not. Another dozen years later, he faced a crisis in Taos, New Mexico, when he found the Pueblo people living their myth as the proud sons and daughters of the sun. They believed their worship helped the sun to rise every morning for the sake of the whole earth. They knew themselves to be partners of God, and their confident, well-grounded demeanor spoke eloquently of the effects this mythic knowledge had upon their daily lives. It was no wonder they saw white Americans as hollow-eyed, restless searchers.

An echo of the numinous relationship Mountain Lake's people had with the rising sun occurred for Jung just a year later on Mount Elgon in Kenya—where he, the Elgonyi and a troop of baboons were all caught up simultaneously in a worshipful state of mind at the dawn of every day. The fact that the ancient Egyptians carved lines of worshipping baboons into the frieze of the Temple of Abu Simbel more than three millennia ago testifies to the timelessness of our primate religiosity in the face of the rising sun. Moreover, it emphasizes the nature of the collective unconscious and hints at why we ignore it to our own peril.

Modern archaeology and its new techniques for dating its discoveries have allowed us to extend Jung's view of the history of human consciousness many millennia into the past. What we have found reveals that Jung's guesses have again been quite accurate. We have documented the importance of altered states of consciousness for human ritual behavior and found that shamanism is nearly a "hard wired" capability of the human nervous system and therefore the "natural religion of the human mind." The evidence shows that shamanism flourishes in a maximally polyphasic society, while forces of greed, conformity and ambition distrust the unpredictability of what a shaman might find. Consequently, various powerful elites have, over the millennia, gradually chipped away at the free exploration of altered states of consciousness, to the point that our modern Western culture has become almost thoroughly monophasic, in that it trusts only left-brain linear thinking.

We in the West generally believe in a powerful ego capable of virtually any worthwhile feat, while the reach and attainments of our ever advancing technology seem to be proof that we are right. These fundamental assumptions, however, leave no room for individuation, the natural tension that always exists between the wholeness of a human organism and the necessarily narrow focus of its conscious attention. The tension exists whether we know it or not. Furthermore, it generates dreams, flights of ideas and symptoms whether or not we "believe in" the unconscious. In many cases, ignoring such disturbing psychological data can lead to breakdowns and misery. We do not merely resent our irrational feelings and thoughts, we fear them.

Evidence for the inadequacy of our mainstream attitude is not hard to find. Global warming may be the most striking indication that single-minded reliance on exploiting the earth's resources for technological advancement has become measurably dangerous as the sea warms and rises to flood low-lying islands and coastlines and huge numbers of species go extinct. Meanwhile, dissatisfaction grows among the human populations of the earth. Frightened by the speed of progress, loss of livelihood and changing mores, many find themselves attracted by the illusory comforts of militant fundamentalisms, while other strata of the population explore altered states of consciousness as New Agers or through a variety of possession-trance religions like Umbanda and Santería. Feeling trapped by the linearity of mainstream thinking and a subjective lack of depth, our restless species is casting about for at least a minimally polyphasic approach to life.

But these are minority movements that have failed to find—or perhaps even to look for—commonality, a coherent rationale by which they might discover unity of purpose. It seems they are in need of a perspective like Jung's that would legitimize their aspirations while critically examining their methods. Here, however, is precisely where Jung's reputation has suffered the most. Because he urges us to embrace the irrational and discover the multiphasic nature of human consciousness, he opposes a crucial stand that has characterized Western culture for some 500 years. This is why he has been dismissed for being a "mystic," in the trivial sense of being an irresponsible and muddle-headed thinker. But if a "mystic" may more properly be one who is experienced in and has learned to use altered states of consciousness as essential tools for psychological and spiritual growth, Jung really *was* a mystic.

Volume 1, *Evolution and Archetype*, demonstrates that Jung was anything but an irresponsible and muddle-headed thinker. He was deeply cognizant of scientific issues and chose his concepts with wisdom and perhaps good luck. Now, however, in Volume 2, *Synchronicity and Science*, we take up the other side of Jung, the psychologist who thought that science has been too timid to investigate matters that are unmistakably real, that confront us daily but that have traditionally been treated with embarrassment and largely avoided.

The first of these is the realm of altered states of consciousness and the irrationality we typically resent. In his call for a polyphasic approach to human consciousness, it may seem to some—observers who are more familiar with Jung's reputation than with any exposure to his writing—that he is asking for us to relinquish everything we have accomplished in the West with our left-brain rationality. If so, there would be reason enough to call him a mystic in the unflattering and trivial sense of the term. But if, on the other hand, altered states of consciousness can be mastered and become tools of psychological investigation analogous to the left-brain empirical and conceptual tools we have spent the past 500 years honing, it will become clear that the accusation of muddle-headedness is unjust and made on the basis of unexamined assumptions.

We take up this project in Part I of *Synchronicity and Science*, where we will survey a broad array of altered states of consciousness, showing that there are already well known and even technological professions that use them to very good effect, that all of us are already using them far more than we are aware, and finally that techniques for mastering shamanic states of consciousness have already been documented to some extent. Here is perhaps the best evidence that altered states of consciousness do not represent merely a "going unconscious" or "believing six impossible things before breakfast." Indeed, it is possible to develop and master altered states and use them to complement the linear thinking with which we are already familiar. This would seem to be the next logical step in the history of consciousness—a future in which we shall deliberately accept and take advantage of the whole array of psychological tools we inherit with our DNA. Meditation practices are another source of non-linear states of consciousness that have proven to be reliable and transformative but need far more study.

In Part II of this second volume, we take up Jung's more serious challenge to science—the idea that science has been shirking its responsibility to take seriously the phenomena it treats as inexplicable or non-existent. There are four: life, consciousness, intentionality and parapsychology.

Even before his university years, Jung had familiarized himself with the literature of spiritualism and the table-tipping parlor fad that had taken the West by storm at the turn of the twentieth century. He initiated experiments at his mother's kitchen table, where his younger cousin Helly showed great promise as a medium for entities believed to be souls of the dead eager to communicate with the living. In his first year at the University of Basel, he urged his fraternity brothers to use their training in science to tackle the phenomena of spiritualism and come up with an explanation for such uncanny occurrences. Throughout his career as a psychiatrist, he kept in touch with the field of parapsychology and observed many telepathic, clairvoyant and psychokinetic events that took place in his consulting

room and in the vicinity of his residences. In the final decade of his life he proposed the theory of synchronicity as a way of describing such phenomena.

The idea of synchronicity is widely misunderstood and taken to be an indication of Jung's superstitious and gullible nature. We will see, however, that it was
a serious proposal of a metaphysical nature, and well within the style of thinking
that science has historically employed to solve problems like gravity and magnetism, which first appeared to be impossible instances of "action-at-a-distance." In
parapsychology, when we know things at a distance telepathically or clairvoyantly, our sensory organs have been bypassed and no chain of material causes will
ever be found to explain how we know what we know. Indeed, parapsychology
experiments have repeatedly demonstrated that distance has no effect on the
outcome. This is why most scientists are comfortable dismissing such events as
impossible or merely coincidental. They seem to be absurd, and not worthy of
further consideration.

It is not that science *proves* them impossible, rather it is merely unable to
explain them. Jung identifies our folk metaphysics as responsible for the confusion. Common Western assumptions about the nature of reality (folk metaphysics) shared by both the uneducated and the scientist declare that only material
things are real and that if any one of them changes in shape or position it must
have interacted with some other material thing. Following the model of billiard
balls or gas molecules colliding with one another, we look for the cause of material change in the vicinity of the object undergoing change. Fundamental to this
expectation is the folk metaphysical assumption that every material body, insofar
as it is matter, is inert and insensitive. It requires something else to make it change.
This makes life itself a mystery, if not an impossibility; for what allows a collection of molecules to spring into life as soon as they are gathered into a biological
cell? A tenet of our folk metaphysics *not accepted by science* attempts to answer
this conundrum, too: we say life, consciousness and intentionality are evidence
that a separate "spiritual substance" like Descartes' soul is at work. This creates
our mind-body problem: for we have no way of explaining how a spiritual substance can bring about changes in matter—or even what a spiritual substance
might be. This is why life, consciousness, intentionality and parapsychology
remain inexplicable.

Jung's proposal of synchronicity as a non-causal principle asks us to stop
looking for chains of material causes and not to assume that if two things are
meaningfully connected they must be found interacting in the same locality. Just
as Faraday concluded that magnetism and electric current change the properties of
space, and Einstein concluded that gravity is a property of spacetime, so Jung has
implicitly proposed that spacetime is characterized by relatedness. He calls this
property the "psychoid" nature of reality, meaning that everything in the universe
has a psyche-like dimension in that it is not inert, as our folk metaphysics believes,
but is always receptive.

The inspiration for this idea comes from quantum mechanics, which Jung
came partly to understand through his conversations and exchange of letters with

Wolfgang Pauli, one of the founders of quantum mechanics, and from the meta-physics behind the Chinese "Classic of Changes," the *I Ching*, which claims everything that happens in a particular moment is characterized by the moment in which it occurs. In short, the universe is relational, everything is always in relationship with everything else.

Faraday, Einstein and Jung have all relinquished folk metaphysics in the same way. In every case, a field theory gives up trying to explain a whole as the sum of its parts and instead describes the whole (a field) as imposing conditions on its parts. Thus gravity, a consequence of spacetime's tendency to bend in response to the mass of a heavenly body, organizes the heavens into regularly orbiting planets, stars and galaxies. Similarly, a psychoid field imposes cooperation upon the enti-ties that comprise it, making them function holistically. The appropriate analogy would be a biological cell—for cells organize all their component molecules holistically, just as a mammalian body organizes its liver, lungs, heart and so forth, for the good of the whole organism. The universe, therefore, resembles an organism, somewhat as the earth is pictured according to the "Gaia" hypothesis. Matter is not inert, as the West has believed for some 400 years, but psychoid in the minimal sense of being receptive to influence. "Psyche" is simply the name we give holistic process. It is relatively simple in the protozoa and far more complex in primates. In the universe at large, it facilitates synchronicity.

Like most of Jung's theoretical constructs, considered in *Evolution and Archetype*, synchronicity represents an intuitive leap that science appears to be catching up with. Quantum mechanics had not yet revealed the universe to be rela-tional in 1952, when Jung published his article on synchronicity. Perhaps, however, the author of the Pauli Exclusion Principle had some sort of intuition along these lines, for he was very aware both of the "uncertainty" of the behavior of subatomic particles and yet how "symmetrical" that chaotic quantum sea had proven to be.

Twelve years after the publication of "Synchronicity: An Acausal Connecting Principle" (*CW8*: ¶816–968), in 1964 physicist John Stewart Bell argued that the logic of mathematics requires that subatomic particles be governed by a relational principle.[1] He called it "non-locality." It concerns what are called "entangled pairs" of particles like electrons and photons. "Entanglement" simply means that both members of the pair have been involved in a previous interaction together. Bell's Non-Locality Theorem predicts that, once entangled, two particles will undergo precisely the same changes simultaneously—even if they are too far apart for a chain of causes to connect them. Alternately expressed, the identical changes occur too quickly to allow any "message" to travel from one partner to the other, even at the speed of light. The principle of non-locality, if applied to parapsychological events, would describe how Emmanuel Swedenborg famously became aware, clairvoyantly, of a devastating fire in Stockholm when he was 300 miles away. His psyche was operating non-locally with a place where he was emotionally "entangled."

In 1982, more than two decades after Jung's death, Alain Aspect directed an experiment at the University of Paris-South that proved Bell's Non-Locality

Theorem. Menas Kafatos, physicist at George Mason University in Fairfax, Virginia, who specializes in astrophysics, general relativity and quantum theory, draws a conclusion about non-locality that seems to back up Jung's intuition of three decades earlier:

> Non-locality is a shocking discovery because it appears to subvert the bias that the world is composed most fundamentally of individual objects and their non-relational properties. . . . It appeared as if these results had provided final confirmation that the classical view of the relations between physical theory and physical reality [our folk metaphysics], which quantum physics had been challenging for some time, was no longer supportable.
>
> (Kafatos and Nadeau 1990: 1f)

Kafatos and his co-author, historian of science Robert Nadeau, go on to speculate that if "entanglement" is the heart of the non-locality issue, everything that comprises the universe must be entangled and in relation with every other, because at one point, the moment of the Big Bang, every particle was in the same infinitely small location and participating in the same explosive interaction.

Synchronicity, therefore, appears to challenge the same metaphysical assumptions that quantum mechanics challenges. We relinquish our faulty assumptions reluctantly, even though they blind us to current realities. We must presume, therefore, that physics is slowly moving toward accepting the view that the universe is relational, like a proto-organism. Philosopher and mathematician Alfred North Whitehead made a similar argument in extraordinary detail in 1929, with *Process and Reality: An Essay in Cosmology*. Furthermore, as we shall see in Chapter 11 of this volume, evolutionary biology is also searching for a relational principle to complete Darwin's account of evolutionary process. Thus it may well be that synchronicity, Jung's most outrageous proposal, will eventually be supported just as "archetype" and "complex" are today.

Part I

Shamanism and the mastery of altered states

Our survey of the history of consciousness, while much broader than Jung's, essentially backs up his view that the development of a reflective ego capable of linear, directed thinking and an internalized sense of morality has alienated us from our archetypal, instinctual roots. We have found that the process of birthing our individual selves from a deep but meaningful *participation mystique* in the mythic world explored through altered states of consciousness was gradual and took place over the course of some 40,000 years. As primates and Archaic Humans, altered states generated in rituals bound us into functional societies and defined our intra-societal relations. In the case of our species, the mythic world first taught our ancestors how to manipulate the empirical world, and successes there taught later generations how to manipulate the mythic narrative itself for aggrandizing purposes. It has been the collaboration between economic/political power and mythic narrative that has enforced our species' movement from a maximally polyphasic to a monophasic world. The greatest success in this collaboration is represented by the cathedrals of the Gothic period, which stand along with the Ice Age caves as bookends in the process. When the Gothic contract fell apart with the Renaissance, the core of our social agreement swung to the individual, the conscious, the linear and the empirical. We have become the hollow-eyed searchers Mountain Lake perceived us to be.

Jung urges us to recover our polyphasic roots, re-explore altered states of consciousness and learn to integrate directed thinking with archetypal wisdom. To our monophasic mentality this seems to be lunacy, for our world believes that only directed, empirically based thought is trustworthy and that anything less "rational" (dreams, myth and other altered states) is childish, delusional, naive, even pathological. His stance on this issue is a major reason Jung has been dismissed as a "mystic."

Part I of *Synchronicity and Science*, therefore, takes up the question of whether altered states of consciousness can be mastered and turned into dependable sources of information. To do so, we look primarily to shamanism, the "hard-wired" capability we all have to tune our autonomic nervous system (ANS), alter our consciousness and explore what appears before our inner eyes as a greater cosmos. Shamans have had to learn how to operate dependably in such an alternate universe; and because the techniques they have developed are quite sensible and available to us all, the possibility of integrating realizations brought back from the greater cosmos is a real possibility.

In Chapter 2, we survey Jung's views on altered states. Chapter 3 provides an overview of shamanism as it has been seen in academic studies and as it is now understood through neurobiology. The techniques of mastery will become understandable in such terms. Then in Chapter 4, we consider a form of shamanism that has been explored in great detail by Western scientists, the use of ayahuasca in the Amazon, to see how such techniques of mastery are employed by living shamans. Finally, in Chapter 5 we survey meditation techniques for altering consciousness and how meditative states can be mastered.

Chapter 2

Jung on the mastery of altered states

The history of consciousness from the Upper Paleolithic to the modern world can be briefly described as a one-way trend from maximally polyphasic societies that valued altered states of consciousness for the vital information they provided about self, world and transformation to monophasic societies in which materialism and linear thinking are the sole source of legitimate meaning and where transformation seems to be an impossible dream. Twenty thousand years ago, shamanistic practices were universally available and widely employed, but as society became more complex and hierarchical they were gradually replaced with less effective rituals. Personal encounters with transcendent experience became rare, and religion began to consist of symbolic dramas that portrayed a world of *belief* for people who no longer knew or even imagined that direct numinous *experience* was possible (Walsh 1990: 47). Even in the theocentric European Middle Ages, mysticism aroused suspicions of heresy. Today, altered states of consciousness are so misunderstood and underappreciated that to most people they suggest pathology, gullibility or deliberate deception.

Along with William James, C. G. Jung was one of the earliest psychologists and remains today one of the very few to have vigorously opposed this sad trend toward a flat and lifeless mechanical world so devoid of transcendence and wonder that even religion seems powerless to transform it. Indeed, Jung found it "probable that any one who has immediate experience of God is a little bit outside the organization one calls the Church" (*CW11*: ¶481).

> The Churches stand for traditional and collective convictions which in the case of many of their adherents are no longer based on their own inner experience but on *unreflecting belief*, which is notoriously apt to disappear as soon as one begins thinking about it. Belief is no substitute for inner experience.
> (*CW10*: ¶521)

In an atmosphere where even the Churches cannot be counted on to support inner experience, the most ordinary sort of altered state, the dream, has little value. "Even Freud, while recognizing the utility [of dreams] in therapy, saw the material as reflections of the culturally aberrant. Only Jung saw them as a vehicle of transcendence" (Laughlin *et al.* 1990: 268). A major aim of Jung's Complex Psychology has been to reintroduce polyphasic consciousness, where "certain doors and windows [are left] open to [the reality] of other worlds" (Ibid.: 269). This is not a call to "go unconscious," but rather a challenge to the West to become as clear about our psychic capabilities as we are about the objective world—to effect an unprecedented integration.

In the past three or four centuries, the West has learned how to investigate the empirical world. We have taught ourselves how to think precisely and how to measure differences that are too fine to distinguish with our unaided senses. Having learned in principle how our senses work, we have invented machines to extend them. For example, with telescopes we can "see" nearly as far away in space and time as the postulated Big Bang, and to "see" with segments of the electromagnetic spectrum that our sense organs cannot register, such as radio waves and microwaves. In the other direction, we have mapped and measured the movement of subatomic particles. Western science has been unrelenting in mastering our extraverted senses of sight, hearing, touch, taste and smell. In the 1600s it was still possible to wonder what good could come of experimenting with telescopes and microscopes. But not today, for three and a half centuries of "steady work" have gone a long way toward mastering our powers of extraverted investigation.

In contrast, we have hardly begun to imagine that other powers might also be susceptible of mastery, namely our *introverted* capacities for altered states of consciousness. We have yet to determine what they are good for, how we might use them, how we might extend them, in what ways they are reliable and when they ought to be distrusted. The modern West has not subjected shamanism, meditation and other uses of altered states to the "steady work" that might finally "throw off our unconsciousness" in this domain. A great deal remains to be done, and probably will not be done as long as our society stays rigidly monophasic; but there is evidence from anthropology, neuropsychology, and various schools of meditation to suggest that when we do take up this work we will open a rich field for investigation.

Jung on the mastery of altered states

Mastery is not a word that Jung was inclined to use. In fact, he emphasized *letting go* of our Western tendency to identify with our ego and to try to control everything in our lives, for relinquishing ego-centered control helps us to discover aspects of our unconscious wholeness. It is the first step in becoming aware of non-ordinary states of consciousness and the fact that thoughts are simply "given" to the ego, that they come from somewhere unconscious. It leads, in short, to "original thinking." Jung avoided mentioning mastery, evidently, lest he seem to imply that more monophasic ego-control was desired rather than less.

My Toronto colleague in the study of mysticism, however, Dan Merkur, has convinced me with his book, *Becoming Half Hidden: Shamanism and Initiation*

Among the Inuit (1992), that a shaman's accomplishments cannot be understood without addressing the issue of mastery. Merkur makes it clear that shamans distinguish themselves from the ecstatically gifted laity by the degree of control they exercise over their altered states. "Shamans neither passively enjoy nor passively suffer their trances. Rather they actively employ them, more or less consciously, to serve their own religious goals" (Merkur 1992: 157). While an apprentice, the shaman-to-be is guided in her altered states by the suggestions of a master shaman. The goal of the training is to help her gain a degree of voluntary control over what happens when she journeys through the greater cosmos.

This kind of mastery is quite different from what our monophasic society is apt to appreciate. To the extent that a shaman is taken on cosmic journeys in which he seems to leave his body behind, his observing ego is a passive recipient of the ecstatic experience. But because he learns to go where he wishes in that larger cosmos and because he deliberately seeks out and obtains important information, he retains a significant measure of initiative. Shamanism, therefore, requires a peculiar balance between deliberate choice and submission to an agency that is quite foreign to our ego. This ambiguous region is precisely the area that Jung's work addresses, and it is why I believe I am being faithful to Jung's intentions when I call it "mastery of altered states."

We have already encountered several of the techniques Jung recommends for gaining mastery. First and most obviously, he urges us to attend to the state of our consciousness and to take note of the subtle changes that indicate our unconscious is expressing itself. Dreams, especially, are to be recollected and recorded, for they represent visions of ourselves and of the world that are likely to clash with and befuddle our ordinary assumptions. These first two techniques amount to catching our everyday consciousness in the act of changing. Normally, we Westerners preserve the monophasic illusion when we ignore these changes or dismiss them as absurd. Jung urges us to bring them into focus and learn from them, and that cannot be accomplished unless we discipline ourselves to relax our ego-centered vigilance while sharpening our attention.

In active imagination, Jung's most characteristic exercise for exploring non-ordinary consciousness, we can distinguish at least three techniques: first, to still the chattering mind that would belittle the images and thoughts that manifest in our altered states, second, to attend to the "original thinking" that manifests as a curious gift from elsewhere, and third, to get involved emotionally and morally in the visionary events that unfold within us.

In dealing with potentially neurotic issues, Jung would have us recognize our complex reactions for what they are, stereotyped altered states that play themselves out under the cover of a powerful and habitual emotional bias that is inadequate to the situation at hand. He would have us observe the operation of the complex as the ego-alien automatism that it is, thereby providing some opportunity for the more rational cerebral cortex to get involved.

By attending to dreams and subtle changes in our waking consciousness, by practicing active imagination, and by managing our complexes, we also train ourselves to utilize the "transcendent function" that makes psychological transformation possible. When we find ourselves faced with irreconcilable opposites, powerful conflicting tendencies that must be taken seriously, it is important to know that these are autonomous inner forces that deserve respect but cannot be acted upon directly. In this situation, Jung urges us to "hold the tension" between the opposites and observe them as they grow stronger. The task is to allow ourselves to feel pulled this way and that, while resisting the temptation to end the conflict with an arbitrary decision that would accomplish little more than to relieve the tension in the short run. In this way, we can induce the transformative/unitive state of consciousness that is characterized objectively by rhythmic harmony in the brain and subjectively by the emergence of a reconciling symbol in consciousness (*CW8*: ¶131–93).[1]

A sixth and final technique of mastery that Jung employed might be called "active imagination in tandem" (cf. Haule 1999c). This is a practice that is not described in the *Collected Works* but rather in Jung's addresses to the students of the C. G. Jung Institute in Zurich during the 1950s (*Speaking*: 359–64). He implies that the analyst and analysand inhabit a mutual emotional field during their analytic sessions. He says that if the analyst does not hide behind a professional persona but remains "natural, spontaneous, open, and vulnerable," images, ideas and feelings will emerge out of the shared emotional field just as they do out of one's own personal emotional state when one is practicing active imagination in private. Within the mutual field of analysis, the "original thinking" that emerges is relevant to both parties. Jung says it is as if a two-million-year-old man were to enter the room with the wisdom of the human race at his disposal. If they are open to it, the two parties will come to know themselves against the wisdom of the Great Man. It is very much as though a shaman's spirit familiar were to appear. The danger for the analyst is that she may be tempted to think that it is her own wisdom that she articulates. Jung insists, therefore, that the essential discipline is to remember that the Great Man is an other, a visitor from the unconscious who is very much *not* the ego.

Chapter 3

The nature of shamanism

The word *shaman* derives from *šaman*, meaning "ecstatic one" in the Siberian Tungus language.[1] Today, shamanism refers to a loose collection of techniques for altering consciousness that is found in remarkably similar forms the world over. Indeed, it is so widespread that the only reasonable conclusion is that shamanic practices did not so much diffuse from a one-time invention as to be repeatedly discovered as a capability of the human neuro-psychic organism. Indeed, evidence that we have already considered shows that shamanic practices are at least 40,000 years old, and possibly much older (M and S Aldhouse-Green 2005: 62). Shamanic techniques for altering consciousness amount to a powerful expansion of the human psychological repertoire: "Shamans understand things in a way that other people just do not, they understand them better and more profoundly" (Narby and Huxley 2001: 263).[2]

> There is no agreed cross-cultural definition of "shamanism." Indeed, it is characterized by a chameleon-like elusiveness. . . . There is, nevertheless, a certain combination of key characteristics[:] . . . a layered cosmology, with the flight of the shaman's soul to other levels of this cosmos, and the power to use this journey to fight, command and control spirits which inhabit these realms and affect human destinies. Thus shamanism is both an epistemology, that is a system of contemplative thought with an implicit set of propositions, and a blueprint for action, as in the location of game animals or the retrieval of kidnapped souls.
>
> (Narby and Huxley 2001: 263)

Shamanism, understood and misunderstood

Eliade

The classic study of shamanism, and still the only worldwide survey, is Mircea Eliade's *Shamanism: Archaic Techniques of Ecstasy* (1964), first published in Paris in 1951.[3] The general structure of shamanism is that, although the shaman sometimes inherits his office, the best and most representative shamans are "called by the spirits." That is they spontaneously fall ill and undergo an initiatory ecstasy in which they experience their body being dismembered and reassembled. They thereby acquire a more powerful identity and eventually the ability to gain some mastery over their ecstasies. Typically, they experience their "soul" traveling between the three worlds, or cosmic planes we have often discussed, to retrieve the lost or abducted souls of those who have fallen sick or to conduct the souls of the dead to their final destination. Shamans are usually assisted by spirit familiars they may have had to conquer (an aspect of gaining mastery); and they may frequently be entangled with other shamans in battles that take place in the greater cosmos of ecstasy. Such battles may have serious consequences on the material plane.

Eliade's book has been criticized on two counts: first, that it emphasizes the shaman's upward journeys to the heavenly world over downward journeys to the lower world, presumably due to the author's Christian bias (e.g. Rozwadowski 2001: 63),[4] and second, that it claims the use of psychedelic substances by shamans represents a degenerate and profane form of shamanism. On this second point, Eliade retracted the claim after R. Gordon Wasson and Virginia P. Wasson's work proved the ubiquity of consciousness-altering mushrooms and herbs in the history of the human race.[5] Regarding the complaint about overemphasizing upward shamanic journeys, it has always seemed to me to apply more aptly to Eliade's book, *Yoga, Immortality and Freedom* (1954; English trans. 1969), where his aim is to show that yoga doctrines and practices have their roots in shamanism. He seems to have succeeded in this latter aim (e.g. Ripinsky-Naxon 1993: 20), even if it also appears to be the case that shamanic journeys to the lower world are far more common and significant than upward journeys.

Jung

Jung makes only one reference to shamanism before the publication of Eliade's book. In 1918, when he located the origins of depth psychology in the spiritualism craze at the end of the nineteenth century and French theories of dissociation that can be traced as far back as Mesmer's "animal magnetism," he describes the whole intellectual movement as a "rebirth of the shamanistic form of religion" (*CW10*: ¶22). From 1952 onward, in the last nine years of his life, Jung makes upwards of a dozen references to shamanism, each time citing Eliade's book. He says that the ideas and rituals of shamanism "far from ever having been invented, simply happened and were acted long before they were thought" (*CW11*: ¶410). He calls shamanism "the original model of the individuation process" (*CW11*: ¶460; *CW13*: ¶462). He also describes shamanism as the foundation of "medical psychology" (*CW18*: ¶578) as well as a numinous, archaic form of prophecy, priesthood, philosophy, and religion (*CW11*: ¶448).

Jung was particularly impressed with the theme of dismemberment and re-creation (*CW11*: ¶246, n. 9; *CW13*: ¶91, n. 4), for it implied a mythology of trans-formation parallel to that of individuation. And he often mentioned the theme of the shaman's spiritual marriage to a spirit-guide of the opposite sex (*CW9i*: ¶115, n. 8; *CW14*: ¶2, n. 5), for it shows the importance of the anima figure and eros in the process of encountering the wholeness of the self. He found the shadow, too, in the shaman's trickster qualities, the malice and vengeance of spirit battles, and the grueling and painful initiations that he thought might well leave psychic scars. He believed that this shadow material added the missing element to the "phenomenology of spiritualism," which at the beginning of the twentieth century displayed a good deal of "sickish sentimentality" (*CW9i*: ¶457).

Misunderstandings

Despite the views of anthropologists and others who have carefully investigated shamanistic phenomena, the majority in our monophasic society continues to exhibit hostility and fear. Psychiatry tends to classify mystical states as pathological. Behaviorist and materialist approaches favored by a good many scientific investigators tend to dismiss the employment of altered states of consciousness as irrational, undisciplined, and superstitious. Ecstatic cults that emphasize personal experience of the spirit realm are generally seen to be threatening to doctrinally organized religions and even to society at large—much as Christianity has almost always suppressed the indwelling Holy Spirit, a part of the divine Trinity that is rarely discussed because it is too dangerous. The government's "war on drugs," another manifestation of the collective hysteria that altered states arouse, appears to be unstoppable despite its ineffectiveness and its deleterious effects (Winkelman 2000: 3).

Having been forgotten for tens of millennia, shamanism was rediscovered in Europe in 1672 by a dissident Russian Orthodox priest, Avvakum Petrovich, who had been banished for heresy to Siberia. There he encountered a shaman predicting victory in a war against the Mongols; but Petrovich said, "My soul saw that [the army] would be massacred," and opposed the war. The army marched off anyway, and only two soldiers returned. Narby and Huxley (2001: 23–6) point out that the priest ironically and unconsciously used a shamanic state of consciousness to oppose the shaman he found so abhorrent. The incident inspired 150 years of stories and rumors in Europe about animism, spirits, other worlds, and altered states of consciousness (Price 2001b: 3–6).

In the same period, reports from missionaries in the Americas interpreted the use of tobacco and other means of altering consciousness to obtain information and effect cures as somewhere between "jugglery," i.e. charlatanism, and "dealing with the devil" (Narby and Huxley 2001: 23–6). A century later, shamanism had become a topic to conjure with; for the Enlightenment had greatly reduced people's fears of satanic involvement, leaving them free to worry about what was real in the stories and what deceitful (Narby and Huxley 2001: 21–5). Artists like Goethe (whose *Faust* portrayed the dilemma of "Modern Man" in Jung's view) and Mozart (*Magic Flute, Don Giovanni, Idomeneo*, etc.) found shamanic themes to be powerful sources of inspiration (Flaherty 1992).

Growing understanding

The earliest anthropological reports on shamanism were published in the late nineteenth century, where the central theme was that shamans claimed to communicate with "spirits" for the sake of their communities. Such an approach gave shamanistic phenomena an underlying coherence for the first time, and led to sympathetic portraits of shamans as people very much like ourselves. If they were given to trickery in much larger measure than we, at least their intentions were honorable, for they meant to be helpful to their communities (Narby and Huxley 2001: 39–73).

The twentieth century opened with accounts of shamanism as a pathological condition based on "arctic hysteria," which the successful shaman nevertheless learned to master. Data collection became much more careful; consciousness-changing techniques, such as drumming, were identified; and the dangerous, vengeful dimension of shamanism was recognized. Peter Elkin emphasized the shaman's discipline and training. Lévi-Strauss saw shamans as primitive psychoanalysts (Narby and Huxley 2001: 79–107). In his book, *The Savage Mind* (1962, English trans. 1966), Lévi-Strauss attempted to overcome European cultural bias by showing "that magic and science require the same mental operations and complement one another. He made it thoroughly acceptable to take shamanism seriously" (Narby and Huxley 2001: 244). Thus by the end of the twentieth century the fact of altered states of consciousness had ceased to boggle professional Western minds and we could begin to appreciate that it is the mastery of such states that is the essential thing.

About this time, anthropology began to experiment with "participant observers." Bronislaw Malinowski had developed the method in 1910, but a half-century of the Standard Social Science Model forbade subjectivity and contamination of scientific reports with naive native perspectives. Gordon Wasson, the American banker and mushroom enthusiast, broke the ice with his highly respected studies that began in the late 1950s. Carlos Castaneda popularized the practice—whether his books be seen as anthropology or as fiction. Barbara Myerhoff and Peter Furst were the first anthropologists to take peyote under Huichol supervision. Michael Harner and Gerardo Reichel-Dolmatoff took *jagé* with the Native Americans of the Upper Amazon. Holger Kalweit studied with Tibetan shamans in refugee camps in India (Narby and Huxley 2001: 135–83). American anthropologist Edith Turner published this report of participant observation in 1992:

> I saw with my own eyes a large gray blob of plasma emerge from the sick woman's back. Then I knew the Africans were right, there is spirit affliction, and it isn't a matter of metaphor and symbol, or even psychology. And I began to see how anthropologists have perpetuated an endless series of put-downs in regard to the many spirit events in which they have participated—participated in a kindly pretense. They might have been obtaining valuable

information, but they have been operating with the wrong paradigm, that of the positivists' denial.

. . . Thus for me, "going native" achieved a break-through to an altogether different worldview, foreign to academia. . . . We anthropologists need training to see what the natives see.

(E. Turner 1998: 83f)

How shamanism works

The essential piece in shamanism is that shamans tune their autonomic nervous systems so as to experience what lies below ordinary consciousness, namely "neurognostic structures," the neural structures that make "knowing" (gnosis) possible (Winkelman 2000: 78). Myth, and the archetypes that comprise it, simultaneously affect physiology and meaning. They are said to "conflate" biology and meaning and to "collapse the false dichotomy" that Western thinking makes "between objective and subjective knowledge" (Winkelman 2000: 241). With this language, Winkelman comes very close to Jung's metaphor, whereby instinct and archetype comprise a spectrum. Instinct, the bodily end, occupies the infrared region, while archetype, with its numinous spiritual implications extends into the ultraviolet.

Jung's metaphor implies there is a bottom-to-top continuity between inherited behavior patterns and the mythic images that express their intentions. This whole entity is what we have been calling an archetype. And it is the reason why archetypal images "entrain" physiological responses. Image generation is found in the same package with neural networks, hormone release, and all the rest. At the bottom end, we inherit a set of genes which build bodily structures that interact with the environment to produce certain behavior patterns. Near the top end, we cannot avoid recognizing the conditions that entrain that behavior. One form of such recognition is what the biogenetic structuralists call "penetration," whereby a symbol at the violet end activates unconscious neural networks at the infrared end. When we encounter archetypal images in literature, in ritual or in dreams, the entire chain of events is set in motion and we find ourselves moved, intrigued, aroused, and ready for more. We are engaged from the lowest bodily level to the highest spiritual dimension of experience.

Winkelman had the biological discoveries of the entire twentieth century to draw upon for his description of this bottom-to-top archetypal structure.[6] Jung's sources, however, lay mostly in the nineteenth century and were summarized by Pierre Janet (1903), who sought to understand human psychology in terms of stages of evolutionary development as well as he could construe them at a time when the disciplines of genetics and molecular biology had hardly been imagined.[7] Thus, when Janet spoke of a "drop in mental level" (*abaissement du niveau mental*), he meant that an individual's psychic functioning had dropped to that characteristic of an earlier stage of personal development, or even to that of a less evolved animal.

Trance induction

We have already discussed how the autonomic nervous system can be tuned with (a) extensive motor behavior, such as dancing, (b) auditory driving, such as drumming, (c) fasting, (d) sensory deprivations, and (e) other austerities, such as pain, injury, and extreme cold. In Chapter 4, we discuss the use of hallucinogens. In all cases, the balance is altered between the sympathetic system that arouses us for emergencies and the parasympathetic system that slows us down for nourishment and sleep. Generally, the sympathetic system is stimulated to the point of exhaustion, generating a spillover effect upon the parasympathetic. This generates high-voltage, slow EEG-waves in the emotion-governing limbic system which synchronizes the entire brain from the very primitive brain stem to the frontal cortex, which is primarily responsible for ego-function. The brain becomes hierarchically integrated, bringing neural networks that are normally unconscious within the reach of self-conscious awareness, harmonizing the limbic system and the cortex, and synchronizing the left and right cerebral hemispheres. Brain-wave patterns slow to alpha and theta rhythms, inducing a sort of "waking-dream" state that promotes "integrative processing" (Winkelman 2000: 128–30).

Shamanism and integration

Once the integrative state of shamanic consciousness is attained, the bottom-to-top archetypal organization of the brain becomes open to the shaman's awareness. Lower brain centers are engaged, but no longer fully unconscious. To greater or lesser extent, they become available to the shaman's observing consciousness. This brings with it a sense of insight, understanding, certainty, conviction and truth. One has the sense that all of this surpasses ordinary understanding, and memories of the insights achieved tend to persist into ordinary consciousness when the shamanic state has passed (Winkelman 2000: 4). In addition to the bottom-to-top integration, there is also a "horizontal" assimilation of separate archetypal patterns into a larger model of self based upon deep structures that operate independently of language. The shaman thinks analogically rather than in a language-based manner, and this leads to animistic and anthropomorphic thinking. The animals talk. Everything seems to be alive and guided by a human-like soul (Winkelman 2000: 2).

   The deepest and most integrative of neurognostic structures are those associated with the shamanic initiation, when the individual faces death and dismemberment and is then reassembled and reborn. The shaman-to-be faces the most central terrors of human life and survives, an experience that would transform anyone's outlook (Winkelman 2000: 82). Such deep, universally human issues, which appear to be related to the theta-wave pattern of whole-brain stimulation, are central to the survival of the species (Ibid.: 136f). The altered functioning of the brain in integrative mode, therefore, is tuned to the fundamental issues of human survival and the psychocultural beliefs of the shaman's own society.

Winkelman points out that these integrative achievements are not merely bio-psychic, but "bio-social"; they are universally human, cross-cultural characteristics "that constitute the primordial basis for religion," that is for ultimate explanations that are inevitably generated when our brain's "cognitive imperative" applies itself to the most fundamental and comprehensive "zone of uncertainty" (Winkelman 2000: 71). Here is where the deepest and broadest integrations occur. Shamanism is "the mechanism by which the distinct modules for human thought were integrated" (Ibid.: 58). The dynamic of shamanism reveals the limitations of Mithen's model of psychic integration (opening the doors between the side chapels of the Paleolithic mind). Mithen's view is too much oriented to conscious, language-based thought. "Shamanism contributed to this integrative cognition through the systematic neurophysiological, psychological, psychosocial, and symbolic effects of the altered states of consciousness which produced integrative brain states" (Winkelman 2000: 102). In other words, the caves give us evidence of a deeper process than Mithen has described, a reorganization of the human psyche that paved the way for all that has followed.[8]

Healing and transformation

In the course of a life of shamanizing, an individual repeatedly activates deep neurocognitive structures through altered states of consciousness and the use of symbols—those of the shamanic costume, the induction procedure, the healing rituals, and those of society's mythic narrative. All of this restructures the brain and psyche at levels below theoretical and operational thinking. Ritual and the shaman's journey through mythscape repeatedly restore and reexamine the structure of the mythic cosmos. And these activities, performed in altered states of consciousness, realign neural networks, and harden their "wiring," so that eventually the myth reestablishes itself automatically every time the shaman undertakes a consciousness-altering exercise. Mythscape, repeatedly explored, "serves as a bridge between the iconic and the verbal rational levels by including elements of both domains" (Winkelman 2000: 88).

In short, the bottom-to-top structure of the archetypes is regularly exploited by shamanism. Although everyone's brain-and-psyche is structured archetypally, shamans exploit this structure to firm up the neural "wiring" that links image with physiology. Years of practice will potentially bring the shaman to the point where every incident in life is instantaneously appreciated for its mythic significance. Ideally, the experienced shaman lives in mythscape all the time, the archetypal structure of reality functioning as a background that lurks out-of-focus in waking consciousness but remains always available. Nevertheless, Eliade's stories of shamans who become sick unless they have regular opportunities to shamanize attest to the ongoing importance of immersing oneself in mythscape and activating deep neural networks that carry with them a sense of wholeness in self and cosmos.

Shamanic healing rituals have a similar effect upon patients. The ceremony itself evokes opioid (endorphin) release which alters autonomic nervous system balance and generates an emotional charge. The same endorphins that build mother-infant and lover-lover bonds constitute the foundation of all social bonding. They foster social interaction, play, and the comfort of having a place in society, and provide a sense of belonging (Winkelman 2000: 198). Endorphins work on the whole ritual community, whose social cohesion favors the entrainment of certain physiological processes in the patient, and prepares them all for the effect of mythic reenactment. Myth "molds, stabilizes, and integrates the patient's experience, giving it meaning." In this way it facilitates the integration of ego-identity within the mythscape of the group, while strengthening the top-to-bottom archetypal structure of brain-and-psyche (Winkelman 2000: 231, 245).

> Ritual healing produces cures through entraining deep levels of neurocognitive organization, evoking repressed structures and psychodynamic complexes and re-elevating them into consciousness. These repressed structures can produce conflict and collapse the ego in development of a different relationship of self to the world. Integration of this previously unconscious material into the conscious network may result in profound changes in the individual's experience of self and world, including alteration of behavior, personality, self-understanding, and autonomic balance.
>
> (Winkelman 2000: 245).

The shaman has been called the expert in a non-ordinary "grammar of mind" (Jordan 2001); for the shaman remembers and reestablishes the reality of the greater cosmos that interrelates the ecology, the economy, the social structure, and the source of collective meaning. Illness, both personal and social, is often understandable in terms of alienation from the greater cosmos. Temporal concerns draw people away from the timeless foundational reality of the myth, and it is the shaman's duty to restore the connection.

> Equipped with an impressive corpus of empirical knowledge (ethnoscience) and a profound grasp of human behavior, the shaman fulfills the vital role of a psychocultural adaptive mechanism, not merely as a healer of diseases, but as a harmonizer of social and natural dysfunctions and imbalance.
>
> (Ripinsky-Naxon 1993: 9)

To accomplish such goals, the shaman must be something of a showman and manipulate the "set and setting" of ritual, to address the current psychosocial reality of the community as well as that of the patient. Conditions must be right for the mythic imagery to have its full effect.

Chapter 4

Mastery of shamanic states of consciousness

Showmanship, arranging the "set and setting" within which altered states of consciousness will be experienced, even perpetrating the illusions for which shamans the world over are renowned—all in the best interests of individual healing and the revitalization of society—have little to do with the *mastery of altered states*. All of these activities can be performed by a shaman in ordinary consciousness. By "mastering altered states," we mean learning to gain some control over what happens when one is in a trance state. The question before us is whether altered states can be refined and developed somewhat analogously to the way Western science has refined, developed, and extended our sensory capacities. Are "inner" discoveries and manipulations possible that would parallel the techniques of an "outer"-directed science?

If altered states of consciousness are useful for healing and transformation, can we learn to use them dependably; or must we, perhaps, induce trances and then just hope for the best? Is it possible to gain some mastery over what happens to our consciousness *while we are entranced*? Surely the importance of altered states of consciousness is not simply that they exist, but rather what we can learn to do with them. Anthropologist Piers Vitebsky of Cambridge University, one of the most respected contemporary experts on shamanism, *defines* the shaman as "any kind of person who is in control of his or her state of trance" (Vitebsky 1995: 10). He implies not only that altered states are "an absolutely normal, ordinary, indispensable side of human experience" (Hunt 1995: 1), but also that shamans distinguish themselves in having refined their talent for exploiting this universal human capability. Among contemporary shamanic societies, the San (Bushmen) of southern Africa are one of the most closely studied and frequently cited examples of a *simple* hunter-gatherer culture. For that reason they may resemble our Ice-Age ancestors. There is very little role-distinction in San society, and every San is a potential shaman. Some individuals, of course, display a greater talent for becoming entranced and for controlling their trance, but the San trance-dance involves the whole community, and anyone who enters a trance is authorized to heal. The San say that a form of energy they call *n/um* rises in their bodies as they become entranced. It is a painful experience; but if an individual is to become an effective and dependable shaman, he or she is expected to have mastered the pain of *n/um* by the age of thirty-five (Lewis-Williams and Dowson 1989: 34).

Techniques of mastery

Mastery of altered states begins with exercises undertaken in ordinary consciousness. This is true not only for such seemingly exotic activities as shamanism, but also for everyday altered states, such as those employed by athletes. For example, golf champion Arnold Palmer has said that you have to *know* that you will make your putt: "The hardest thing for a great many people is to win. They . . . *doubt*. Which gets them into trouble" (Murphy and White 1978: 99). He implies that a state of supreme confidence had to be cultivated, that he had to learn to master his state of mind. Decades of success on the golf course demonstrate that he has done so, but he does not tell us how—and perhaps does not know himself what he did.

Role of the conscious ego

Perhaps many shamans, too, have gained mastery without knowing how they did it, but some general principles of mastering our conscious states may be enunciated. Not unlike learning how to drive, chip, and putt a golf ball, consciousness-training inevitably involves a good deal of habituation, i.e. repetition of some simple actions to the point that they become automatic. Consciousness-training, just like athletics and musicianship, requires "steady work" to "throw off an unconsciousness" most of us do not know we have, for we have never imagined gaining control over our altered states.

The biogenetic structuralists refer to the habituation process as "*relegation*." When we practice an activity over and over, we establish new neural networks in the brain; and the better "wired" those networks are (on the principle that "neurons that fire together wire together") the more capable they are of functioning outside of conscious guidance.

A pianist in the midst of performing a concerto does not have to *think* which keys to strike or by which technique. Practice has rendered such motor activities highly automatic, leaving consciousness free to attend to the general form of the musical passages and to the nuances inspired by this particular performance. While he plays his part in the concerto, the pianist is in an altered state of consciousness in which he may be said to "inhabit" the music, to live in the world of the concerto, while a certain capacity to introduce subtle changes in timing, mood, and emphasis reveals his mastery over unconscious networks, giving the performance its unique character.

Extended, conscientious repetition "wires" a neural network so solidly that it can be trusted to function without conscious attention. As this degree of dependability is achieved, the network will automatically be "disentrained from the [larger] conscious network" of the ego, and "relegated" to the lowest functional level of the nervous system capable of performing it well enough (Laughlin *et al.*

1990: 98). Such "demoted" networks are not lost. Rather they can be "rediscovered," at first with effort, and eventually quite naturally. "If there is sufficient interest, consciousness will actively, even persistently search for the requisite network" (Laughlin *et al*. 1990: 99). Searching for and finding unconscious networks is part of what "mastery" means.

Some of the simplest examples of such searching and finding have to do with the influence the conscious ego can exert over subsequent sleeping states. For example, J. Allan Hobson, the Harvard dream researcher, says that experiments done with lucid dreaming (i.e. dreams where we *know* we are dreaming) show that it is possible to influence the content of dreams by concentrating on some issue while falling asleep (Hobson 2002: 20). In this case, a conscious intention seems to be "held," even as the conscious ego disappears into sleep. Somehow, despite the physiological upheaval of switching from waking consciousness to the dream state, something that just a moment before was conscious is now "searching out" networks in order to investigate the issue in question. Meanwhile, the very fact that we are capable of lucid dreaming (though it may not be a common experience) implies some sort of control, namely the ability to see the dream *as a dream* and not to believe it is waking reality. A critical function of the waking ego is retained despite our passing over into a state of sleep.

A second issue is implied by Hobson's comment on lucid dreaming. The very idea that we may intend to have a lucid dream while we are awake and thereby influence our brain-and-psyche to achieve lucidity implies a certain conscious influence over the dreaming state. Most people have to train themselves to achieve this small degree of mastery. A standard technique, in fact, for learning to become lucid while in the dream state is to develop the habit of asking oneself repeatedly during the day whether one is dreaming right now or awake. In the beginning, the would-be lucid dreamer will have difficulty remembering to ask herself at odd moments during the day: "Am I dreaming now? How can I be sure?" The habit has to be developed until the thought will come to mind unbidden and repeatedly during the day. It must become sufficiently automatic as to be "relegated" to a much lower functional level, and thereby available also during sleep.

A similar claim is made by Lewis-Williams and Pearce (2005) when they report that we can gain far more control than we may have imagined over our hypnagogic imagery—those fleeting and fragmentary images and impressions that pass through our minds while we are falling asleep. If we make an act of will to attend to those images, we can increase their duration and frequency. Furthermore, this greater stability of attention will persist into the dreaming state and teach us "to control and prolong both [our] hypnagogic experience and [our] dreams" (Lewis-Williams and Pearce 2005: 44).

What replaces the waking ego

In all these instances, the notion of a part of our consciousness "searching" for unconscious memories, capabilities, and other associations, seems quite apt. But the "consciousness" that "searches" for the relegated network is surely not quite identical with the ego of ordinary consciousness. It must resemble, rather, the ego of "original thinking," the one that has relinquished the illusion of being in charge and is aware of being given to. This is the experience that inspires Jung to say, "I think unconsciously," and "My thoughts are given to me, I do not invent them" (*Speaking*, 166). From the perspective of the ordinary ego, the ego that emerges in "original thinking" seems strangely passive and withdrawn from the empirical world. Yet it clearly does "search out" unconscious networks. It performs an activity that the ordinary ego can only dream of doing.

For instance, Jung sometimes describes active imagination as a technique for getting our moods to speak to us. Perhaps we are out of sorts and do not know why. Withdrawing from the concerns of everyday life—including the constant chatter by which the ego of everyday consciousness maintains its narrow perspective on world and self—and redirecting our attention to the meditative field of active imagination, we permit images to emerge "out of our mood." The activated neural networks that belong to the general state of brain-and-psyche that *is the mood* are drawn into the conscious field and appear as images and fragments of dramas. The mood is supported by deeper levels of the top-to-bottom structure of the archetype, while the imagery is produced by the top layers.

As we argued in Volume 1, in the same year that Jung discovered his method of active imagination, or "original thinking," 1913, Edmund Husserl published his own account of having developed a similar technique for catching consciousness in the act. Again, he describes a "strangely passive" agent, in contrast with the ordinary behavior of the ego. The advantage for us of Husserl's account is that the ego that functions in his "phenomenological *epoché*" is much more precisely described than is Jung's "original thinker."

Husserl calls this agent the "transcendental ego." But it only *seems* passive to us, because we are identified with our ordinary, empirical ego, the one that believes it is in charge of our careening and thoughtless course through a world that exists outside of me as a set of independent objects. When we look more closely, however, we see that absolutely everything is given to us by the transcendental ego—the whole world and even ourselves. *It* is the truly active agent: "The Objective world . . . with all its Objects, derives its whole sense and its existential status . . . from me as the transcendental Ego, the Ego who comes to the fore only with transcendental-phenomenological *epoché*" (Laughlin *et al*. 1990: 33).[1]

Laughlin *et al*. (1990: 31f) describe an exercise by which we can learn to experience Husserl's transcendental ego. First, we must learn to concentrate stably on a single object in the conscious field (perhaps a blue vase). It will take some practice to keep the concentration steady. Then, we must switch to a second object (the table it sits upon) without losing the first, and practice until both objects can be held steadily in mind. The third step is to alternate the focus of our attention from vase to table and back again without losing either object. The final and crucial step is to attend not to the objects themselves but to the *effort* required by these acts of attention. This shift "brackets" the "existence" of the objects, which is what Husserl means by *epoché*. Object and subject—no longer separate entities—are revealed to be what they are in consciousness, two aspects of the same phenomenon.

Husserl's shift is the essential move in all mystical practices. One attends not to the object itself, existing in the world out there, but rather to the act of consciousness by which the object is held. This shift sets aside the naive "empirical ego" and reveals the transcendental ego that has been there all along. Like the ego of active imagination, the transcendental ego emerges when the habitual constraints of the everyday waking ego have been bypassed. When the shaman makes this shift, it "allow[s] him to immerse himself and participate in a broader more destructured phenomenal field" (Laughlin *et al.* 1990: 341), i.e. a field of phenomena no longer structured by everyday expectations.

Learning to "steer" a trance state

If "the goal of shamans is to find the correct balance or equilibrium point between tapping into sacred forces and the ability to control them" (Hayden 2003: 59), the equilibrium point surely is closely related to Husserl's transcendental ego and Jung's original thinking. Furthermore, it seems obvious that shamans must possess sufficient "ego strength" to tolerate conflicting themes, structures, demands, emotions, and the like, and to trust that a non-conscious force like Jung's transcendent function will be able to resolve their discrepancies. The empirical ego is incapable of such integration, and the transcendental ego is simply handed the resolution in symbolic form (cf. Winkelman 2000: 83). But still, some "steering" of the altered state is required. "The shaman's art is to consciously bring about the state of trance and to steer it" (Müller-Ebeling *et al.* 2002: 39).

Dan Merkur (1992) describes such "steering" of trance states using the language of hypnosis. He says that an entranced apprentice shaman is guided by "hetero-hypnotic" suggestions made by the master shaman in charge of the training. After sufficient guidance by another, the apprentice begins to learn some techniques of "auto-hypnosis," i.e. to guide the course of her own trance. Merkur (1992) does not justify his choice of hypnosis as a metaphor or explain how the transition takes place, from hetero- to auto-suggestion. Nevertheless, he nicely sets the parameters for any discussion of mastering altered states. Furthermore, his descriptions accord very well with those of archaeologist and rock art specialist David S. Whitley, describing puberty ceremonies among the Native Americans of California: "Shamans tried to manipulate the initiates' visions to ensure the proper, culturally prescribed supernatural experiences" (Whitley 2000: 86). Brian Fagan, Professor of Anthropology at the University of California, Santa Barbara, describes similar "hetero-suggestions" among the San:

> During the trance dances, shamans might draw each other's attention to things they can see, such as a spirit-eland standing in the semidarkness beyond the fire. Participants look in the same direction and share the same

vision. When everyone has returned to a normal state of consciousness, the visions are described. The shaman is then able to manipulate these visions for the audience, using such things as dance, flickering lights, or paintings, to direct his narrative.

(Fagan 1998: 65f)

The biogenetic structuralists bring us closer to understanding the interior process of "steering" one's own trance state. The first step in gaining mastery is learning to attend to consciousness itself. That is, we have to learn to "exit the natural mind" by making a phenomenological reduction like that of Husserl. The natural mind— whether it looks out at the outer world or in at the inner world—can only see what happens to appear. With my natural mind in the waking state, I look out the window and see cars passing by on the street, leaves trembling in a light breeze, sparrows squabbling over a crust of bread someone has dropped on the sidewalk. Or in the natural mind of the dream state, I see a girl on a bicycle collide with the mailman's letter-cart; papers begin to blow everywhere, and I run to help pick them up. In either case, the natural mind is heedless of the consciousness that makes these things appear. We have to make some sort of phenomenological reduction, some turn to "original thinking," if we are ever to "learn that what we perceive is a pattern of neural activity," that it belongs to us, and that we potentially have the power to exercise some influence over it (Laughlin *et al.* 1990: 108f).

The "warps" in our stream of consciousness

The biogenetic structuralists describe consciousness in terms of a nested hier-archy: modes, states and phases. The largest "nests" are the modes, the four bio-logically based gross types of mammalian function: wake, dream, dreamless sleep, and transpersonal consciousness. These same categories are distinguished in the Hindu Upanishads, where transpersonal consciousness is called *turiya*; and the first three are self-evident to us all. While in the waking (or sleeping) mode, we find ourselves in various distinct "states" of consciousness, each of which is "based upon sociocultural learning and psychosocial needs" (Winkelman 2000: 124). Lucien Lévy-Bruhl's distinction between "primitive thinking" and the "theory-based" thinking of the monophasic West describes extreme examples of socio-cultural learning. The "primitive's" conscious state is based in being alert for archetypal patterns or "collective representations," while we in the West are attentive to theoretical explanations for why events occur (Lévy-Bruhl 1922).

Certainly different cultures favor different states of consciousness, but accul-turation and psychosocial needs do not restrict each of us to a single waking state. We would be wrong to think that a university physicist is always in the same con-scious state. Surely she is in a highly focused physical-science state of mind while working in her laboratory or teaching her students. But she is in a familial state of mind while picnicking with her husband and children. Indeed, each of us knows a variety of familial states of mind, ranging from bickering to bliss. There is probably no end to the list we could make of familiar states of consciousness—all without entering the murkier region where altered states are to be found. Each psychosocial state is a way of being a psyche-in-the-socialized-world.

We pass through a number of states of consciousness in the course of a day: a groggy period at the beginning, quiet reflection while reading the paper, irritated competitiveness during the commute, and so on. But no one of these conscious states is uniform. In each one we go through *phases*. Take reading the morning paper. For a few moments, we read the story behind the headline, and our imagination takes us into the mayor's office, where several individuals hurl accusations at one another. Then disjointed memories of these local political figures flit through our minds as we follow the article with skepticism. There are moments of fumbling for our coffee cup, rearranging ourselves in the chair, suddenly remembering an appointment made for 11:15, and so on. Each of these is a different "phase" within the same general "state" (quietly reading the paper). A phase is a "discrete, cognized strip of unfolding experience" (Laughlin *et al.* 1990: 142).

Phases of consciousness are separated from one another by gaps where, for instance, my feelings about the mayor fade out as I find myself fumbling for my coffee cup. The biogenetic structuralists call these in-between moments "warps." Consciousness is "warping" from one state to another, and these "nowhere moments," the warps, are the handles by which the transcendental ego can grab hold and steer a state of consciousness. Warps are the secret behind the mastery of altered states.

What the biogenetic structuralists call "warps" have long been known in the literature of Eastern meditation as the empty moments between thoughts, whose discovery is crucial for transforming consciousness. They are momentary and so evanescent that in most cases we have to train ourselves to notice them. There are some warps, however, that are easier to detect, and paying attention to the easier ones helps us to begin noticing subtler instances. For example, the warp between a drop in blood sugar and the feeling of being tired and irritable is characterized by familiar physical signs. Learning to become aware of the warp before we fall into a phase of touchy exhaustion can be very useful, for it allows us to take a little timely nourishment and thereby eliminate or diminish the undesirable phase. The warp between wake and sleep is another—called "hypnagogic" while falling asleep and "hypnopompic" on awakening. Sharpening our awareness of these transitions can increase dream-recall (Laughlin *et al.* 1990: 142–4).

Jung's idea of becoming conscious of a feeling-toned complex relies upon the reality of warps. Experience shows that once we become aware of the stereotyped pattern of experience and behavior that a complex produces, we can identify it as a typical "state of consciousness" that seems to "get into us." At first we will recognize the complex-behavior only after the fact and with chagrin. Practice in attending to our conscious states, however, enables our catching a complex-reaction in the act, and at progressively earlier moments. Finally, if we become sharp enough to catch the warp before the complex-state becomes established, we can learn to reduce its effects or even to avoid it.

Steering through the warps

Shamans generally wish to induce certain novel states and phases of consciousness rather than avoid others that are dysfunctional and all too common. Using ritual to tune their autonomic nervous system and those of other participants is the prime example by which shamans create a warp and steer themselves and others-not into just any altered state, but into a desired mood, one that is conducive to healing, transformation or discovery (Laughlin *et al.* 1990: 147; Winkelman 2000: 124). Consciousness can be steered into specific states by employing the principle of "symbolic penetration" to the warps. Symbols introduced in the warps penetrate to unconscious neural networks and evoke experiences with a mythic or numinous tone, and inspire a conviction of truth, awe, curiosity and vulnerability (Laughlin *et al.* 1990: 229). Shamans take advantage of the warp's lack of form to trigger unconscious networks that structure the next phase into which consciousness passes.

A shaman's practice at employing the transcendental ego to attend to the states and phases of consciousness begins during an apprenticeship when the beginner psychic traveler is steered by a master shaman who drops suggestions into the novice's warps. Repeated experiences of trance states and warp transitions under different circumstances and with the penetration of different symbols exposes the apprentice to a wide range of conscious phases. Any one of them might solidify as a sort of complex, the distinctive source of an extraordinary power. Seen as supernatural authorities from another realm of the cosmos, i.e. as "spirit-guides," such stereotyped phases of consciousness are experienced as autonomous agents. They can bring about dissociations in the shaman's personality. But by learning to control these phases through symbolic and ritual devices applied to the warps, "a young shaman learns to integrate alternate phases into a single personality" (Laughlin *et al.* 1990: 147). Shamanic mastery of altered states of consciousness is essential—first to preserve the shaman's own sanity, then as a means of taking charge of journeys through mythscape as a "free soul," and finally to manipulate the patient's state of consciousness in the direction of health.

Acquiring shamanic mastery

The process of acquiring shamanic mastery over altered states has been described by the biogenetic structuralists as comprising three stages. In the future shaman's initiatory sickness, a previously habitual structuring of brain-and-psyche as that of an unremarkable ordinary citizen is subjected to extraordinary pressures that cause it to fragment. The center no longer holds while radically new, extremely vivid imagery and emotional reactions intervene, causing confusion and panic. Images of dismemberment are highly appropriate to this first phase. When the shaman-to-be finds an experienced mentor who can help to contain this efflorescence of frightening material, guided journeys into mythscape force the novice to become accommodated to the new psychic landscape. Growing familiarity with this expanded cosmos and with the warp manipulations that make it possible begin the process of reassembling the fragmented brain-and-psyche into a new and expanded form. If the initial phase is *fragmentation*, the middle phase is *assimilation*, and the final phase is *consolidation*. For:

> With guidance and experience, the shaman gains mastery over his new realm of experience. He becomes expert at cross-phasing warps and transcending levels of his own internal structures. What was earlier experienced as dismemberment and madness now becomes exploration.
>
> (Laughlin *et al*. 1990: 272f)

The biogenetic structuralists cite Jung's disciple Erich Neumann's *The Origins and History of Consciousness* (1949) as support for this three-part description of a shaman's maturation. They might also have cited the central theme of Jung's studies in alchemy, expressed in the Latin motto, *solve et coagula*, and also in the Greek name for alchemy, the *spagyric* art.[2] Every psychic transformation begins with the fragmentation (or "dissolving") of an old synthesis. Elements, old and new, are then experienced in isolation from one another, rather chaotically, before they "coagulate" into a new, stable configuration.

Chapter 5

Shamanic mastery

Ayahuasqueros in the Amazon

The use of psychoactive drugs to induce shamanic states of consciousness has been widespread in human history. Some of the best documented material comes from the shamanic use of a drug mixture variously called ayahuasca, jagé, or daime in the Upper Amazon basin, involving parts of Venezuela, Colombia, Ecuador, Peru, Bolivia, and Brazil. We will call it "ayahuasca." Evidence for its use in shamanism is very ancient, and it is used today by more people and by more classes of people than ever before. Originally, it was used by very simple hunter-gatherer societies, so that its use may closely parallel the shamanism of our Ice Age ancestors. Today, it seems that only the highest social classes in the Andes remain ignorant of ayahuasca. The main advantage for our purposes of investigating ayahuasca rests upon its thorough documentation, especially by participant-observer scientists. This provides us with a wealth of information to help us closely consider how South American shamans attain mastery over their altered states of consciousness. What we learn from them tells us a good deal about how traditional practitioners have manipulated the warps in their consciousness.

Ayahuasca: general introduction

Ayahuasca is a psychedelic tea made by boiling together pulped pieces of a vine found widely in the Amazon jungle together with one or more other herbs. *Ayahuasca* is the name of the brew in the Quechua language, which is the Native American lingua franca of the Andes. Much of the evidence that follows comes from Ecuador and Peru. *Aya* means "bitter," "dead person," and "spirit"; *huasca* means "vine." It is the drink of the vine that is bitter to the taste and turns its drinkers symbolically into dead people and experientially into spirits—in the same sense that our ancestors in the Upper Paleolithic linked the ideas of dying and entering trance. Although its ingredients are somewhat variable, depending upon locale and the purpose of drinking it, ayahuasca is ubiquitous in the Upper Amazon, and known by other names, including *yagé* by the Tukano people of Colombia (Luna 1986: 9).

Anthropologist Jeremy Narby says that ayahuasca use in Western Amazonia stretches back without interruption some 4000 or 5000 years. The natives and

Western "participant observers" describe ayahuasca as a "school" and a "teacher." It is a much older school than the European university system, which is not yet 900 years old (Narby 1999: 154). Somewhat more conservatively, Dennis McKenna (1999: 190) reports that archaeologists have found evidence of figurines and drug delivery systems for an inhaled version of ayahuasca in the Ecuadorian Amazon that date to 3500 or 4000 years ago. The first European to encounter ayahuasca was the English botanist Richard Spruce, in 1851; the earliest written report of first-hand experience was made by an Ecuadorian civil servant named Villavicencio, in 1858 (Shanon 2002: 19).

What impresses most investigators is the universality of the experience: certainly not socially or culturally determined (Shanon 2002: 318f), and "most plausibly ... because we *Homo sapiens* are [all] wired the same" (R. Siegel 1989: 235). Psychedelic researcher Stanislav Grof is particularly struck by the precision of this archetypal universality:

> I had never suspected that the ancient spiritual systems had actually charted with amazing accuracy, different levels and types of experiences that occur in non-ordinary states of consciousness. I was astonished by their emotional power, authenticity, and potential for transforming people's lives.
>
> (Grof 1992: 17)

Universally, ayahuasca is said to reveal the "real world," the world of the spirits, i.e. the greater cosmos from which all true and valuable knowledge comes. The brew itself is described as a powerful spirit being that enables its users to know this and other worlds, past and future, and the natural environment (geography, flora and fauna); to diagnose illnesses; to discover game animals, the plans of enemies and lost objects; to communicate with distant relatives; and to travel in time and space (Luna 1986: 60–2).

Although some of the earliest and most influential accounts of ayahuasca use were published by participant-observer anthropologists working with fairly remote tribes of Native Americans (Harner 1972, 1973; Reichel-Dolmatoff 1971, 1975), most of the material gathered here comes from more recent observers who have studied with *mestizos*, who call themselves *vegetalistas* more frequently than *ayahuasqueros*. Although *mestizo* literally means a person of mixed race, it is used by these researchers as a socio-cultural term. Whatever their race, mestizos, in this sense, are individuals who have Spanish as their mother tongue and are at home throughout the thousands of square miles that comprise "the large and diffuse Upper Amazon cultural complex" (Luna 1986: 15). The extensive interchange of information across such huge geographical regions, nations, and local cultural traditions means that shamanism effectively transcends all social boundaries (Luna 1986: 35). It combines ideas and imagery from several Native American traditions with European religious traditions. Indeed, each practitioner develops a uniquely personal syncretism (Luna 1986: 41). In Brazil, there are three legally recognized Churches that imbibe ayahuasca as a sacrament; they call the drug *daime* (literally, "give me") (Shanon 2002: 21–6).

Most mestizo vegetalistas have worked in the jungle during their youth, usually tapping rubber trees, learned the flora and fauna of the forest, and been in contact with local indigenous cultures. Some have moved to cities and absorbed a good deal of the esoteric literature of Rosicrucianism, Gnosticism, and Far Eastern traditions (Luna 1986: 158). In the Peruvian Amazon, Luis Eduardo Luna (1986: 73) reports that only a very small portion of the upper middle class and the upper class lead a life that is ignorant of ayahuasca and the forest. Apparently this most European layer of society is insulated by its wealth from the attractions of ayahuasca use. For:

> Demoralized by the shock of acculturative forces, mestizo inhabitants of Iquitos [Peru] suffer from high rates of stress-induced anxiety and associated psychosomatic disorders. The use of ayahuasca, as supervised by mestizo healers, is incorporated into complex healing ceremonies.
>
> (Grob 1999: 224)

Cave painters redux

Parallels between the Upper Paleolithic cave painters and the ayahuasqueros of the Amazon are striking and extensive. Both sorts of shamanism are practiced by simple hunter-gatherer societies, both understand becoming entranced as a symbolic form of dying, and both embrace the notion that the shaman's free soul travels through a greater cosmos that makes this empirical world more tractable. Both use altered states of consciousness to heal, find game animals, and the like. Both paint and etch into stone characteristic images associated with their trances.

It appears that drug use probably does *not* distinguish South American shamans from their forebears in the Upper Paleolithic. The likelihood is that the cave painters did employ drugs for trance induction. Duke University anthropologist Weston LaBarre has argued in his book, *The Ghost Dance: The Origins of Religion* (1970), that "hunters and gatherers, rather than farmers, were probably the first to learn much about hallucinogenic plants" (cited in Dobkin de Rios 1990: 7). Gordon and Virginia Wasson (1957) report that the use of the hallucinogenic mushroom *Amanita muscaria*, also called "fly agaric," began at the end of the last Ice Age. Indeed, it appears that since Amanita grows in symbiotic relationship with birch and pine trees, that the mushroom followed the retreating ice cap northward along with the trees (Wasson and Wasson 1957: 34f). Its use has long been associated with Siberian shamanism, which may well be the historical successor to Upper Paleolithic shamanism. It is also believed, however, that the Upper Paleolithic people probably used ergot, a more dangerous drug, which is found in a blight on grain, and is often associated with the late-antique cult of Eleusis.

The classic three stages of trance are widely reported with ayahuasca use—although Benny Shanon, the researcher who has had the most extensive personal familiarity with the drug, says that the sense of passing through distinct stages diminishes with cumulative experience (Shanon 2002: 277). Psychopharmacologist Ronald K. Siegel believes the experience of the tunnel is a common illusion caused by the fact that the center of the visual field produced by ayahuasca is so bright that the images there are obscured, while images outside the center retain their distinctness (R. K. Siegel 1989: 232). Imagery from the visions, however, especially the phosphene designs, are unmistakable in body paint, textiles, ceramics, and other utensils. Reichel-Dolmatoff's (1987) study of the Eastern Tukanoan people is the most densely documented volume, but studies of Native American rock art from both continents show the close relationship between shamanism, myth, and art (cf. Grant 1967; Patterson-Rudolph 1990; Whitley 2000).

The most impressive statement, however, is a series of shamanic paintings by the former ayahuasquero, Pablo Amaringo, published in a large format book with text by Luis Eduardo Luna (1993) *Ayahuasca Visions: The Religious Iconography of a Peruvian Shaman*. Pablo Amaringo's story is somewhat typical of mestizo shamans. Born in 1943, he declared himself an atheist at the age of 15 because the Catholic Church wanted nothing to do with a poor man who wished to become a priest. He worked as an assistant Harbor Master in Pucallpa until he was discovered to have a heart condition. Then he found he could draw and went to jail for counterfeiting currency. He escaped, and his father cured his heart problem with ayahuasca. Believing his life was now reformed, he went back to jail to serve out his sentence and was released for good conduct in 1969. He practiced as a vegetalista until 1977 but abandoned shamanism on account of spirit-world battles with an angry curandera who believed that her spirits had left her as the by-product of Pablo's cure of his sister's hepatitis.[1] Having been hurt by an act of her sorcery, Amaringo went to a vegetalista to be cured and was told that he would never escape the attacks of the vengeful woman unless he use his own shamanic powers and kill her. Unwilling to become an unscrupulous sorcerer himself, he relinquished ayahuasca and dedicated himself to art (Luna and Amaringo 1993: 25–8).

When he paints, Amaringo "concentrates until he sees an image in his mind" (Luna and Amaringo 1993: 28). Thus, he evidently practices a sort of active imagination in which he gains access to his transcendental ego. Judging from the verbal descriptions he has provided to accompany his published paintings, it appears that every canvas is a record of a well-remembered instance from his shamanic practice. As he sketches the images on paper or canvas and fills them in with color, he sings or whistles the shamanic songs (*icaros*) he was taught by his mentors— human, vegetal, or spiritual. He attributes his powers of visualizing to his experiences with ayahuasca.

The paintings manage to convey a numinous sense of the visionary. Generally, there is a shadowy group of humans, usually painted in gray or black, using ayahuasca in a *tambo* (an open-sided, thatch-roofed platform on stilts, a typical jungle shelter). These humans are almost hard to find, however, for the huge colorful serpents, mermaids and figures from myth and fairy tales that completely overwhelm the scene in the tambo. All of these figures seem to emerge out of dense jungle foliage, as though the squiggles, circles, dots, and zigzags of the phosphenes have coalesced marvelously to suggest jaguars, goddesses, monkeys, armed warriors, and flying saucers. There are cities and castles and humanoid monsters comprised of animal parts from several species, not unlike the so-called shamans in the Ice Age caves.

Anthropologist Jeremy Narby says the paintings strongly resemble his own ayahuasca visions (Narby 1999: 69), and Luna says he has shown them to many vegetalistas who say they have seen the same images themselves. Luna has heard many descriptions of visions from people participating in ayahuasca sessions that sound like the same images and mythic themes that Amaringo has painted (Luna and Amaringo 1993: 43, n. 69).

Ayahuasca: psychoactive principles

The vine (huasca) that gives ayahuasca its name is *Banisteriopsis caapi* and other species of the *Banisteriopsis* genus. It climbs the trunks of huge forest trees as a liana, and attains a woody stem diameter of three or four inches. By itself, it has little potency as an hallucinogen. The hallucinogenic component of the brew is derived from the leaves of a bush, *Psychotria viridis* or *Diplopterys cabrerana*. These supply the most potent of psychoactive drugs, known by its abbreviation, DMT (N, N-dimethyltryptamine). DMT is easily deactivated in the stomach by monoamine oxidase (MAO), which removes the amine group from DMT. Alkaloids called beta-carbolines provided by *Banisteriopsis*, however, function as MAO-inhibitors, keeping DMT active and allowing it to be absorbed into the bloodstream and make its way to the brain (McKenna 1999: 198). Not a few observers have remarked upon the herbal and biochemical acumen or incredible blind luck that induced hunter-gatherers to hit upon such a complex and ingenious solution to achieving altered states of consciousness four or five millennia ago. Vegetalistas say that the vine taught them how to make the brew and everything else they know.

Casual drug users of DMT in the West usually bypass the stomach's MAO barrier by smoking a little of the powdery chemical sprinkled into a pipe of tobacco or marijuana. They receive an "overwhelming immersion in an extremely alien world that lasts less than ten minutes" (Pinchbeck 2002: 140). The smoke is said to smell bad and to cause the room one occupies and one's body as well to "break into crystalline shards" (Strassman 2001: 6). By contrast, the beta-carbolines in ayahuasca produce subtle hallucinations that are "soft and warm." Their effect upon DMT is to "pacify and humanize" the visions and to extend the experience from a few minutes to several hours' duration. It must also be mentioned that beta-carbolines are powerful emetics and purgatives—so much so that ayahuasca is often referred to as "the purge" by its users in South America. The beta-carbolines function very effectively against intestinal microbes and worms (Luna 1986: 59). Most inexperienced users of ayahuasca cannot avoid extensive vomiting and diarrhea.

Dimethyltryptamine (DMT)

Professor of Psychiatry at the University of New Mexico School of Medicine, Rick Strassman, has written an extraordinary account of his research with DMT called *DMT: The Spirit Molecule* (2001). It begins with great hope and ends in morbid terror. He calls DMT "the first endogenous human psychedelic," found naturally in the cerebrospinal fluid and urine and apparently representing an adaptation for dealing with extraordinary experiences (Strassman 2001: 68, 53). Far from barring the way to the DMT molecule, as it does to most other drugs, the brain appears to "hunger" for DMT (Strassman 2001: 52). And, unlike most psychedelic drugs (e.g. LSD, psilocybin and mescaline) DMT use shows little or no "tolerance effect," i.e. none of the tendency to require more and more of the drug to achieve the same original effect. When acting upon the brain, DMT elicits spiritual states, extraordinary joy, timelessness, a sense that what one experiences is "more real than real," the coincidence of the opposites, the conviction that consciousness will continue after death, a vision of the fundamental unity of all things, and a sense of wisdom and love (Strassman 2001: 136, 54).

The body produces its own DMT in the pineal gland, which has the highest levels of the neurotransmitter serotonin of any structure in the human body. Serotonin levels are held high in the brain while we are awake during the day, and seratonin is replaced by melatonin, the neurotransmitter which regulates the brain during sleep. The pineal gland converts serotonin to melatonin and also to DMT. Furthermore, as a sort of inborn ayahuasca production center, the pineal gland also produces beta-carbolines to inhibit MAO, which would otherwise breakdown the DMT (Strassman 2001: 69).

Strassman believes that the primary pathway by which DMT produces visual and auditory hallucinations has to do with little mounds of tissue located directly beneath the pineal gland, separated from it only by cerebrospinal fluid. These "mounds" are the visual and auditory colliculi ("little hills"). Electrical impulses from the eyes and the ears have to pass through these colliculi before they go anywhere else in the brain. Anything secreted by the pineal gland would fall first on the colliculi, and then secondly affect the "emotional brain," or limbic system, which surrounds the pineal gland (Strassman 2001: 61).

Thus DMT seems strategically located in the brain to bring about spectacular results instantaneously. The sorts of incident that provoke DMT production are nearly all moments of life-or-death crisis: the birth process, psychotic crises, near-death experiences, and death itself. A fifth DMT moment occurs when deep meditative states are achieved (Strassman 2001: 68f). Evidence from the final chapters of Strassman's book suggest that spontaneous release of pineal gland DMT may also be responsible for the frightening experiences that have led some people to believe that they have been abducted by aliens. With the exception of this last possibility, it appears that the body supplies DMT in moments when we are in greatest need of unshakable certainty regarding spiritual realities that will put our material existence into a meaningful context—precisely the function shamanism seems designed to provide.[2]

Because DMT competes with serotonin (and melatonin) for receptor sites in the brain (Calloway 1999: 263) and because the pineal gland has some control over their relative concentrations, it seems that there may be at least three different modes of operation that the brain is capable of. Journalist Daniel Pinchbeck (2002) describes this situation after the metaphor of tuning a radio:

> With the "normal" levels of serotonin, the brain is tuned to "consensual reality"—something like the local pop or talk radio station. By substituting psilocybin, ibogaine, dimethyltryptamine, or some other psychedelic compound for serotonin and other neurotransmitters, you change the station and suddenly you begin to pick up the sensorial equivalent of avant-garde jazz, Tibetan chants, or another channel resonating with new and astonishing information. Yet your mind, the perceiving core of the self, remains more or less unaffected. In that sense, psychedelics, unlike alcohol or heroin, are not even intoxicating.
>
> (Pinchbeck 2002: 36)

Managing psychedelic states

Rick Strassman began his study wondering whether pineal gland DMT was the source of the natural psychedelic states accompanying birth, death, near-death, and mystical experiences. He seems to have succeeded in that, and reports that "not one volunteer, no matter how worn out, refused that fourth and final high dose of DMT" (Strassman 2001: 12). It seemed to be a wholly positive experience, with no danger of "habituation" or addiction. "Too much" DMT only meant that the subject could not remember anything after the session except that "something frightening had happened" (Ibid.: 18). But Strassman ended by terminating his research project midstream, resigning from the university, and sending his unused DMT back to the National Institute on Drug Abuse (Ibid.: 307). The reason for this is that he and his subjects came to believe that they were becoming too vulnerable to encounters with alien beings (Ibid.: 219). Several of his experimental subjects had formed a support group because no one else could understand what had happened to them. They wanted to convince themselves that they were not losing their minds (Ibid.: 201).

Strassman was a diligent researcher in that he carefully screened his subjects in advance, and paid a great deal of attention to the set and setting within which the subjects were given precisely measured injections of DMT. He listened to their subsequent reports sympathetically and with close attention to detail. He had a trained medical staff and equipment ready in case of any unexpected difficulty. But he makes no mention of the basic principles of psychedelic research that have appeared in nearly every extensive account that has been published since R. E. L. Masters and Jean Houston's 1966 classic, *The Varieties of Psychedelic Experience*.

Masters and Houston (1966) describe three stages of psychedelic experience. In the first, the subject is exposed to marvelous hallucinations and may have powerful impressions of seeing deeply into the meaning and beauty of natural objects, such as flowers and fruit. Alternatively, these first experiences may in a minority of cases be quite frightening. The second stage is crucial, for then we begin to see that all this imagery has something to do with our own lifestyle, our unresolved guilt, our neurotic complexes, our rigidities and fears. Only those who come to grips with these personal issues go on to transformative symbolic experiences with profound mythic, spiritual, and religious overtones. In short, psychedelic altered states have to be *managed*. The second phase, what Masters and Houston (1966) call the "recollective-analytic stage," cannot be bypassed. In contrast, it seems that Strassman's subjects had only encountered psychedelic imagery and made no attempt to manage their experience by examining what their experiences had to tell them about themselves.

It seems, therefore, that adequate management of psychedelic states requires the two preparations Strassman made: (a) screening and (b) carefully preparing the set and setting. Once the drug is administered, however, there are further steps to follow, and it is the entranced subjects who bear the greatest responsibility for them: (c) familiarizing themselves with the trance state, (d) developing a framework for understanding their own psyche's response to the material and critically examining their own psychology, (e) developing a framework to understand the mythscape they have entered, perhaps even mapping it, and (f) only then learning to guide the altered state by manipulating its warps.

Having not done all the interior work, Strassman found he could not resist taking the visions of alien beings literally. He wondered whether "dark matter" may be the explanation, and began to speculate that DMT tunes the brain to an alternate reality that exists parallel to this one and is comprised of WIMPS (weakly interacting massive particles) (Strassman 2001: 316–22). Of course, such a hypothesis may not be mistaken. But with our present understanding of psyche and cosmos, it is surely premature. There is no way to explore the hypothesis, no way even to collect evidence for or against it. A project that started out as an example of Western science encountered a reality that is "unthinkable" within the Western paradigm. Perhaps this is what the shamanic world has been offering us for 40,000 years, and why we retreat so quickly to the monophasic reality we know so well.

Strassman's fright resembles that of John Mack's alien abductees; and *their* complaint was that if these alien beings can appear whenever they wish, as it seems, then the world is not what we always thought it was. Life and the cosmos became terrifyingly unpredictable for them. If *that* cosmos is real, our Western assumptions are insufficient. All of Mack's abductees began their course of abduction experiences in a state of terror. But those who bravely pursued the experience eventually began to learn something valuable from it. Many discovered that they themselves were "part alien." Their own personal reality was expanding in archetypal directions (cf. Mack 1994; Haule 1999a: 145–222). Strassman failed to stick to it long enough to become thoroughly familiar with the trance state or to develop a framework, either interior or exterior. Nevertheless he is aware of Mack and even points out Mack's observation that many self-described abductees report having been taken from their homes "in the early morning hours when the pineal gland is most active" and that the abduction phenomenon has been responsible for many people "reconnecting with spirituality" (Strassman 2001: 322).

The ayahuasca "diet"

The DMT in ayahuasca is probably responsible for the UFOs in Pablo Amaringo's paintings and in the reports of other ayahuasqueros. Profound DMT experiences—whether following ingestion of DMT from an outside source or from a natural stimulation of the pineal gland—force us to see the world in a radically different way. This appears to be something shamans have known for 40,000 years.

As for those who have experienced DMT in its more natural form of aya-huasca tea (as opposed to Strassman's injections), some claimed to have had no visions at all, and some found the experience unpleasant or even frightening. Precautions are always essential in the traditional use of the tea. The set and setting of the experience are carefully controlled, and all participants are required to follow "the diet," which is variously described in the literature. Most ayahuas-queros insist on the avoidance of carbohydrates, meat and salt. Sometimes rice, manioc and fish are recommended. Sex is usually forbidden. The main thing is to lower tryptophan levels in the bloodstream (usually found in carbohydrates) to prevent "serotonin syndrome," an acute physiological condition of distress that results from an overabundance of serotonin that may occur when the tea's inhibi-tion of MAO removes the main serotonin deactivator (Metzner 1999a: 28f). The symptoms of serotonin syndrome are nausea, vomiting, tremors, elevated tem-perature, cardiac arrhythmia and renal failure. In the most extreme cases, it can result in coma and death (Calloway 1999: 260).

Ayahuasca and the mammalian psyche

The most authoritative treatment of ayahuasca use is Benny Shanon's *The Antipodes of the Mind: Charting the Phenomenology of the Ayahuasca Experience* (2002). Shanon, a cognitive psychologist, is Professor of Psychology at the Hebrew University in Jerusalem. Over the course of a decade, he actively partici-pated in more than 130 ayahuasca sessions. His book is the first cognitive psycho-logical investigation of the ayahuasca experience, the first and only theoretical treatment, and is based on the largest collection of data. He believes that the non-ordinary experiential phenomena that ayahuasca induces present a new and uncharted natural cognitive domain,[3] perhaps something like the new "radio station" Pinchbeck (2002) describes. Shanon spent vacations and sabbaticals in Brazil and Peru because he found ayahuasca to be a "school and a teacher." He has mapped the course of his "schooling" and found that every series of sessions dealt with a different problem—though perhaps not identified until later—that confronted him with himself, produced a struggle he was often tempted to avoid, and ultimately changed him from a "devout atheist" to one convinced of the reality of a spiritual domain (Shanon 2002: 8).

While surveying his fellow drinkers of the ayahuasca brew, he found that asking them about their psychedelic experience was a bit like asking them about their sexual encounters, insofar as they were more likely to be open and generous with the details when they knew their questioner had had comparable experience (Shanon 2002: 43f). He lists the following typical reasons why people drink ayahuasca, and says he identifies with every one of them: for the joy of the experience, because it reveals true knowledge that is elsewhere unavailable, because it yields psychological insight and understanding, because it provides a sense of well-being, personal transformation and transcendence, because it puts one in touch with the sacred, and because it provides social coherence and cultural identity (Shanon 2002: 324–6).

Initial experiences

Joan Parisi Wilcox (2003) gives us a first-person account of initial experiences that she and her friends recall from ayahuasca sessions they had in the United States. Later some of them traveled to the Amazon forest for a more traditional series of sessions in a ritual context. These earliest experiences are valuable for what they tell us about the preliminary lessons to be had in the "school" of ayahuasca: "Bam! Reality shifted . . . I was assaulted with geometry, . . . complex patterns, spinning . . . their immensity was overwhelming, shocking, even terrifying" (Wilcox 2003: 19). With her eyes open, she saw geometric visions (phosphenes) imposed over the "'real world' . . . as if I were seeing two different worlds, both existing independently." She witnessed spheres that were simultaneously alive and mechanical, without personality but possessed of "awesome purpose." Her immersion in that alien world, she believed, was partial; she felt she would "face death" if she were to enter it fully (Wilcox 2003: 20–22). This "immensity" that threatened to "fry my circuits" brought her "the realization that I haven't got a clue—about myself, about the world, about reality, about anything" (Ibid., 55).

All the qualities we have touched upon—wondrous, strange, numinous, yet disturbingly "alien"—reside in Wilcox's early experiences. She seems to be faceto-face with death, evidently a universal feature of DMT. We also see the predominance of phosphenes that seem to have a life of their own and may form themselves into "the fantastic coils of an enormous serpent" to inspire "awe and humility" in the face of its "spiritual power" (Metzner 1999a). But other reporters recall even earlier reactions that were not at all visionary, but violently physical. F. Bruce Lamb (1985), who encountered ayahuasca while working as a forester in the Upper Amazon in 1960, says that a typical first reaction to the drug is a violent discharge of energy through the nervous system that may lead to a few minutes of abdominal convulsions, nausea, and powerful sexual arousal (Lamb 1985: 21).

He found that he could eventually achieve a "smooth and harmonious flow of energy." The ayahuasca "diet" was essential, but he also required "the constant tutelage of a master" to steer his experience by influencing the warps in his consciousness. Later he was able to follow ayahuasca on his own, for the brew itself directed his experience as a teacher (Lamb 1985: 134f). Shanon concurs, saying that the school of ayahuasca "has different classes . . . the notion of relatively ordered stages . . . within sessions and across sessions, over the course of one's accumulative experience with the brew" (Shanon 2002: 289).

Animals and the "fourth drive"

Our monophasic culture treats the use of psychoactive drugs as some sort of recent aberration that is entirely foreign to "nature." But we have seen that our ancestors from the Upper Paleolithic—and possibly much further back than that—have known and used consciousness-altering substances and rituals. Indeed, we have considered the phylogenetic roots of consciousness-changing rituals, with the knowledge that our human brain functions much the same as that of our primate, canine, feline, and cetacean cousins. They must feel pretty much the same as we do when they engage in their rituals; they, too, have learned to tune their autonomic nervous systems. The same is true of consciousness-altering herbs and mushrooms. Those who have investigated the pursuit of intoxication by wild animals believe our four-legged relatives have enjoyed such plants far longer than we have. Many have concluded that humans discovered coffee, tea, khat, iboga, fly agaric, and other mind-altering plants by observing animals seeking them out. We might wish to believe that modern humans lived for millennia in sober ignorance of such things until a few of our perhaps rebellious or reckless ancestors began to watch the chimpanzees, goats and reindeer. But realistically, if we take evolution seriously, we would have to guess that our first human ancestors knew about these things because their parents did—for that "generation" belonged to the species that is ancestor both to us and to the chimpanzees. We knew what all animals knew, both before and after the species-divide.

After examining thousands of non-human animals, psychopharmacologist Ronald K. Siegel (1989: 13) says he is "convinced that seeking intoxication is natural behavior in the animal kingdom." All of us mammals have opiate receptors in our brains. Somewhere along the line of evolution, some early species invested energy in producing those receptors. Because there was already something in the environment to "receive," animals with the receptors had a survival advantage over those who did not. The receptors and the altered states of consciousness they make possible have been favored by natural selection (R. K. Siegel 1989: 100).

Ronald Siegel (1989) and Giorgio Samorini (2000) have collected hundreds of stories of animals deliberately seeking out certain leaves, roots, flowers and fruits for their ability to alter consciousness. For example, gorillas, boars and porcupines dig up the bitter roots of the iboga shrub for the ibogaine they contain.

Ibogaine is a tryptamine-based molecule, a relative of DMT, as are most psycho-active alkaloids. The biochemistry of these animals is essentially the same as ours, and their willingness to tolerate unpleasant tastes and symptoms in order to change their consciousness also resembles ours (R. K. Siegel 1989: 65). Reindeer not only seek out the fly agaric mushroom, but also are aware that the urine of those who have eaten the mushroom contains an even better form of the active ingredi-ent. Thus travelers are warned against urinating in the open when reindeer are present, and every Koryak man carries a sealskin vessel of his own urine to attract "refractory reindeer" (Dobkin de Rios 1990: 32; R. K. Siegel 1989: 66f). One final example: the huge, heavy durian fruit of Asia falls to the ground and ferments, where it is eagerly sought by elephants, monkeys, orangutans, honey bears, squir-rels, flying foxes and tigers, as well as humans. Tigers have been known to attack children carrying the fruit, but only to steal the source of intoxication, leaving the children unharmed (Samorini 2000: 29).

The abundance of such evidence has led Siegel to describe a "fourth drive," alongside the basic three of hunger, thirst, and sex. The fourth drive is the desire to rapidly change one's mental state through the pursuit of intoxicants. It is "no more abnormal than the pursuit of love, social attachments, thrills, power, or any number of other acquired motives . . . [it] cannot be repressed. It is biologically inevitable" (R. K. Siegel 1989: 209f). Evidently intoxication is a form of "decon-ditioning [that] allows for new behavioral ways to be established in a species." Even if only a few individuals in a species seek out intoxication, they represent an *essential minority* (Samorini 2000: ix–xi).

Many have asked a more fundamental question, not only whether intoxication may be an essential fourth drive for mammals and perhaps birds, but also what is the nature of this evolutionary peculiarity. Those plant alkaloids that provide healing and insight and help us discover new survival strategies are produced at a tremendous expense by plants who appear to derive no benefit for their own sur-vival. The plants build molecules that are close analogues of the neurotransmitters found in mammalian brains, molecules that alter the function of those brains in marvelous ways. But it is not at all clear that the plants need them for their own purposes. This is a "strange symbiosis" (Metzner 1999c: 290)—perhaps "an inter-species communication" (Devereux 1997: 242).[4]

Transformation and the goal

Not all users of ayahuasca have glowing tales to tell. Many people never get "beyond the puffs, bursts and splashes of light" that constitute the first stage, as defined by Masters and Houston (1966). "Only a small minority experience full-fledged visions—often those that do not experience them the first few times, do not consume [the brew] further" (Shanon 2002: 98). Some that do, go on say that after about two years the visions diminish, but long-term drinkers report an increase in insights, and spiritually uplifting perspectives (Shanon 2002: 137). Post-modern anthropologist Michael Taussig (1987) has famously said, "*Yagé* lies" (using the

Tukano word for ayahuasca). Shanon (2002: 246) agrees that ayahuasqueros can find the truth in their visions and or be misled by them. Clearly it is not the psychoactive plant molecules that bear the truth. Rather truth and falsity belong to what we choose to do with the experience. In similar fashion, Jung is believed to have said, "Intuition is a hundred percent reliable fifty percent of the time."[5]

Benny Shanon (2002: 95–111, 293ff) outlines fourteen "progressive stages" in the school of ayahuasca. More simply, he tells us he divides his work into three "cycles" of sessions. His first sixty-seven sessions comprise the first cycle, when he appears to have gone through the stages outlined by Masters and Houston (1966). First he was exposed to a general idea of the wonders that were in store for him, then he had to learn to handle the experiences. This would be the first stage of mastery. Then he learned to heal diseases—first hand, since he was the patient cured of his malaria. At the end of the first cycle, he had begun to learn shamanism by serving as an apprentice. In his second cycle, roughly the next sixty sessions, he became a director of ayahuasca sessions, learned to become attentive to changes in consciousness through observing others, and learned about the nature of the mind, consciousness, and mysticism. At the time his book was published, he had just begun his third cycle of sessions (Shanon 2002: 302).

Strassman (2001) summarizes his follow-up conversations with DMT volunteers by saying that they had developed a strong sense of themselves, a diminished fear of death, and a greater appreciation for life. Some said they were better able to relax and were less driven in everyday life. Some said they drank less alcohol, others that they had a greater certainty that reality is much more layered, that their perspectives had become broader and deeper (Strassman 2001: 274). Metzner says that ayahuasca helps people see one another and themselves better. They learn to think more clearly about relationships, the nature of the cosmos, and their own place in it (Metzner 1999c: 278).

Shanon reports that, overall, ayahuasca makes people think and reflect and integrate their insights into a comprehensive, unified picture of self and world (Shanon 2002: 162). Ayahuasca has the specific effect of interesting people in the origin of the universe and the laws that govern the natural world (Shanon 2002: 169). Clearly, their thinking begins to take on a mythic quality, in the sense that their "cognitive imperative," as the biogenetic structuralists would call it, begins to try to assimilate all the visionary experiences they have had and to integrate them with the empirical world they live in every day. Ayahuasqueros become aware that consciousness is not merely personal, but also transpersonal and non-individual, and that the inner and outer worlds are not distinct (Shanon 2002: 206–8).

These are views that Jung insists upon throughout his *Collected Works*. Ayahuasca clearly takes people in the direction that Jung believed we need to go, but most of our authors seem to miss this. Thus Shanon (2002: 391) says: "Empirically the Jungian data parallel those revealed by ayahuasca visions, yet theoretically, the Jungian archetypes fail to explain the concrete commonalities of contents in both ayahuasca visions and other materials that Jung himself investigated." It is hard to imagine what Shanon objects to, here. If archetypes are understood as we have described them, as top-to-bottom structures, in which the "ultraviolet" top imagines and recognizes in terms of collective images and the "infrared" bottom is comprised of inherited neural networks and other structures that are common to all human beings, then ayahuasca visions ought to have much in common with the mythology, dreams, and Gnostic and alchemical images that fill Jung's writings. And they do.

If Shanon, however, wonders why ayahuasca visions feature so many "serpents, palaces, and objects of gold," these have been consistently identified by Jung as images of the self; and as such, they suggest that ayahuasca visions will probably have the effect of revealing the transpersonal and impersonal nature of consciousness and the fact that inner and outer worlds are not distinct.

They lead, in short, to ultimate visions concerning the nature of the self and the cosmos. But this is precisely what Shanon (2002: 164) says of ayahuasca experience: that it provides a metaphysical perspective that resembles Hindu philosophy and perennial philosophy. He also reports that several of his informants said that they had "discovered that God was beyond good and evil, or that he encompasses both good and evil (2002: 178). As we have repeatedly seen, this is precisely Jung's conclusion (*coincidentia oppositorum*).

Ayahuasca and mastery

At a typical mestizo vegetalista ceremony, people gather two to four hours in advance of drinking the brew, and the leaders tell stories to prepare the participants for the visionary experiences they may have. Here the "set and setting" for altered states is established as dignified, spiritual, belonging to ancient tradition, and open to visions of deep import. Luna (1986) says: "The shaman is not only the one who 'sees,' but also the one who knows how to tell what he has seen, and to do it in such a way that people will also see it" (Luna 1986: 142). Storytelling itself is a powerful means of altering consciousness.

Depending on the devotion of the leader, there may be prayers to Christ, to God the Creator, and to the Virgin Mary, invocations that invite the highest representatives of the sacred realm to be present. Then each participant is given about 50ml of the thick tea and all but one of the lamps are blown out. When the shaman begins to feel the effects of the brew, 20–30 minutes later, he starts to shake his rattle and whistle an ayahuasca song (an "icaro"). For the next 40–60 minutes, people view their visions in silence and near darkness. Occasionally people will leave to vomit or defecate and return. When the hallucinations begin to come in waves, chants begin under the leadership of the shaman, with an invitation for the participants to join in if they know the tunes (Luna 1986: 146–8).

Preliminary requirements for mastery

Such preparations are designed to shape the expectations of the participants toward having a healthy and positively transforming experience filled with visions. The shaman provides suggestions designed to ease the participants into an experience that is safely contained by social cohesion (the physiological and cognitive effects of the preliminary ritual) and by the sense that they are in the hands of a benevolent deity, with a personified Ayahuasca taking that role for those who do not impose a Christian structure on the experience. Autonomic nervous system tuning is the underlying goal of the preliminaries. Even so, when the drug takes effect, one is apt to feel a very strong "Bam!" Violent physiological reactions are the rule, especially for those who are least experienced, and the imagery itself is usually terrifying. People may find themselves turning into jaguars against their will, being devoured by boas or having boas crawling into their mouths. In the face of such assaults, "it is necessary to be calm and not to be afraid of the visions" (Luna 1986: 153). There is much that will be terrifying, but it is essential "to master one's hallucinations" (Narby 1999: 147). The shamanic "gnosis must be earned" (Pinchbeck 2002: 143).

Calmly submitting to an onslaught that would be overwhelming for any unassisted human ego is a common requirement of certain religious practices. In the tantric traditions, a practitioner may heroically dare everything that is terrifying, disgusting or sexually provocative—anything that threatens to arouse the sympathetic nervous system to the limit, that is to the point of spillover, when the parasympathetic system begins to take over. During this time, it is essential for the aspirant to steadily and calmly observe her own consciousness (cf. Haule 1999b: Chapters 6 and 7). In a much quieter manner, the same approach was taken by St. Francis of Assisi (Haule 2004). The essential piece in profiting from such over-stimulation is to manage an attitude of equanimity. Jung calls it "holding the tension" in expectation that the "transcendent function," one's own principle of balance and wholeness, will provide a transformative vision. This is the first requirement of mastery: calm contemplation of an over-stimulated situation.

Finding a balance

Holding the tension sufficiently to view potentially overwhelming imagery without losing one's equanimity is a notable achievement, but it is inherently passive. When describing active imagination, Jung argues that one must not simply observe the imagery but get actively involved. This, he says, is the essential difference between passive and active imagination (*CW7*: ¶368f). Pablo Amaringo, the Peruvian shaman-become-painter, makes very much the same point, when he says:

> It is only when the person begins to hear and see as if he/she were inside the scene, not as something presented to him, that he is able to discover many things. . . . I saw how the world is created, how everything is filled with life, how great spirits intervene in every aspect of nature and make the universe expand.

> (Luna and Amaringo 1993: 27)

Getting involved in the action, however, has to be done with a certain restraint; otherwise ordinary ego-consciousness may obstruct the process. Over-reliance upon ordinary mental states is very likely the reason so many who participate in ayahuasca ceremonies fail to see visions at all, or find that after a time they disappear. There appears to be a fine balance one needs to find between an active participation that goes too far and reestablishes ordinary consciousness, on the one hand, and a passive letting-be in which one never learns anything on the other.

Pinchbeck (2002) addresses this issue in saying that he searched for a "psychic space between willing and letting go." Too much of either extreme resulted in his losing the visions altogether. "There was, I realized, a skill to perceiving them, an initial effort that required utilizing a form of visionary seeing that was disconnected from normal sight" (Pinchbeck 2002: 142). Those who learn to find this balance and can return to it with some confidence may have arrived at a point Shanon (2002) describes. He had been an amateur pianist since childhood, but he had never been able to play without pages of printed music. After a few ayahuasca sessions, however, and the training they provide in holding a psychic balance, he suddenly developed a spontaneity at the piano that allowed him to improvise endlessly upon Bach variations. He describes it as a balance and a flow between two poles: deep immersion in piano playing together with a reflective distance. To master ayahuasca, he says, is pretty much the same. One must find a balance between fear and vanity (Shanon 2002: 252f).

Tuning the warps

The primary means by which American shamans tune their own warps and those of ritual participants and patients is through song. Songs, understood as gifts from the spirit realm—acquired in altered states of consciousness while on vision quests or while practicing shamanism—are nearly universal among the native peoples of the Americas. In the Andes, the word for a shamanic song is "icaro," from the Quechua verb *ikaray*, which means "to blow smoke in order to heal" (Luna 1986: 100). Becoming a vegetalista is nearly synonymous with learning a large number of icaros and how to use them. The melodies and words of a shaman's icaros modify the effects of ayahuasca by applying emotional pressure to the warps in people's consciousness. Luna (1986: 105) tells us the intensity of visions can be increased or diminished, their colors changed, their emotions shaped—even the *structure* of the visions altered. Shanon (2002) says that in the use of ayahuasca, music functions as an *axis mundi*, a "world axis," which not only joins the three cosmic planes into a single experiential unity, but also provides the pathway by which shamans move from one plane to another while entranced (Shanon 2002: 313; cf. Eliade 1964).

Shamans master their own entranced consciousness by using their icaros in a manner that Dan Merkur (1992) would surely describe as "auto-hypnotic." They are a means of manipulating for oneself the intensity, imaginal content, and emotional engagement with the visions. Luna says that a shaman's repertoire of icaros has its own hierarchy, with the individual's "principal icaro" at the top—the song that represents the essence of the shaman's power. One of Luna's shaman-informants, Don Alejandro, told him that "if a vegetalista manages to learn the main icaro of another practitioner, he will inherit his knowledge upon the latter's death (Luna 1986: 109).

Protective songs, "icaros arkanas," are used by the shaman to reduce the danger of exposure to powerful spirit entities inevitably encountered during a cure: "When a vegetalista is healing or when he enters other dimensions through the ingestion of psychotropic plants, he is particularly vulnerable and exposed to the attacks of agents that cause illness" (Luna 1986: 107). Even if we retain our Western monophasic mentality and assume all illnesses that are curable by shamans must be essentially psychosomatic, we can still appreciate that entering an imaginal realm where the psychosomatic forces exist would be dangerous for doctor as well as patient. Without trying to name such agents, apart from acknowledging that they must be archetypal, it is easy to see that what infects the patient might also carry the danger of contagion for the doctor. Recall how contagious we find lust, depression, hilarity and anger to be when we are in ordinary states of consciousness. Psychoanalysts are keenly aware of the fact of contagion. Jung mentions it frequently (cf., also, Haule 1993; Searles 1979).

F. Bruce Lamb's informant, Don Manuel Córdoba, a mestizo who had been captured by Native Americans earlier in his life and learned shamanism from them, says clearly[6] that he uses icaros to tune his warps:

> They actually initiate and channel the flow of visions. Later as the scene progresses, it seems that half-learned, half-spontaneous chants sway the sequence and content of the internal vision message. My impression is that all this material flows from a pre-conscious level or perhaps even from some outside source.
>
> (Lamb 1985: 135)

The shaman Don Manuel also demonstrates his ability to tune the warps of others' consciousness when he uses his icaros to give a man named Izidoro the experience of being transformed into a black jaguar—in return for Izidoro's teaching Córdoba how to make curare:

> Imitating all the jaguar sounds my Indian captors had taught me, interspersed with precise songs and chants, I brought the black jaguar into our visions. . . . Gradually, Izidoro seemed to blend with the body of the black cat. They wandered off into the forest and I followed in my dreams. . . . that big cat showed my Tikuna friend things you would not believe.
>
> (Lamb 1985: 135)

Joan Parisi Wilcox (2003) provides a distinctly layperson's perspective. She says she found the icaros of her teacher, Don Luis, to be "mesmerizing"—even when she had not drunk any ayahuasca. Although she did not understand the words of the songs, for they were a mixture of Spanish and Quechua, she found that her consciousness was steered in the direction of "a dreamy sort of state." "The sounds and rhythms, complemented by the steady swishing of his *schacapa*-leaf rattle, were sonorous and undulating, and they lulled me into a place within that was unfocused, malleable, less defined by ego" (Wilcox 2003: 15). The singing, humming, and whistling of Don Luis became strongly associated in Wilcox's mind with the altered states induced by ayahuasca, and she found that she had learned unconsciously to tune her awareness: "I often find myself whistling [such icaros] under my breath, and whenever I do, it is almost as if I can taste ayahuasca, which inevitably causes my body to involuntarily shudder in revulsion" (Wilcox 2003: 17).

The shadow-world of ayahuasca

An apprentice shaman who learns to cultivate equanimity and remain calm in the face of physiological and visionary shocks, one who reliably finds the balance point between activity and passivity while in altered states, and one who learns a repertoire of icaros to fine-tune the warps between phases of trance: such a one is not necessarily a success. The first and most basic danger of establishing a reliable connection with the spirit world is that one may forget or even relinquish the world of ordinary consciousness and never return to family and friends. Luna (1986) says this lamentable state can be described as a permanent alliance with a malignant spirit that makes one lose interest in the ordinary world. Regardless of the explanation for it, this condition represents a significant psychological danger. Widespread acquaintance with such cases is implied by the rock art of North and South America where an individual who has never returned is depicted with feet turned back-to-front (Luna 1986: 87). One can learn, then, to negotiate the spirit world while losing this one. It is a condition indistinguishable from madness.

Thus the first lesson to learn from the existence of the shadow-world is that one needs to find a balance between life in the two worlds. It is surely more crucial than learning to negotiate the spirit world itself. Ayahuasqueros say that the spirit world is hostile to humans, and a shaman has to learn a great deal about relating to spirits if real benefits are to be gained (Luna 1986: 120). The *second*, and related, lesson the shadow-world imposes is the obligation to manage one's own self-centeredness. The knowledge and power a shaman acquires constitutes its own pitfall, for the more power one has, the greater will be the temptation to misuse it (Luna 1986: 118). Misuse generally takes the form of self-aggrandizement, using acquired powers for one's own fame and fortune or in the interests of vengeance. The power to do good is always accompanied by an equal power to do evil; increasing that power through mastery of altered states only increases the danger.

> Don Emilio says that the spirits of the plants offer the neophyte great powers and gifts with which he may cause harm. If the apprentice is weak and accepts them, he will become a witch. Only later the spirits present other kinds of gifts, for healing or for performing love magic.
>
> (Luna 1986: 116)

The yoga tradition is aware of this danger, too. Extraordinary powers (*siddhis*) are often acquired as one gains mastery over one's meditative states. They are a danger to spiritual progress, for the temptation to use them for short-term gains may become too great, and the aspirant will fail to reach his mystical goals.

We have seen this theme already in the story of Pablo Amaringo, who relinquished shamanism and ayahuasca and took up painting his visions when it became obvious that a vengeful woman would lose no opportunity to injure him through her manipulations of the spirit world. It became clear to him that if he did not wish to suffer more attacks, he would have to kill the woman. He refused to do so and gave up shamanizing instead. In a less drastic incident, Luna (1986: 125) reports that the shaman Don Emilio would refuse to treat a patient if he discovered that the shaman who caused the illness was stronger than he. He would advise such a patient to find another vegetalista.[7]

The practice of shamanic healing itself is often experienced as a great struggle on the spiritual plane with the forces of darkness. Shamans, however, take on such battles only when ordinary means are insufficient. Luna (1986: 122) tells us that the preliminaries of a shamanic cure involve diagnosis to determine whether the illness is "natural" or "magical." The patient is questioned about his own condition, and then his family is questioned about his financial and emotional condition. Only when the illness is found to be magical does the shaman consult the "doctores," the plant-teachers and spirits. Ideally in the course of treatment, the patients will be "forced to self-reflection about their lives as a whole, and the emotional and social tensions to which they are subject" (Luna 1986: 122).

Even so, the cure may be a harrowing experience for the shaman. Lamb's informant, Don Manuel, says, "Ayahuasca, it tells you how, but by itself it cures nothing directly" (Lamb 1986: 127). When Don Manuel determines that a session with ayahuasca is necessary for a cure, he retires to his hammock and brings his wife, Nieves, who sits in her cane rocking chair, keeping an all-night vigil over her entranced husband. He drinks ayahuasca, lies down, and begins humming his icaros. He describes the experience of a typical night:

> a soft ringing in the ears, sometimes a slight muscular shock, and then color visions progressing into a shimmering golden aura. . . . with songs and chants I only half remembered afterwards—I directed the course of my visions to my young patient. In the heightened state of perception brought on by my trance, every function of her body was apparent to me.
>
> (Lamb 1986: 85)

The next morning at breakfast, Nieves tells Lamb that she saw some of her husband's visions, particularly the patient's black and swollen liver and then the flowers Don Manuel was to use in treating her. "Many times, dozing there as he chanted to himself, I have seen his visions, also. It is an awesome and frightening thing just to experience a part of it (Lamb 1986: 158).

Chapter 6

Meditation and mastery

We have considered shamanism at some length because, first, it is a continuous tradition extending back at least to our Upper Paleolithic ancestors and very likely much further back in human history, and second, shamanism is not possible unless altered states of consciousness can be mastered. Our Western monophasic culture wishes to marginalize or invalidate altered states with what looks superficially like hard-headed scientific realism. In fact, however, our culture's attitude constitutes an unexamined form of dogmatism that cavalierly excludes a use of human consciousness that has been vital to human survival for 40,000 years at a minimum. Our sketch of the history of human consciousness in Volume 1 showed that altered states were fundamentally responsible for the integration and expansion of the human mind in the Upper Paleolithic and also for many insights into daily living and the management of the empirical world during the Neolithic—as appears to be the case regarding the domestication of plants and animals. A trend, however, away from reliance upon altered states began before the agricultural revolution, when hunter-gatherer societies started becoming complex, and economic and political power began to marginalize spontaneous discoveries by individual shamans. The trend grew with the rise of empires, including the ecclesiastically driven Holy Roman Empire, and really took off with the empirical-science revolution of the last 350 years. We have learned much by applying our analytical skills to the empirical world, but our understanding of ourselves and our place in the world has seriously suffered.

Monophasic culture's rejection of altered states as a legitimate field of inquiry is as blind as the fundamentalist religious movements that would forbid certain fields of scientific inquiry. In view of this situation, our overview of shamanic techniques for mastering altered states is meant to serve as a call to a greater scientific openness. We need a vigorous investigation of the nature of altered states and the means by which they may be mastered; we need to discover how to use them reliably and what they can contribute to our human existence on a planet that is truly becoming a global village. It is time to turn our Western analytical consciousness back upon itself. It is time to study, to map and to experiment with our capacities for non-ordinary consciousness in a rigorous manner. Personal transformation, the re-enchantment of the world, finding a balanced way of understanding ourselves and our planet have become matters of life and death, now at the beginning of the twenty-first century. Our neglected talents, if developed, will be important assets in finding our way forward.

Shamanism, however, is not the only tradition to demonstrate that non-ordinary states can be mastered. Meditation does, too, and it has very deep roots in our past. By some interpretations of the evidence from archaeology and India's sacred ancient texts, the Vedas, a yogic type of meditation may be more than 6000 years old (Feuerstein *et al.* 1995). It is very likely, in fact, that the meditative traditions are rooted in shamanistic practices that are typical of hunter-gatherer societies and may, therefore, stretch much further back into our history as *Homo sapiens* (Hunt 1995: 282).[1]

Mastering meditative states of consciousness

Meditation, like shamanism, achieves altered states of consciousness by tuning the autonomic nervous system. But meditation tunes it in the opposite direction. Shamanic ritual induction ceremonies typically begin by stimulating the sympathetic nervous system with a rhythmic beat and dancing. Most participants in the ritual experience a brief ecstasy within which a problem characterized by a disparity between myth and the issues of daily life finds a solution that satisfies ordinary consciousness (d'Aquili and Laughlin 1979: 177). The shaman, whose sympathetic arousal proceeds to the point of spillover, remains in the entranced state much longer than other ritual participants and finds much more detailed solutions. By contrast, meditators stimulate the parasympathetic nervous system by sleep deprivation, fasting, sensory deprivation, and other austerities (Winkelman 2000: 125). Reliance on the parasympathetic system enables adepts in the meditative disciplines to maintain their ecstatic states. In the most successful instances, the spillover is from the parasympathetic to the sympathetic, which eventually results in a strong discharge from *both* parts of the autonomic system (d'Aquili and Laughlin 1979: 176f). When stimulation begins with the sympathetic system, as in shamanism, spillover usually involves exhaustion of the sympathetic system so that strong discharges come only from the parasympathetic system. In contrast, the dual discharges that occur in the most successful of meditative states are more likely to provide unitary states, such as oneness with God or the cosmos (d'Aquili and Newberg 1999).

Training our attention

Most of us human beings, most of the time, live in a mindless and unconscious manner. We identify with our ego, which is only a small part of our whole being. We maintain our ordinary consciousness by constantly talking to ourselves about our habitual preoccupations, and rarely if ever catch ourselves in the act of doing so. We are extremely vulnerable to the suggestions and expectations of our society and culture, and tend to think and act as "everyone" does, thoughtlessly participating in a collective mindset that resembles a "culturally induced hypnosis." By contrast, meditation trains our attention and enables us to attend to the moment with greater concentration and awareness (Winkelman 2000: 169). Seen from this angle, the difference between shamanism and meditation is huge; for shamanic states of consciousness are characterized by immersion in an overwhelming vastness and complexity of image and emotion, while meditative states are more likely to be detached and stable (Laughlin *et al.* 1990: 277).[2]

The first effect of training our attention by years of meditation is that we more easily become aware of the state of our consciousness in everyday life. We are more sharply attuned to moments when our attention wanders, when it picks up collective notions from the social world in which we live. We become more aware of who we are beneath the kaleidoscopic ideas, images and emotions imposed by our environment. Winkelman (2000: 228f) lists a variety of specific conscious traits that a meditation practice promotes: increased refinement and sensitivity in our visual and auditory perceptions, increase in the speed and accuracy of perceptual/ motor skills, and increased awareness of mental processes that are usually unconscious in people who do not train their attention with meditation. These improvements in ability to attend also have important implications for improving our lives. They provide us insight into areas where we have been "stuck" and assist in "self-actualization," i.e. becoming the unique individual that each of us potentially is; for we discover a larger context within which to understand the pressures of our social conditioning and related anxieties. All these results make it clear that meditation helps us increase the stability and precision of our attention, opening up a larger field of consciousness, not only during periods of meditation but also in the rest of our waking life.[3]

The decision to remain in the temple

John McManus (1979), one of the biogenetic structuralists, reports that beginners at meditation typically alternate between sympathetic nervous system dominance—which is normative for ordinary waking consciousness and characterized by rapid and erratic beta EEG waves—and a desired condition, when the parasympathetic system dominates and everything slows down, as brain waves fall into a more regular alpha pattern. At some point, after long effort and steady discipline, "a decision is made at some level" and "the mind remains in the temple" (McManus 1979a: 210f). The "decision" is not made consciously, we find it made *for* us, and we simply find ourselves the recipients of some "grace."

Clearly the "decision" to remain in the temple of slow brain waves and inter-hemispheric harmony is not made by the conscious will and has nothing to do with the language area of the left hemisphere. Still, words may be involved in setting up the brain-and-psyche shift. One thinks, for example, of meditation techniques that require us to count our breaths and even to visualize the numerals as we breathe. McManus' colleague in the biogenetic structuralism project, Barbara Lex, tells us that the repetition of a mantra (a short phrase usually given by one's teacher) monopolizes the left hemisphere, preventing it from dominating brain function and allowing the right hemisphere to function freely (Lex 1979: 126). Mantras and similar activities are, therefore, tuning exercises.

Jungian analyst and long-time meditator Walter Odajnyk (1993) refers to this process as "deautomatization." He means that we do many things automatically and without thought. Daily routines that maintain the familiar waking world function largely outside the range of our attention. They have been "relegated" to lower levels of brain-and-psyche and keep us in a relatively low state of awareness that may seem almost robotic to those who have trained their attention with meditation. To bring our habitual activities out of the automatic zone, therefore, is "to free up the psychic energy that normally flows into our habitual responses," and to cut the ego loose from automatic supports that allow it to operate at a low level of attention (Odajnyk 1993: 57). He gives us an example of what such de-habituating does for the meditator by citing an experiment that compared non-meditators with Zen monks. Both groups were subjected to the sound of a click repeated every fifteen seconds. The lay people habituated to it within five minutes; that is, they automatically tuned it out of their awareness. But the Zen monks did not. After five minutes, their response to the last click was the same as to the first.

The phenomenon of habituation or automatization has much to do with the unconsciousness of our everyday lives. We screen out whatever our worldview or habitual attitude disregards as irrelevant. This keeps the world artificially constant and free of surprises, dulls our attention and limits our ability to remain fully aware in the moment. Therefore, what McManus (1979a) describes as the decision to remain in the temple of meditation may also be called maintaining a steady state of alert attention or refusing to allow our attention to be dulled by habituation. Meditation masters a non-ordinary state of consciousness, hones it well and renders it more effective than the familiar states of awareness our culture erroneously believes to be normative for sanity and definitive of an adequate orientation to reality.

Mastering terror

Much of meditation training has to do with dethroning the everyday ego, the center and primary agent of ordinary consciousness. What was said above makes such demotion seem to be a wholly desirable undertaking. But when the ego's habitual supports are successfully removed, terror is the usual response. As with apprentice shamans, profoundly altered states of consciousness are apt to provoke a crisis in a novice meditator. But while the terror in shamanic training is usually associated with an overwhelmingly full visionary field, the terror experienced in meditation is often provoked by radical emptiness.

Odajnyk (1993) reports on an experiment done with meditators advanced enough to hold their attention steadily on a blue vase. For one female subject, it soon became clear that "decisions" were being made by someone other than her ego. She experienced the vase disappearing into a diffuse blue visual field. Apparently she was not disturbed by this first alteration, as she continued to keep her attention steady. Terror overtook her, however, as soon as she found herself merging with the blue field. Incipient merging made her feel she was falling into emptiness and caused her to be overwhelmed with feelings of loneliness and isolation. The shock brought her back to ordinary consciousness. Odajnyk (1993: 58) comments, "Had she overcome her anxiety and let herself merge with the emptiness, she would have had an enlightenment experience, and the fear would have turned to awe."

Odajnyk (1993) claims that merging with emptiness would amount to becoming "egoless." But it might be well to examine that claim. The woman's experience of terror proves that her ego is still with her, observing something unthinkable and quaking at the prospect. If she had somehow overcome that terror and merged with the blue field, the observer would presumably have disappeared. Logic would seem to tell us that there would be blueness but no observer to see it, in which case we could say that she would be "egoless." But if so, who is experiencing the "awe"? It would probably be more accurate to say that the woman experienced terror at the prospect of her familiar ego's having lost all its habitual supports. Its sense of being a stable entity, separate from all other persons and objects, seemed about to disappear.[4] The moment everything familiar and supportive falls away, we face an existential crisis, similar to that of the near-death experiencers, those who believe they have been abducted by aliens, and Strassman's DMT subjects.[5]

Success in meditation can be as profoundly unsettling as a series of ayahuasca visions. The terror it inspires is the subjective experience of a highly aroused sympathetic nervous system. Meditators who can maintain their equanimity in the face of such arousal will experience the spillover effect of parasympathetic arousal, and their fear will turn into awe. But they will not necessarily have lost their ego. Biogenetic structuralists d'Aquili and Newberg (1999) have a lot to say about unitive experiences but not much about becoming egoless. Nelson Pike (1992: 162–6), however, engages the question seriously and concludes that real mystic union, where oneness thoroughly overcomes the duality of subject and object, has to be blank, like being knocked out by a baseball. The mystic differs from the ordinary individual by knowing what happened to him after he returns from the blankness, because he remembers what he was doing when it happened and has an explanation for having gone blank.

The identity of the meditator

Ego is clearly a vague term that is used for a variety of overlapping and sometimes even conflicting realities. It may not make sense to talk of becoming "egoless"; and, indeed, it often seems that when mystics talk of becoming egoless they may simply mean to describe a way of living that renounces being "attached" to the "fruits" of their actions as the Bhagavad-Gita puts it (XVIII, 9).[6] The Gita seems to mean that while an ordinary everyday ego acts in hopes of achieving specific results and becomes elated if those results are attained and depressed or angry if they are not, the mystic seeks to replace this "I-maker" (*ahamkara* in Sanskrit) and trains his attention to observe without the attachments caused by ordinary desires and assumptions. This is why the first rule in meditation is neither to oppose nor to hold onto the disturbances that inevitably arise when one tries to meditate. Just observe; let distractions come and go; do not pursue them.

Edmund Husserl sought to become relatively egoless, too, when he philosophized. He came up with the expression "transcendental ego" to name a conscious agent that had placed ordinary reality in "brackets," suspended everyday functioning with its reliance upon unexamined socio-cultural conditioning, in order to attend "to the things themselves," precisely what comes to presence in our conscious field. He claimed this meditation-like move—insofar as it requires training in holding the attention steady—liberates us from the everyday illusion that we are isolated subjects encountering isolated objects. Rather, what is *real* is the encounter itself, the moment of seeing and being seen. Having developed the psychological technique of the *epoché*, Husserl wished to proceed to its application: what is a blue vase or a passing moment, when seen from the perspective of the transcendental ego?

Training himself to use the transcendental ego is an introvertive move insofar as Husserl's attention is removed from the object of everyday interest (the blue vase that everyone can see sitting on the table) to his *consciousness of* the blue vase. But he then deliberately introduces into this field of examination a variety of matters that philosophy traditionally considers. This abiding interest in the world at large resembles, in a strange way, what the ayahuasqueros sometimes do with their psychedelic states of consciousness. First, sometimes they add an unknown herb to the ayahuasca brew with the intention of learning what that herb has to teach them about itself. They say that their extraordinary knowledge of plants has been taught them by the plants themselves, while they were in altered states of consciousness. Second, in healing ceremonies like that of Don Manuel Córdoba, described above, the shaman enters an ayahuasca trance to survey the physical and mental condition of his patient.

Therefore, while Husserl's transcendental ego resembles the ayahuasquero's shamanic consciousness in its employment for extravertive purposes, Jung's actively imagining ego is more radically introvertive. His move away from ordinary consciousness to learn that he does not create his thoughts but has them given him is very similar to Husserl's. But Jung's intention was to retain the introvertive stance and to learn what it is that is given to him autonomously. In active imagination, we are the recipients of processes that are mostly unconscious. Activated neural networks that pass largely unnoticed by the everyday ego—except perhaps for unaccountable moods, sudden hunches, slips of the tongue, and the like—occupy the field of active imagination and are seen by this "other ego." Probably the main difference between Husserl's transcendental ego and the observer of Jung's active imagination is that Husserl wished to *choose* the objects his transcendental ego would encounter and learn to describe, whereas Jung's active imagination was radically open for whatever would appear. Jung wished to learn what new and unexpected internal processes would reveal themselves, and for this reason began with an empty conscious field.

Thus it appears that in shamanism, meditation, Husserlian phenomenology, and active imagination, the fundamental move is not to "become egoless" but rather to train up another observing agent, an alternative or transcendental ego, one whose gaze is fixed upon consciousness itself. The existence of this new form of ego becomes the primary factor in "changing the nature of identity," as Winkelman calls it. Its existence helps to deconstruct the sense of permanence the "I-maker" ascribes to itself. It aids in our unlearning the socio-cultural conditioning and automatic processing that have narrowed the scope of our awareness and made it "monophasic." And, finally, it assists us in our attempts to become aware of unconscious processes that normally underlie our ordinary and unreflective consciousness of being an ego (Winkelman 2000: 172). We always do return to a form of ordinary consciousness. But if exercises in training our attention have been successful, everyday consciousness is bound to expand. "After some proficiency in meditation, most people report that upon their return to ordinary reality the world looks new—brighter, cleaner, more vivid and alive" (Odajnyk 1993: 55).

The new observing agent that is trained and installed during an apprenticeship in meditation, shamanism, active imagination and phenomenology operates very much like a complex. It takes on a quality of reliability to which we can gain easy access. Odajnyk (1993: 51) describes what every meditator experiences, once a certain minimal facility has been gained, "The concentration continues subliminally and of its own accord even after one has stopped meditating." Meditation begins with effort, creates stable neural networks and then "relegates" them to a position of reliable automaticity. Those who meditate on their breathing, for instance, will find that eventually their breathing happens on its own. In ordinary consciousness, when we are aware of our breathing, and even of counting our breaths, we have the sense that *we* are doing it, that we are directing every inhalation and exhalation. But when the switch has been made to that other agent, the meditation complex, we discover that "we are being breathed."

Mastering attention in meditation, then, can usefully be described as deliberately creating a complex that has its own autonomous characteristics. Just as the neurotic complexes we discussed in Volume 1 become easily "constellated" when a typical situation arises that stirs up a familiar feeling-tone, so the meditation complex begins concentrating its attention effortlessly. Repeated sittings in meditation provide a history of meditative experiences, solidifying the meditation complex—as do repeated shamanic journeyings and repeated forays into active imagination. The meditation complex, therefore, is built up by accumulated experience, much as are the neurotic complexes. But while neurotic complexes narrow and distort reality, the meditation complex opens, broadens and deepens us to a larger reality. Furthermore, it remains open to more unconscious regions of the brain-and-psyche: the "decision," for example, to attend to the diffuse blue field rather than to the vase; or the icaros that come readily to mind from "elsewhere" when a shaman needs to tune her warps.

Meditation: tool for a potential science of consciousness

Now that we have reviewed a variety of ways in which altered states of consciousness can be mastered, we will enquire whether meditative states of mind may be used to develop a "science of the mind" itself. As Jung frequently repeats, the difficulty in any study of the mind is that the object of study and the tool for studying it are one and the same. In contrast, the objects of our five senses are separate from the sense organs and from the brain-and-psyche. Western empirical science has capitalized on this separation to devise instruments to enhance the acuity of our sense organs and to describe the world with remarkable precision. In contrast, we have barely begun to investigate what the mind perceives. Although it seems unlikely that we will ever have instruments to enhance the acuity of our mental perceptions, it is clear that the mind can be trained—both to enter a variety of conscious states and to attend more steadily to whatever appears in the conscious field.

B. Alan Wallace outlines what he calls a *Contemplative Science* (2007), on the foundation of his fourteen years' training and practicing as a Buddhist monk as well as his more recent work as the founder and president of the Santa Barbara Institute of Consciousness Studies. He writes from the Tibetan Buddhist tradition of the Great Perfection School (Dzogchen). The basic idea is that an untrained consciousness lacks luminosity and steadiness. It limits what we can see much as a dim lamp that flickers in the wind casts dancing obscuring shadows around the object of our attention, impairing our vision. Meditation trains the mind to settle down to a still and steady luminosity (Wallace 2007: 59). Luminosity is lost when the attention goes slack, and stillness is lost when the mind is agitated by compulsive attachments, desires, fears and the like (Wallace 2007: 136). Even the Western mystical traditions failed to discover the powerful mental tool of steady stillness. The Christian mystics did achieve high states of unitive/transformative consciousness, but they were fleeting; and the West's tradition of exploring the nature of mystical consciousness went into serious decline after the Protestant Reformation and the scientific revolution (Wallace 2007: 53).

Wallace (2007: 62, 91) admits that habitual thinking in both the East and the West stands in the way of developing a "contemplative science." In the West, scientific materialism holds sway, with its dogmatic adherence to the idea that nothing exists outside of the measurable material world. In the East, adherents of the various meditative traditions hold just as dogmatically to the infallibility of their scriptures. They are generally more concerned with proper meditation technique than with a rigorous exploration of the nature of the mind. Wallace (2007) attempts to bring the best of the West's analytical inquiry together with the East's introversion and interest in mapping states of consciousness. He outlines, therefore, one richly suggestive way that the next era in the history of consciousness may proceed: the integration of science with a robust multiphasic consciousness.

Settling down to the bottom

The Great Perfection School holds that steadiness and luminosity can be achieved only if the meditator can get below all the turmoil and fluctuation of ordinary consciousness—all the way down to the substrate of consciousness itself, which it calls *ālaya*. It is the blank unthinking void into which all mental contents and activity dissolve when we fall into dreamless sleep and out of which all psychic phenomena reemerge when we wake up (Wallace 2007: 18). The Great Perfection School attributes a "substrate consciousness" (*ālayavijñana*) to this ground of the psyche. Substrate consciousness is said to be empty and luminous (Wallace 2007: 16). It is simply an essential aspect of the psyche, and it exists whether we know it or not. The substrate is the place to go if we wish to see things clearly—rather like the mirror of the observatory telescope or the screen of the electron microscope.

To get to the substrate, one must attain an advanced degree of *samādhi*, which can be described as "enstasy," that is, an altered state in which one does not stand outside oneself, as in ecstasy, but rather inside oneself. It has been called the "perfect forgetting" of the state of meditation which precedes it;[7] its object is consciousness itself in which subject and object are merged. The Paingalā-Upanishad (III.4) likens samādhi to "a lamp laced in a windless [spot]" (Feuerstein 1990). The Great Perfection School calls this advanced state of samādhi *śamatha* ("quiescence"). A fascinating and compelling fact about the substrate as it is experienced by a meditator in the state of *śamatha* is that it is a continuum of awareness comprised of successive "pulses" of cognition, each lasting about one millisecond. This corresponds amazingly to the pulse-driven nature of brain-function that we considered in Volume 1 of this book.[8] The Buddhists say that objects appear in each of these millisecond moments, but are not consciously recognized due to inattention. The quiescence of *śamatha* is necessary to bring them into awareness (Wallace 2007: 137).

From the personal to the transpersonal

Apparently Wallace has not himself attained such excellence in meditation as the Great Perfection School proposes, for he speaks in terms of what "is said to be possible" in the state of *śamatha*.

> Once a contemplative's mind has settled in this silent, luminous state of awareness through the achievement of *śamatha*, it is said to be possible to direct the attention to the past, bringing to consciousness distinct, detailed memories of events that occurred many years earlier in this lifetime.

> Then, through rigorous training, one may allegedly retrieve memories that precede the current life, remembering, like Pythagoras, the circumstances of preceding lives.
>
> (Wallace 2007: 17)

It seems that *śamatha* may not be used in the same way Husserl used the transcendental ego, that is to contemplate objects and issues that are dragged into the meditative field from outside. Rather it seems that the advantage of *śamatha* is that it enables one to examine one's own mind at work, as "objective appearances" arising from the substrate. The claim about personal memories suggests that one can theoretically examine anything that is already "in" one's own mind.

The reference to preceding lives, however, goes beyond one's "personal unconscious," the memories which, remembered or not, constitute one's biography. Transpersonal memories—those that putatively belong to previous lives—are "stored," Wallace says: "in the continuum of substrate consciousness which carries on from lifetime to lifetime. This conclusion is based on the experiences of highly trained contemplatives who have refined their attention in ways unknown to modern science" (Wallace 2007: 17). In this Buddhist theory, one can also go beyond the individual substrate to "the absolute space of phenomena" (*dharmadhātu*), which Wallace describes as "the timeless, infinite vacuum of absolute space." Although this expression seems to mean what we usually call "outer space," the vastness of the universe, we ought to be cautious, for the expression "absolute space" is often used, especially in Tibetan Buddhism, for the total freedom and spontaneity of liberating consciousness[9]—personified by the *dākinī*, "a female figure that moves on the highest level of reality; her nakedness symbolizes knowledge of truth unveiled" (Fischer-Schreiber *et al.* 1989). In any event, consciousness of "absolute space" is "non-dual," in the sense that absolute space and the primordial consciousness that contemplates it are "an intrinsic unity" (Ibid.: 20).

Wallace appears to be describing an experience that others—including the bio-genetic structuralists—attribute to transformative/integrative states in the brain-and-psyche. Various schools of Hinduism and Buddhism describe ultimate reality in similar terms, perhaps as a cosmos of dancing points of light, each of which is a grain of consciousness. The mystic is said to pulse back and forth between seeing the cosmic vision (which looks remarkably similar to what quantum mechanics might propose) and then seeing nothing, as one merges with the dancing field of vibrations (cf. Dyczkowski 1987; Panda 1995).

If such states are possible, and there is no good reason to think that they are not, we are better off knowing rather than dogmatically denying them. We would also be better off for knowing how to attain them and what the brain is doing when we get there. If a profound and steady quiescence can be achieved that enables our studying our own psychic processes, we would be better off knowing it from all angles, the subjective-experiential as well as the objective-instrumental. The employment and critical study of the altered states of consciousness that our organism makes possible is an important topic for scientific investigation. If we learn under what conditions we can trust our altered states, we can begin to recover what we have lost that our cave-painting relatives used in their everyday struggle for survival. Perhaps such talents will enable us to survive the ecological and political disasters we have been creating for ourselves.

Part II

The border zones of exact science

To demonstrate that Jung's theories and concepts of nearly a century ago are con-silient with recent developments in the biological sciences, we have been content in previous sections of this book to accept today's dominant philosophical per-spective: that psyche and brain operate in parallel because in some sense they are the same thing. While the brain is a complex physiological organ that can be studied from the outside with the instruments of science and described in third-person terms, psyche is the first-person lived experience of everyone who has a brain. Having a brain in the first-person, subjective sense allows us to live a world, wander in dreamscape, form emotional alliances and become a "personality."

The brain-mind identity hypothesis has allowed us to establish the neural sub-strate that produces the complexes, namely the "convergence zones" of the limbic system. It also allows us to see how archetypes are both inherited with our genes and yet have their "wiring" completed through familial and cultural interactions. We have come to appreciate as well how the compelling "numinosity" of arche-typal experience results from an autonomic nervous system that has been "tuned" by emotional encounters or ritual enactments. Altering ANS balance generates state-transitions in the brain which are characterized by specific altered states of consciousness, including identification with mythic figures and situations. When the two cerebral hemispheres are harmonized with the limbic system, unitive/transformative states of awareness can be brought about. These are the experi-ences for which Jung reserves the terms "self," "transcendent function" and "hierosgamos" (the wedding of the gods).

Over the past 40,000 years of human history, the employment of altered states of conscious has assisted our discovery and mastery of the natural world and facilitated the hierarchical organization of societies. Shamans and their descen-dants have learned techniques to master trance states, and aggrandizers have learned to manipulate ideology derived from myth to subjugate large segments of the population and produce immense surpluses of food and treasure. These, in turn, have led in the West to the development of an ego preoccupied with empirical discoveries, leading to modern science and technology, as well as the devaluation of "non-ordinary" conscious states as pathological or at least irrele-vant for "real life."

On account of this cultural prejudice, Part I of this volume, on shamanism and mastery, has run to some length in order to demonstrate that altered states are common and varied and that they can be managed and put to good use. If evolution means anything for us humans, it is that the talents that led our distant ancestors to paint the walls of caves and to build magnificent cathedrals are very much a part of the genetic endowment that has ensured our survival as a species. We have not so much outgrown as learned to ignore this inheritance.

Border zones

The topic of shamanism and mastery, however, has introduced reports from seemingly reliable observers that implicitly challenge the hypothesis of brain-psyche identity. Anthropologist Edith Turner (1998), for instance, saw a tooth extracted from the back of a native sufferer. Turner was herself in an altered state at the time and did not initially identify what she saw as a tooth, but rather saw some sort of ectoplasmic projection that seemed to be forced out of the patient's back by the shaman's thumb. Later the captured "tooth" was displayed in an empty Vaseline jar and appeared quite ordinary. The patient was genuinely cured. Turner had no explanation to satisfy herself but remained convinced that she had witnessed something extraordinary. Similarly, Amazonian shamans inflict injuries and effect cures with "darts" that lodge in a strange sort of "phlegm" that also resembles the ectoplasm of European spiritualistic séances. Such stories imply that psyche can have effects on matter. For if ectoplasm is not a "materialization" itself, changes seem to have been made in human bodies and personalities. They have been cured or attacked.

Amazonian vegetalistas claim that the "vine" taught them everything they know. Originally it showed them how to brew the complex psychedelic tea itself, and it continues to teach them what herbs are useful for healing and how to use them. Most impressively, it enables them to survey the physical and mental condition of an ailing patient, showing them how to remedy what is wrong. Their claims and their cures resemble those of the North American healer and so-called prophet, Edgar Cayce—who used hypnosis rather than a psychedelic drug to alter his conscious state. In these cases, it appears as though the psyche of the healer makes a tour of the patient's body. No doubt the shaman's brain is functioning in some sort of rhythmically harmonized fashion. But what appears to the psyche does not arrive through the sense organs. The whole procedure seems impossible, and yet the information provided appears to be remarkably accurate. Furthermore, while an ayahuasquero like Don Manuel is making such a tour, his wife keeping watch over him says she has witnessed his other-worldly activity and been horrified by it. If we accept her story, and we have no reason to suspect her of lying, we have to wonder how her psyche-and-brain—if they are one and the same thing—can have simultaneous access to the patient's body and her husband's mind.

Jung's position

This material takes us into "The Border Zones of Exact Science," the title of Jung's first presentation to his college student fraternity, the Zofingia Society, in November, 1896. Although officially pursuing the study of science and medicine, Jung was an avid student of spiritualism as well. Popular spiritualism—as it appeared in table rapping, visitations by ghosts of the departed, and serious investigations by people like William James and the members of London's Society for Psychical Research—belonged to the "somnambulism complex" of phenomena whose psychological investigation by Janet, Binet, Flournoy, Prince, and others constituted the informal "French School" of psychology that Jung so often cited as the primary source of his psychological theories.

As a 21-year-old university student in that first lecture, Jung demanded that science extend its empirical methods and analyze the data of hypnotism and spiritualism. He wanted his fraternity brothers to join him and leave the safe paths of established philosophy and science and "make our own independent raids into the realm of the unfathomable, chase the shadows of the night" (*CWA*: 23). Entering these "border zones," therefore, implied that Jung wanted to find a middle way "between the scornfully skeptical [as the majority of scientists and citizens at that time were and today still are] and the eagerly superstitious," a phrase that describes most parlor spiritualists of a century and more ago as well as New Agers today.[1]

Jung never lost his interest in those border zones. He wrote his medical dissertation on mediumship and took up the theme of somnambulism (a.k.a. dissociation) empirically in his Word Association Studies. A few years later, he had an important disagreement in Freud's study when he accurately predicted poltergeist phenomena in the master's bookcase and Freud called it nonsense (*MDR*: 155). He paid close attention all his professional life to non-ordinary events and in his last decade published his theory of parapsychology in collaboration with one of the founders of quantum mechanics, Wolfgang Pauli, "Synchronicity: An Acausal Connecting Principle" (*CW8*: ¶816–968).

The consequences of Jung's "chasing the shadows of the night" are chiefly two. In the first place, Jung had to develop a broad enough conception of the psyche to include all the non-ordinary events and experiences that manifest themselves despite their alleged impossibility. His view of psyche more adequately accounts for what we experience; and it will require less revision to accommodate itself to a future that surely lies before us—though not so near as William James imagined it to be—the day when mainstream science overcomes its hesitations and prejudices and seriously undertakes studies in parapsychology and related phenomena. Second, and regrettably, "the black tide of occultism," as Freud called it (*MDR*: 155), has injured Jung's reputation, leaving him vulnerable to the charge of being a "mystic," in the derogatory sense of being a soft-headed and superstitious investigator. This last section of *Synchronicity and Science* will be an investigation of where Jung wanted us to go in those "raids into the realm of the unfathomable."

The project

We begin with an overview of Jung's relationship with the "borderzone" phenomena of parapsychology and the logic of his proposal of synchronicity (Chapter 7). Chapters 8 to 10 present a review of parapsychology, discovering that non-ordinary experiences like clairvoyance and telepathy are neither supernatural nor impossible. Surely they are far more occasional and less dependable than more familiar experiences that originate in our sense organs. But their manifestation appears to rely on human talents that can be developed and refined in ways that closely resemble what we have already seen concerning the mastery of trance states.

These things happen. They are real, and it is not accurate to say that they violate the laws of physics. The laws of physics can neither prove nor disprove them. What they violate are our metaphysical assumptions—but no less than do twentieth-century developments in physics. We do not have a metaphysics that "works" to adequately account for the reality we actually experience. We need a general account of the world that can make even quantum mechanics intelligible, to say nothing of parapsychology. Indeed, although no one doubts that life and consciousness also belong to the real world, we have no adequate account of them, either.

In the process of making such raids into the realm of the unfathomable, it will become clear that, first, psyche cannot be identical with the brain, and this on biological grounds alone, regardless of parapsychology; second, effects in the real world cannot always be understood on the analogy of colliding billiard balls; third, process, incessant change, is fundamental but neglected when we try to understand it in terms of a series of stop-action snapshots; and fourth, the best analogy for the structure of reality is *organism*, parts integrated into a whole whose process is a higher order of reality, transcending the sum of its constituents.

Consequently, Chapters 11 to 13 articulate the implications of Jung's theory of synchronicity to redraw our picture of reality. Jung and Pauli would add a fourth ("psychoid") field to our understanding of the universe—alongside the gravity field of space-time, the electromagnetic field, and the quantum field. The modest metaphysics proposed here will be in line with both the general trend in physical science over the past three or four centuries and Jung's appeal to Chinese metaphysics to clarify his proposal of synchronicity as a fourth principle. It renders parapsychology far less mysterious and potentially has useful application elsewhere.

Chapter 7

The lawful irrationality of synchronicity

The centrality of extrasensory perception (ESP) experiences for Jung's understanding of the psyche can easily be underestimated—either by dismissing it as some sort of naive belief in spirits, as Harvard dream expert J. Allan Hobson puts it (Hobson 2002, 2005) or by viewing the theory of synchronicity as some late development in Jung's career that arose only in the 1950s along with his book on UFOs,[1] perhaps nothing but the self-indulgence of an old man. It therefore seems important to demonstrate that a deep concern with "border zone" phenomena was constant throughout Jung's professional life.

In 1900, when he began his psychiatric career, parapsychological claims were deemed to be either naively exalted fantasies, a sort of superstitious religion, or else were seen as pathological symptoms of interest only to the psychiatrist. Jung wanted to understand them in another sense—as legitimate phenomena for psychological investigation, a body of natural but poorly developed talents of the human psyche. He found incidents of ESP to be more common than is generally believed or admitted, although undeniably irregular and unpredictable. He wanted to know how it is that such phenomena sometimes turn out to be extraordinarily useful and how reality must be structured if such things do sometimes occur.

He bravely made incursions into the border zones of exact science, despite the danger to his reputation, believing that the only way to obtain an adequate picture of the human psyche was to exclude none of its capabilities. In that sense Jung's persistence represents what is the best in science. Indeed, as we shall see in this chapter and those that follow, Jung has been as much an unrecognized trail blazer in parapsychological studies as he has in evolutionary and biologically sensitive theories of the psyche. Starting with his roots in the "French School" of dissociation psychology and hypnotic trance, he studied spiritualism with an eye as critical as those of London's Society for Psychical Research (SPR) and agreed with the SPR that some mediums were anything but fraudulent. He followed the laboratory work of J. B. Rhine at Duke University, and was delighted to find that ESP adheres to some basic laws that seemed related to his own archetypal studies. In the end, he found not science but mainstream Western metaphysics to be the obstacle to our accepting and developing our inborn capabilities. In collaboration with Wolfgang Pauli, therefore, he proposed a remedy, namely the idea that our public view of reality excludes a necessary principle of nature—the one he calls synchronicity.

Jung on the irrational

For Jung, the prototype synchronistic event, the one most often cited, has to do with the analysis of a woman he describes as defensively attached to a Cartesian, ego-centered philosophy. In that sense she stands for us all. For the Cartesian subject-object and mind-body dichotomies as well as its mechanistic picture of the world has been the most obstinate problem for biology and psychology. Recently, with the development of quantum mechanics, it has also become a problem for physics.

Jung says his patient was "steeped in Cartesian philosophy" and that her allegiance to it kept her neurotically stuck and unable to get on with her life. Too much of real life was denied and ignored, leaving her brittle and unsatisfied. Jung believed her situation would transform itself if only she could be affected by "something quite irrational" that would "burst through the armor" that was holding her back. He was becoming discouraged by the strength of her resistance, however, when a numinous archetypal reality appeared. The patient was recounting her dream of the previous night in which she had been given a golden Egyptian scarab. Just then a rose chafer began tapping at the window behind Jung's head. He opened it, grabbed the green-gold beetle—Northern Europe's closest analogue to the Egyptian scarab—and handed it to the patient, saying, "Here's your scarab." The monumental improbability, yet striking aptness of the event opened the woman to the larger perspective she needed (*CW8*: ¶843–5).

When a synchronistic event happens, it violates our rational expectations. Jung uses the world *irrational* to mean not that which is counter to reason, but that which lies outside the rational sphere—not counter-to but alongside-of. What were the odds that the Egyptian symbol of death and transformation would appear just at the critical moment in this woman's life, when the death of her old attitude had become essential? Apparently the scarab dream alone would not have been enough to break through her Cartesian armor. The synchronistic appearance of the rose chafer, however, seems to have done the trick. The event was irrational in the sense that there were no grounds at all on which it could be predicted or explained.

Jung uses the term *irrational* also to describe the psychic functions of sensation and intuition. No one doubts that thinking is rational, and Jung counts feeling, too, as a rational means of access to the world. Thinking discovers conceptual order in the world, while feeling orders the world hierarchically, finding that some things feel more pleasant or more threatening than others. With sensation and intuition, on the other hand, there is no rational reason or order to what appears. I look out the window and see a red car turning the corner. Its driver knows where she is going and why. But from my point of view, there is no rational reason there should be a red car going by when I look out the window. The case is similar with intuition—ideas and images simply appear and we do not know how or when they will do it.

Synchronicity is "irrational" in just this sense. These things happen and we don't know how. But they are strikingly meaningful.

Jung: from spiritualism to synchronicity

The early years

Jung's interest in somnambulistic phenomena evidently began in childhood, with a mother whom he describes as a sort of dual personality: a conventional peasant harboring an uncanny witch whose sudden and unexpected pronouncements were alarmingly accurate. By night he would see ghostly figures floating out of her bedroom (*MDR*: 18). Moving a generation back, her own mother had the talents of a gifted spontaneous somnambulist (Charet 1993: 69). In Jung's generation, his cousin Helly's talent for mediumship was discovered in 1895, when the twenty-year-old Jung instituted familial experiments in "table-turning" that provided the material for his doctoral dissertation at Basel University (Zumstein-Preiswerk 1975: 35f).

His interest in spiritualism continued in Zurich where he served his residency in psychiatry at the Burghölzli mental hospital. The *Basler Nachrichten* newspaper carried the text of a lecture he gave in Basel in 1905, where he reports having studied eight different mediums in Zurich. He reviews the history of spiritualism, beginning with the Fox sisters of Hydesville, NY, and discusses a large number of related phenomena, including levitation, clairvoyance and prophecy (*CW18*: ¶697–740). The tone of his talk is given in the introduction:

> The dual nature of spiritualism gives it an advantage over other religious movements: not only does it believe in certain articles of faith that are not susceptible of proof, but it bases its belief on a body of allegedly scientific, physical phenomena which are supposed to be of such a nature that they cannot be explained except by the activity of spirits. Because of its dual nature—on the one side a religious sect, on the other a scientific hypothesis—spiritualism touches upon widely differing areas of life that would seem to have nothing in common.
>
> (*CW18*: ¶697)

He ends his talk with a declaration of faith: "If we wait quietly until the most impressive physical phenomena put in an appearance . . . the exact sciences will surely conquer this field by experiment and verification" (*CW18*: ¶740).

Further evidence of Jung's enduring pursuit of "impressive phenomena" appears from time to time in the historical record. His mentor in the study of mediums, Theodore Flournoy of Geneva, wrote to William James, March 15, 1910, that he had just observed a psychic named Carancini in the company of Jung and others, and all were agreed that the self-styled medium was "an out-and-out humbug" (LeClair 1966: 228). Fifteen years later, Jung's signature as an expert witness, along with that of his former chief at the Burghölzli, Eugen

Bleuler, declared that the famous Austrian psychic, Rudi Schneider, was *not* a fraud (Gregory 1985: 73).

In 1919 Jung made a presentation to the Society for Psychical Research in London in which he described the phenomenon of soul-loss as the loss of psychic energy from the ego due to a complex reaction and contrasted that with the experience of spirit-visitation which he ascribed to the irruption into consciousness of an archetypal image from the collective unconscious. He concluded that such events may be accompanied by "exteriorizations," the same term he had used in Freud's study to describe the poltergeists in the bookcase. He went on to say, "But in all this I see no proof whatever of the existence of real spirits, and until such proof is forthcoming I must regard this whole territory as an appendix of psychology" (*CW8*: ¶600). In a footnote to this statement added in 1948, however, he doubts "whether an exclusively psychological approach can do justice to the phenomena in question." He cites his study of "nuclear physics and the conception of the space-time continuum [which] opens up the whole question of the transpsychic reality immediately underlying the psyche."

The reference to relativity (space-time continuum) and quantum mechanics (nuclear physics) in this statement shows that his work formulating the notion of synchronicity was already well under way, though it would not be published for another four years. His exchange of letters with Wolfgang Pauli—the nuclear physicist who helped develop the theory with his criticism and suggestions—had been under way since 1932, according to the *Pauli/Jung Letters* (*PJL*).

The 1930s and after

From the 1930s onward come most of the stories about Jung's own medium-like behavior during analytic sessions. Some of these accounts are recorded in the documentary film *Matter of Heart* (Whitney and Whitney 1983) in which Jung's still-living students and analysands were interviewed for their recollections of the famous man. Others can be found in published collections of reminiscences. All of the stories mentioned here have been contributed by distinguished and well-published Jungian analysts.[2]

Marvin Spiegelman's experience seems to have be relatively common. He gained an interview with Jung and found himself with nothing to say. Then Jung began "to speak from out of himself somewhere. He spoke of his own life." Strangely, Spiegelman found that Jung's monologue was addressing all of his own "problems, fears, concerns and deep desires" (Spiegelman 1982: 87–9). Hilde Kirsch had a meeting with Jung when he was 85 and, trying to spare his energies in view of his precarious health, told him only the first half of her long dream. In response, Jung "just started to talk . . . and told me the second part of my dream which I had not told him." Liliane Frey-Rohn has a similar story (Whitney and Whitney 1983).

Rix Weaver (1982: 91–5) and Jane Wheelwright (1982: 97–105) tell stories of finding the familiar world dissolve around them when in Jung's presence. The distinction between self and table was lost, everything became "whizzing molecules" out of which emerged "before my eyes and ears and senses a model of the changed person I was meant finally to become."

The situation was apparently no less mysterious for Jung than it was for his patients. Jung's English friend, the physician Eddy Bennet, records an interview with Jung in which he describes how he conducted his analytic sessions. Usually he would just wait for the patient to speak, but sometimes he would begin talking without knowing why. The other day he had found himself speaking "about Africa and snakes . . . then it turned out to be absolutely relevant for he discovered that she [the patient] was deeply interested in these things. So we wait and the instincts guide us" (Bennet 1985: 25).

In addressing the students at the C. G. Jung Institute in Zurich in the 1950s Jung described his method of doing analysis: namely to set the conditions and then wait for what he called the two-million-year-old wise man, the personification of the collective unconscious, to appear.

> Analysis is a long discussion with the Great Man—an unintelligent attempt to understand him. Nevertheless, it is an attempt, as both patient and analyst understand it. . . . Work until the patient can see this. It, the Great Man, can at one stroke put an entirely different face on the thing—or *anything* can happen. In that way you learn about the peculiar intelligence of the background; you learn the nature of the Great Man. You learn about yourself against the Great Man—against his postulates. This is the way through things, things that look desperate and unanswerable. The point is, *how are you yourself going to answer this*? . . . The unconscious gives you that peculiar twist that makes the way possible.
>
> (Baynes 1977: 360–1)

It seems that Jung used the emotional atmosphere of his analytic sessions as an opportunity to practice what might be called "active imagination in tandem." When analyst and analysand enter that meditative space that Husserl called the transcendental ego, images and memories relevant to their joint emotional reality are apt to appear to either or both participants. When they give voice to them, the process intensifies. The collective unconscious constellated in the space between has the wisdom of two million years of human experience, from *Homo erectus* on down to the present.

In the material just mentioned, Jung's mediumistic behavior has to do with mind speaking to mind—what the parapsychologists would call telepathy, if they agree that something para-normal has occurred. There were also incidents in which non-human events spoke to mind. A subjective (mental) event could be meaningfully connected with an objective event occurring in the world outside, as was the case when the rose chafer tapped on the window. Whenever these sorts of things happened during an analytic session, Jung interpreted the objective event as a contribution to his dialogue with the patient. His long-time disciple and biographer, Barbara Hannah, gives us a vivid picture of being in analysis with Jung in the garden room of his house on Lake Zurich, where he was attentive to every natural event that might add synchronistic commentary: "insects flying in, the lake lapping more audibly than usual" (Hannah 1976: 202, n. k). He had come to the view that the psyche is not so much a factor locked inside our bodies but "more like an atmosphere in which we live" (*Letters, i*: 433).

Synchronicity

By the mid 1940s, particularly after his heart attack and near-death experiences, Jung must have realized that his patient, quiet wait for the day when the exact sciences would "conquer the field" of parapsychology was a dream that would not be satisfied in his lifetime. He had to come up with his own provisional theory and was encouraged by his dialogue with Wolfgang Pauli, who bore tidings from quantum mechanics: that matter is an evanescent condition of energy and that the observer always affects what is observed. Both men became convinced that psychology and "microphysics," as they called the study of subatomic phenomena, were somehow mutually implicated.

The principle of acausality

The essential element in Jung's definition of synchronicity is that two or more events may have a meaningful connection without being causally related to one another. According to classical science and common sense, a cause can be identified only when the producer and the receiver of an influence find themselves in the same place at the same time. On a billiard table, for instance, a rolling cue ball strikes a stationary ball and sends it rolling in a particular direction with a particular speed. No cause at all can be discovered in synchronicity, and Jung takes this as definitive, and that is what is difficult to grasp about synchronicity.[3]

Whenever something happens, we look for a cause: "we cannot imagine events that are connected acausally" (*CW8*: ¶820). This is why we come up with fanciful explanations for telepathy. We speak of sending and receiving "vibes," for instance, and leave the nature of those vibes undetermined. Someday, we think, someone will discover what they are. In fact, no one has discovered vibes of any sort to explain telepathy. Indeed, if there were some vibratory wave-like transmission, the signal would have to diminish with distance; but distance is not a factor in telepathy or clairvoyance. Jung saw no way out of this unthinkable dilemma and had to admit that there is nothing resembling a cause lying behind synchronicity, even though its occurrence is "not unusual at all, but relatively common" (*CW8*: ¶441).

In synchronicity, one of the two linked events can be explained causally while the other cannot (*CW8*: ¶855). In the case of telepathy, related images or feelings occur in the minds of two separate people. One of them knows why she is excited, anxious or sad or that she is gazing on a glorious scene; the other does not know why, but may very well intuit that the feelings and images belong to his friend. In clairvoyance, the causally explicable scene is a devastating fire in Stockholm, while the scene that cannot be explained causally is the terrible vision of that fire in the mind of Swedenborg, 300 miles away (*CW8*: ¶912).

Some lawful elements

In spelling out the essential characteristics of synchronicity, Jung gives predominance to the work of J. B. Rhine (1895–1980) in the Parapsychology Laboratory at Duke University where, "Decisive evidence for the existence of acausal combinations of events, has been furnished with adequate scientific safeguards" (*CW8*: ¶833). Rhine experimented with telepathy using decks of "Zener cards,"[4] each with one of five images on them. One subject gazed on a card, while the other, isolated in another room, attempted to imagine or guess which image it bore. In psychokinesis experiments, subjects tried to influence the roll of dice with their minds. Small but statistically significant results were obtained with both types of experiment. Pauli pointed out the obvious fact that Rhine's data were far less interesting than Jung's spontaneous psychic phenomena, and more importantly lacked evidence of archetypal involvement (*PJL*: 36). He was evidently thinking of such examples as Swedenborg's vision, the rose chafer or Jung's waking in a hotel room at two in the morning thinking of the suffering of a depressed patient when he felt a pain shoot through his skull as though he had been shot. A telegram arrived at dawn confirming his surmise that the man had killed himself with a pistol (*MDR*: 137f).

Humdrum though they were in comparison, however, Rhine's results gave Jung some essential, scientifically verified information with which to work. First was the fact that double blind laboratory experiments had proved what Jung himself had not the means to prove, that subjects could regularly score significantly better than chance at ESP tasks (*CW8*: ¶833). Second, it was discovered that distance had no effect upon performance: neither between separate subjects in telepathy experiments nor between subject and scene in clairvoyance experiments (*CW8*: ¶835). Third, *time* had no effect. Subjects could gain reliable information, mentally, both before and after an event occurred in the physical world or in the mind of another (*CW8*: ¶836). Jung summarized these last findings by saying that synchronicity reveals the "psychically conditioned relativity of space and time" (*CW8*: ¶840). It was impossible, therefore, that ESP could involve some sort of energy transmission (*CW8*: ¶839). Space and time, Jung gathered, consist of nothing at all. We only think they have objective reality because our knowing apparatus, as Kant argued, requires them (*CW8*: ¶840).

Probably Rhine's most significant discovery was "the decline effect": the observation that one's level of performance in ESP experiments declines as one's boredom increases. Interest and emotional involvement turn out to be of primary importance (*CW8*: ¶838), and this is surely the reason spontaneous synchronicities are experienced as huge, numinous events compared to what is produced in the laboratory.

Altered states

A strong point of agreement between Jung and Pauli was precisely that some additional principle, other than causality, is required if we are to understand the nature of synchronicity and that "the psychic state [that is to say the level of interest] of the subject and the investigator" is the best candidate to play that role. Pauli wanted to include it in the definition of synchronicity (*JPL*: 53f). Jung, who ultimately resisted the suggestion, agreed in principle that strong emotions, and particularly those associated with the archetypes, play at least a facilitating role. "Synchronistic phenomena can be evoked by putting the subject into an unconscious state (trance)" (*CW8*: ¶440). "Every emotional state produces an alteration of consciousness" (*CW8*: ¶856). Jung explained that, in the case of the archetypes, numinous emotional effects produce what Janet called a "lowering of the mental level." This means that psychic energy drains away from consciousness, causing the conscious field to shrink, and the individual's orientation in the here and now to be reduced. The lost psychic energy flows into the archetypal matter at hand giving it a "supernormal degree of numinosity," and producing "a favorable opportunity" for something to slip in from the unconscious (*CW8*: ¶841). "The subject's response . . . is the product of pure imagination, of 'chance' ideas which reveal the structure of that which produces them, namely the unconscious" (*CW8*: ¶840).

When Jung speaks of "chance" ideas, he means to emphasize only that there is nothing "causal" about their entering the conscious field: no clacking billiard balls, no vibes of any sort. But in no sense is there anything arbitrary about them. They are meaningfully connected to something else, and often crucially so. How is it possible that by "pure imagination" and "chance" exactly the right information should appear? When we ask questions like this, we expect an answer that satisfies our search for causes, and Jung has none. Instead he speaks mysteriously of "absolute knowledge,"[5] an "*a priori* causally inexplicable knowledge of a situation" (*CW8*: ¶857), "a knowledge not mediated by the sense organs" (*CW8*: ¶948) but that is "immediate" and characteristic of the unconscious (*CW8*: ¶856). He seems to be saying (here and elsewhere) that the unconscious, by its nature, is capable of knowing anything in the universe, and that this is the foundation of synchronicity. Furthermore, to be in touch with absolute knowledge, one must usually be in an altered state of consciousness. When an archetype is constellated, we are in an altered state that may on occasion be open to absolute knowledge.

The synchronistic nature of "psychoid" process

The archetypes do not only open the mind to absolute knowledge by altering the conscious state, but also have an organizing function. They work out of sight of the ego, setting lower level (unconscious) operations in order and gathering them into a shape that later may become visible to the conscious mind (*CW8*: ¶440). The archetypes have, in short, the very nature that we have been calling top-to-bottom structure. It is only as we approach the ego-conscious "top" that numinous patterns are recognized or projected. "Below" that are neural networks, autonomic nervous system balance, hormones, and the like. Because such lower-level processes are incapable of becoming conscious, in the late 1940s Jung began referring to them as *psychoid* activities. They are psyche-like but will never become conscious.

On introducing the term *psychoid* he was careful to note that it is only to be used an as adjective, so as not to suggest that some additional entity may be present. The word simply describes those processes in an organism that are "quasi-psychic, such as the reflex-process" (*CW8*: ¶368). In principle, *psychic* process can be represented to the ego in symbolic form, while *psychoid* process is "irrepresentable" (*CW8*: ¶840).

Jung was uncharacteristically careful in his definition of *psychoid*, probably out of fear that he would be accused of promoting "vitalism," the idea that living bodies possess some additional feature, over and above chemical substances and physical forces. It might be a soul, a fiery fluid, or even some principle by which the matter of a body is organized. Hans Driesch (1867–1941), the founder of experimental embryology, had used the term *psychoid* as a noun to mean a directing principle in a living body—and he was a notorious vitalist. On the other hand, Eugen Bleuler had used the term, too, also as a noun, to refer to all of the "sub-cortical processes [in the brain] so far as they have an adaptive function" (*CW8*: ¶368). It appears that Jung wanted to locate his use of the term somewhere between Bleuler and Driesch. Psychoid processes do not have to be confined to the brain, but they have to contribute to an end result that may become conscious. Jung does not wish to add a new element or process to the organism, only to indicate that psyche-like processes go very deep down into the internal workings of the organism. He saw this move as a modest effort to name something that everyone sees but never thinks to mention.

The psychology of an amoeba

How far down psychoid processes may go is suggested by a claim Jung made in 1927, speaking on the evolutionary nature of the psyche at a symposium entitled "Man and Earth." Jung called his contribution "The Earth-Dependency of the Psyche":[6]

> The collective unconscious, however, . . . is not individual but common to all men, and perhaps even to all animals . . .
> This whole psychic organism corresponds exactly to the body . . . still preserves elements that connect it with the invertebrates and ultimately with the protozoa. Theoretically, it should be possible to "peel" the collective unconscious, layer by layer, until we come to the psychology of the worm, and even of the amoeba.
>
> (*CW8*: ¶321–2)

The idea that an amoeba "has a psychology" certainly suggests a new approach to the realm of the psychoid. Evidently we should look to how an amoeba behaves, how it "lives its world." For an amoeba does indeed inhabit a meaningful but evidently tiny world.

How is it that an amoeba, a single-cell organism without anything like neural structure, can have psychoid processes? In his 1952 synchronicity essay, Jung answered that question, "We must ask ourselves . . . whether the coordination of psychic and physical processes in a living organism can be understood as a synchronistic relation" (*CW8*: ¶948). As a form of synchronicity, psychoid process would be acausal. The standard Western view is rather different. It conjures up a Cartesian type of "soul," a separate and radically different kind of substance when it considers the mind-body problem. In our need to find a cause, we imagine the mind somehow piloting the brain, much as we imagine vibes in telepathy. Jung wants to say there is no separate mind substance and no billiard-ball or vibratory causality. There is synchronicity harmonizing acausally, according to the principle of meaning.

Thus the internal process of an amoeba, which we usually describe as evidence of its life and which mainstream science analyzes in causal terms (the interaction of proteins, amino acids, electrolytes, and the like), Jung says ought to be seen as synchronistic. As a medical man himself, he surely does not wish to deny that molecules are interacting in a causal fashion, according to the laws of physics. All that is true enough. Jung points, rather, to what mechanistic science overlooks, the organismic process of the amoeba: the fact that it seems to "know" that nourishment is nearby and "knows" how to extend its pseudopodia to move in the right direction and engulf the morsel when it gets there. As a whole organism, it also "knows" how to metabolize the food it has found. Jung wonders how the amoeba manages to organize its millions of simultaneous chemical interactions in a manner that always serves its wholeness if it does not possess psychoid capabilities. There has to be some sort of primitive proto-knowing, a teleological factor in all of biology (*CW8*: ¶931).

If "proto-knowing" and "teleology" seem dangerously absurd, Jung struggles to remind his readers that psychoid process is too primitive ever to become conscious and it cannot look forward further than the next instant. Its working is limited to the roughly immediate now. Hence the term *syn-chron*-icity (together/in time/ness).

Unconscious "absolute knowing" is inherently synchronistic, both when a human psyche has a vision of fire in a distant city and when the molecules that comprise an amoeba organize themselves for the good of the living whole. In the case of the amoeba, however, Jung wonders whether "meaning" is the right word to name the connecting principle. Perhaps it should be "equivalence" or "conformity" (*CW8*: ¶942, n. 71). Jung's struggle to find the right language to avoid giving the wrong impression makes it clear that he is trying to describe a continuity of psyche-like functioning in all life forms. With the term *synchronicity*, the acausal ordering principle, he attempts to describe the living *process* of beings living their worlds.

Pauli objected to the term *acausal*, calling it "imprecise." He said that Jung's ordering factor itself "could be taken as the cause and that synchronistic events just *appear* to be acausal." Apparently he was trying to save Jung's position from being ridiculed by physicists, who would find "acausality" to be the sticking point, for he goes on to say that there are no causal chains to be followed in quantum mechanics. And this, he admitted, might well bring twentieth-century physicists closer to acknowledging "meaning as an ordering factor" than they had been in Schopenhauer's day (*JPL*: 38).[7] Evidently, Jung was striving to avoid ridicule from biologists, while Pauli had the scorn of physicists in mind. Pauli did, however, agree that the "freedom from strict determinism" that characterizes the quantum realm also suggests a potential connection between physics on the one hand and biology and parapsychology on the other (Lindorff 2004: 172).

Psyche and brain are not identical

The idea of biological processes as humble as those of an amoeba having a psychoid nature surely leads to a rejection of the standard Western view that psyche and brain are identical in substance but separate in experience. For the notion of psychoid process implies that even "irrepresentable" activities can have a kind of proto-subjectivity. Jung does not avoid the issue but makes it clear in the concluding section of the synchronicity essay, "We must completely give up the idea of the psyche's being somehow connected with the brain, and remember instead the 'meaningful' or 'intelligent' behavior of the lower organisms, which are without a brain" (*CW8*: ¶947).

In 1952 he could make the claim on evolutionary and biological grounds, through the theory of psychoid processes operating synchronistically, but the phenomena of parapsychology had long inclined Jung to assert the psyche's "independence" of the brain. In 1896, F. W. H. Myers had listed nine reasons for rejecting neural explanations for ESP, including evidence that brain waves cannot explain clairvoyance, that telepathy is unaffected by distance, that the physical processes of the brain can not produce precognition, and that telepathy often takes place when the organism is in an enfeebled state (Gauld 1968: 295).

Very likely Jung was familiar with some of these arguments, when as a freshman at Basel University he told his Zofingia brothers, "The soul is an intelligence independent of space and time" (*CWA*: 29). Almost forty years later, in an article titled "The Soul and Death," he said: "The psyche's attachment to the brain can be affirmed with far less certainty today than it could fifty years ago. Psychology must digest certain parapsychological facts, which it has hardly begun to do as yet" (*CW8*: ¶812).

Strictly speaking, psychoid processes alone cannot make psyche as "independent" of the brain as some of Jung's statements seem to imply, for many of them are found in the brain. Because psyche belongs to the body as a whole—just as the organismic processes of amoeba function holistically to constitute a sort of proto-self—the brain must be merely a very significant *contributor* to psyche. At the very least it sorts out and analyzes with its parallel and redundant circuitry all the psychoid activities going on in a vertebrate life form, as it responds to its environment and to its internal states. Surely the causal processes of the brain play a significant role in making the psyche conscious—or at least in refining what it is conscious of.

This last possibility was the choice William James favored. He called it the "transmissive theory." He thought the brain works by molding pre-existing consciousness into various forms—either by gathering scattered "particles" of consciousness or by responding to an already unified psyche (Barnard 1998: 176). Perhaps this is what Jung had in mind when he remarked at the end of *Memories, Dreams, Reflections* that the brain may function as a "transformer station."

An appeal to Chinese metaphysics

As a philosophy, synchronicity challenges Western assumptions, not only on account of its mind-boggling notion of non-causal influence, but perhaps especially because of the quality that I (not Jung) have called "organismic." This is the notion that in every instant everything that happens is meaningfully connected to everything else. This principle is probably least objectionable when applied to an amoeba, where everything occurring inside its cell wall and just outside it holds together as an interconnected whole. The amoeba acts as an organism, and the molecules that comprise it all act as one, even as they fulfill their separate functions.

It requires a much greater stretch to accept the challenge that some synchronistic "organismic" structure lies behind telepathy or clairvoyance. What organismic unity connects Swedenborg's mind with a fire 300 miles away? We may be able to countenance the instantaneous unity of an amoeba's molecules, but what is it about a man's mind and a distant city's fire that they should be united? What is it about their synchrony—their merely occurring at the same time—that welds them into a kind of organism?

Jung's efforts to avoid being labeled a vitalist will probably fail to convince most mainstream biologists. No one doubts that a protozoan is an organismic whole. But Western science ignores this fact or postpones considering it in the hope that someday someone will explain it employing nothing but the mechanics of its chemical subunits, following the laws of cause and effect. Our unexamined metaphysics tells us that causal mechanics is the only acceptable explanation for any scientific problem. This means we must always begin with the smallest parts, as close to the ultimate units as we can get, and hope eventually to find how they constitute a whole. This procedure has not worked for consciousness, for parapsychology, for the phenomenon of organism, or indeed for life itself. There are huge gaps in our understanding of reality. Jung's doctrine of synchronicity introduces a new descriptive principle alongside causality, one that addresses all four gaps. But, however modestly he has put it forward, it is a *new* metaphysics, and the Western world has a hard time with it. Indeed, the fact that synchronicity gives priority to the organism over its constituent parts—and what the whole has that the parts do not, namely life and consciousness—probably means that most mainstream biologists will see Jung's proposal as a symptom of vitalism.

Aware of the metaphysical challenge he was bringing, Jung devoted a section of his essay on synchronicity to alternative metaphysical systems (*CW8*: ¶863–71). Primarily, he appeals to the metaphysics of the *I Ching*, the ancient Chinese "Classic of Changes." In place of Western atomism, our concern with analyzing things down to the building blocks that comprise them, the Chinese begin with a holistic assumption. "Unlike the Greek-trained Western mind, the Chinese mind does not aim at grasping details for their own sake, but at a view which sees the detail as part of a whole" (*CW8*: ¶863).

I Ching

The *I Ching* is a divination tool founded on the idea that everything that happens in a given moment has the same character. It proposes an orderly rule-bound method of producing a chance event (counting yarrow stalks or tossing coins). Each result produces a "yin" or a "yang" cipher, a single short line that is either continuous or broken. The procedure is repeated six times, and the resulting six lines constitute one of sixty-four possible "hexagrams"; the book itself contains symbolic commentaries on each of the sixty-four. They speak of the weather; the seasons of the year; difficulties in politics, the family, or the army; or the relationship between features of the landscape, mountains, chasms, lakes, and the like.

One consults the oracle by carefully composing a question, perhaps about the nature of some challenge one is facing, then throws the coins and ponders the commentary. Generally the serious user of the *I Ching* will find the practice brings new dimensions of the issue to mind, allowing it to be seen with new eyes. The earliest layers of contribution to the commentaries probably were shamanic, but the original ideas have been largely overlain and reinterpreted with Taoist, Confucian, and Buddhist ideas. They reflect the traditional mind of China.

According to the Taoist component of the *I Ching*, everything that happens in the cosmos is a momentary expression of the ever-changing relation between the Tao's two constituents, yin and yang. In every moment, therefore, the cosmos is like an amoeba and its molecules: all the pieces contribute to a whole that vastly transcends their sum. For this reason, the personal issue I bring to the oracle belongs to the same moment in which my coins fall into particular combinations of heads and tails. Those combinations point to a particular commentary which describes the moment.[8] When I read the commentary, I read it as a description of my issue, a contribution from a school of wisdom that will help me appreciate the matter in a broader context and raise to consciousness aspects of my previously unexamined attitude.

Regarding the fact that "the coins fall just as happens to suit them," Jung explains:

Two Chinese sages, King Wen and the Duke of Chou, in the twelfth century before our era, sought to explain the simultaneous occurrence of a psychic state with a physical process as *an equivalence of meaning*. In other words, they supposed that the same living reality was expressing itself in the psychic state as in the physical.

(*CW8*: ¶865)

It will be difficult to find a more perfect fit for the theory of synchronicity than the metaphysics of the *I Ching*.

Other metaphysical precursors

Jung discusses the *Tao Te Ching* according to the interpretation of his friend, the German Sinologist Richard Wilhelm, who said that in "the Chinese view there is in all things a latent 'rationality.'" Jung takes this to suggest meaningful coincidence; but I think it goes further than that and suggests that all matter has some sort of inherent aptitude for belonging to organism, for entering the psychoid sphere of nature. In the Western view, consciousness is completely foreign to matter; and this is what makes it impossible to imagine how consciousness can appear when matter's organization becomes highly complex, as in the human brain. If there were no latent capacity for consciousness in the parts, how could it appear in the whole? In the Chinese view, apparently, what Jung calls psychoid potential is latent in all things (*CW8*: ¶917–24).

Jung also cites Western writers from the ancient Greeks to the Renaissance, and especially Johannes Kepler and G. W. Leibniz, in his overview of alternate metaphysical systems. For example, Hippocrates: "There is one common flow, one common breathing, all things are in sympathy. The whole organism and each one of its parts are working in conjunction for the same purpose." The alchemist Agrippa von Nettesheim says: "As in the archetypal World, all things are in all; so also in this corporeal world, all things are in all, albeit in different ways" (*CW8*: ¶925–46).

Primarily, however, Jung speaks of Leibniz and his doctrine of pre-established harmony. The "monads" that are the units in Leibniz's philosophy—also called "souls" in the case of living organisms—are "windowless." They have no conscious perception of what is outside of themselves, and yet they do not fall into chaos, for they move in a universal harmony set by God. Jung says:

The synchronicity principle thus becomes the absolute rule in all cases where an inner event occurs simultaneously with an outside one. As against this, however, it must be borne in mind that the synchronistic phenomena which can be verified empirically, far from constituting a rule, are so exceptional that most people doubt their existence. They certainly occur much more frequently in reality than one thinks or can prove, but we still do not know whether they occur so frequently and so regularly in any field of experience that we could speak of them as conforming to law. We only know that there must be an underlying principle which might possibly explain all such (related) phenomena.

(CW8: ¶938)

This passage leaves little doubt that Jung really would like to claim synchronicity as a universal principle, and not merely an explanation of parapsychology. Synchronistic events are more common that anyone can prove, but we cannot claim they *occur* regularly despite being *noticed* only occasionally. In a footnote to this passage, Jung wants to "stress the possibility that the relation between soul and body may be understood as a synchronistic one." That would make synchronicity common rather than rare.

Synchronicity as a cosmic principle

There are other indications that Jung wanted to make synchronicity a cosmic principle but feared that he had insufficient evidence. In fact, if it is not a cosmic principle, it has nothing to say to the gaps—consciousness, organism, life and parapsychology—in the Western metaphysics that has dominated our thinking since the collapse of alchemy in the seventeenth century. In *Mysterium Coniunctionis* (1955/56), his last great work, Jung described the rise of empirical science out of alchemy as "the great schism" (*CW14*: ¶101). Imagination was severed from sensory perception as matter became dead and the mythic realities of the alchemists became superstitions or deliberate obfuscations. Something crucial was lost when we turned to empiricism and mechanical atomism. We lost a sense of wholeness and mythic depth, while we gained remarkable mastery. It was very much the same observation Lévy-Bruhl made when comparing "primitive thinking" with that of the contemporary West (Lévy-Bruhl 1922).

Cosmic aspirations

In his essay on synchronicity, Jung presents five lines of argument that imply he saw synchronicity as a cosmic principle and wished to be able to say so directly. When we add to these passages evidence from his correspondence with Pauli, the theme becomes undeniable.

The first argument is from the nature of "absolute knowledge." Jung has demonstrated with numerous examples that the psyche sometimes seems to exhibit knowledge of matters that cannot be available to it by ordinary causal means. Such things happen frequently enough that we have to take them seriously. They are, in fact, "characteristic of synchronistic phenomena, a knowledge not mediated by the sense organs." But if the psyche can, in principle, know anything in the universe, regardless of space and time, some "self-subsistent meaning" must exist. Apparently this means that meaning and the possibility of connection pre-exists the occasional moment when Swedenborg has a vision and Stockholm is burning 300 miles away (*CW8*: ¶948).

The second argument is from the nature of the psychoid dimension. He says that the archetype's psychoid nature makes it "transgressive," meaning that "it does not confine itself to the psychic sphere but can occur in circumstances that are non-psychic" (*CW8*: ¶964). This comment is clarified by a passage in a letter from Jung to Pauli where he calls the archetype's psychoid nature "transcenden-tal." It participates in both the physical sphere and the psychic (*PJL*: 69). In a passage from an earlier letter, he muses on the role the archetype plays in synchro-nistic events. He says there are three possibilities. Maybe "psyche casts a spell on mass . . . or mass bewitches psyche," but more likely the psychoid nature of the archetype allows it to transgress the dividing line between realms and "assimi-late" the physical and the psychic. In "a so-called numinous moment, [it] causes a joint field of tension" (*PJL*: 62f). All of this implies that matter (or mass) is sus-ceptible in principle to the psychoid archetype. Matter, then, is not "dead." Some sort of psychoid susceptibility must be everywhere in the universe, making syn-chronicity a universal principle.

The third argument is based on an analogy with quantum mechanics originally suggested by Pauli (Lindorff 2004: 108). Everything in the quantum realm is in constant flux, energy turning into one sort of particle, which winks back into energy and remerges as another sort of particle. Consequently nothing is definite, one can only speak of probabilities. Similarly, Jung argues, "The archetype repre-sents *psychic probability* . . . It is a special psychic instance of probability in general, which is made up of the laws of chance [and] lays down rules for nature just as the laws of mechanics do" (*CW8*: ¶964). Here the archetype again bridges the psychic and physical realms, organizing both. On account of this psychoid activity, synchronicity would be a universal principle. Matter is always respon-sive to the psychoid archetype.

The fourth argument derives from the correspondence with Pauli in which they frankly speak of two meanings of synchronicity, a "narrower" one and a "holistic" one. The distinction first appears in a letter from Pauli, where the "narrower sense" refers to "a small number of individual cases" when a meaningful connec-tion is noticed. Pauli is surprised by Jung's recent remarks which suggest that "synchronicity . . . comprises every acausal and—I should like to add—holistic system." Jung seems to include even the data of quantum mechanics within the realm of synchronicity (*PJL*: 63). Jung responds that synchronicity in the nar-rower sense is a special case—the numinous moment when an acausal incident "occurs (by chance) in the psychic sphere" (*PJL*: 69). In the end, this view was published in the synchronicity essay (*CW8*: ¶965).

The fifth and most persuasive argument is based on statements and diagrams that clearly claim synchronicity to be a universal dimension of nature. For example, "Synchronicity ascribes to the moving body a certain psychoid property which, like space, time, and causality forms a criterion of its behavior" (*CW8*: ¶947). Later Jung says that synchronicity "supplements" "space, time, and causality, the classi-cal triad of physics" and draws one of his "quaternity" diagrams, crossing vertical and horizontal lines with each of the four ends labeled (Figure 7.1).

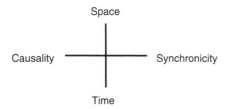

Figure 7.1 Synchronicity as universal principle, first version.

Source: digital diagram by John Ryan Haule in imitation of Jung, *CW8*: ¶961.

Jung says that the vertical space-time axis in Figure 7.1 stands for the "irrepresentable continuum," by which he evidently means Einstein's universe: the gravity field that is usually pictured as a flexible membrane pressed down into bowls here and there by the mass of each sun, planet, and black hole. Acting on the entities of this material universe are the principles located on the horizontal axis, causality and synchronicity. This clearly places the psychoid, organismic effects of synchronicity on a par with the billiard-ball and vibratory effects of causality. Space, time and causality are certainly central principles in Newtonian physics. Jung wishes to "complete the quaternity" by including synchronicity as the acausal principle.

Pauli objected to Jung's diagram of universal principles, saying that a "modern physicist" would find space and time separated at opposite ends to be "particularly unacceptable." He proposed replacing Jung's vertical axis with an opposition between "Energy (conservation)" and "Space-time continuum" (*PJL*: 56f).

Jung accepted and published a wordier version of Pauli's diagram, but without much enthusiasm (Figure 7.2).

In the end it seems obvious that both Jung and Pauli were inclined to see synchronicity as more than an uncertain talent unique to the human psyche. They decided the psychoid principle had to be an inherent quality of the universe. Nothing would be exempt from its effects, although those effects might often go unnoticed.

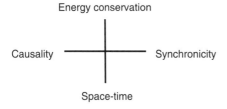

Figure 7.2 Synchronicity as universal principle, second version.

Source: digital diagram by John Ryan Haule simplifying Jung, *CW8*: ¶963.

Field theory and the holistic universe

The idea that synchronicity should be a universal principle, a quality affecting the cosmos as a whole and everything in it, may seem quite radical and even unwise for one whose reputation as a scientist is so frequently questioned. It is worth pointing out, therefore, that the course of Jung's thinking on this matter is very much in line with the way science has solved some of the biggest conundrums it has faced over the past two centuries. This topic will be taken up at greater length in a later chapter, but it might be appropriate to outline the argument here.[9]

Each of the scientific mysteries has had to do with what appeared to be action-at-a-distance, which is the heart of the issue in parapsychology. The first to be solved was that of magnetism. Michael Faraday (1791–1867) performed a number of ingenious experiments that showed magnetic force to be induced by electric current and to occupy a field that takes the form of a doughnut (a toroid). This holistic solution, the idea of an electromagnetic field of force, was inspired by the philosophy of Leibniz, who, in turn, had been inspired by Chinese metaphysics. Historically, the second problem to be solved was Newton's embarrassing discovery that massive bodies like the stars and planets seem to exert an invisible force upon one another across immense distances. Secretly he thought of gravity as "eros" and feared that it must be impossible. Einstein reshaped that problem, under the influence of Faraday's brilliant inspiration. The space-time continuum is a gravity field.

The third problem has to do with the mysteries of quantum mechanics, where everything is thoroughly uncertain: where subatomic particles pop in and out of existence with lightning speed, and each of them spends some of its time as every other type of particle and in every possible combination. Schrödinger's wave equation allows physicists to calculate only the probabilities regarding which type of particle will emerge from the chaos under given conditions. Furthermore, "paired" particles at "impossible" distances from one another act as though they are communicating, though no influence can be transmitted fast enough to make communication possible. The speed of light would simply be too slow. This is called the principle of quantum non-locality. Quanta act as though they are every-where and nowhere (non-local) and so does psyche, as we have seen through our

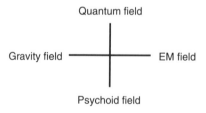

Figure 7.3 The four universal fields.

Source: original digital diagram by John Ryan Haule.

inspection of the amoeba. Physics now makes sense of the chaos of subatomic matter/energy exchanges by conceiving of it as a quantum field.

The progression has been: (a) Chinese metaphysics to (b) Leibniz's universal harmony to (c) Faraday's electromagnetic (EM) field to (d) Einstein's space-time gravity field to (e) Schrödinger's description of what amounts to a quantum field. With this as a background, it seems typically clever of Jung to appeal to the metaphysics of the *I Ching* to describe what we might wish to call a psychoid field. If so, we can complete the Pauli-Jung discussion of synchronicity's place in the universe with a quaternity of *fields* (Figure 7.3).

The visible world and its extension (X-rays, radio waves, etc.) is described by the horizontal axis. It is where locality, the transmission of "vibrations" and billiard-ball causality describe the effects we experience. The vertical axis describes the extremes of non-locality. The top gives us the unimaginable chaos out of which the manageable bodies and radiations of everyday life precipitate. The bottom of the vertical axis is responsible for meaning, consciousness, and organism. Its psychoid nature gives us, as we shall see, an ordered cosmos of nested hierarchies.

Chapter 8

The promise of parapsychology

When Jung addressed Basel University in 1905, calling spiritualism a religious movement that champions a "scientific" hypothesis, and went on to hope that it could ultimately integrate our view of the psyche—if only science would get busy and conquer the field—he summarized the place where we still stand more than 100 years later. We are still divided over what to make of spiritualism and ESP. When we see them as requiring something akin to religious faith, we render their claims "unreal" in the sense of being unavailable for scientific study. When we dismiss them as deliberate acts of fraud or innocent tricks of the unconscious, we render them unworthy of any study at all. When most earnest about parapsychology, we take the position of the thirty-year-old Jung: the phenomena should be studied in all seriousness, and their day will come.

As we shall see in this chapter and the two that follow, that day has indeed come in the sense that a great deal of good scientific work has been done. But it still lies a long way off in the sense that educated, serious-minded people are still expected to "know better." Those who "believe that stuff" are considered gullible. More to the point, as anthropologist C. Roderick Wilson puts it, we have no hypothesis to test, and this leaves us with no way of deciding what our data mean (C. R. Wilson 1998: 197f). Parapsychologists do not doubt that ESP events occur, but they still have no explanation for how they come about, and they do not know what questions to ask. ESP remains unthinkable, even though it clearly happens.

It seems likely that the testable hypothesis will have to come from another field of investigation, probably astrophysics or quantum mechanics. It will have to be a field whose findings are substantiated by mathematics, for this is the only thing we in the West take for proven. Second, it will have to take a holistic shape, like electromagnetism and space-time, a relatively simple picture that has room for everything. Third, it will have to be a principle which includes consciousness in the structure of the universe. Western materialistic science has no place for consciousness. Although it obviously exists, it is an embarrassing reality, an add-on to our picture of the cosmos. When we learn to visualize reality in a manner that includes consciousness, the phenomena of parapsychology will be far less problematic. For, in the end, they are attributes and capabilities of consciousness.

We might begin by observing that consciousness belongs to organisms, seemingly *only* to organisms. Indeed, it seems clear that the degree of an organism's consciousness depends entirely on the complexity of its physical structure. Consciousness would therefore seem to be an organismic function currently missing from our picture of the universe, best described as an organismic field, like Jung's psychoid field.

An organismic field may be just the sort of holistic image necessary to make sense of quantum chaos, the paradox of non-locality and the well-known fact that the observer affects what is observed in the micro-realm. At the other end of the scale in the macro-realm, astronomy struggles to understand the expansion of the universe and the clustering of galaxies—problems that have led it to postulate the existence of dark matter and dark energy. If the cosmos itself turns out to resemble an organism that gathers galaxies into clusters and solar systems into galaxies, many problems may be solved.

When we have a testable model of a single organizing field that unites galaxies, planets, ecosystems, primates, protozoa, molecules and subatomic particles, it will become clear that the everyday realities today's science has no place for— life, consciousness and parapsychology—all arise from qualities inherent in a universal principle, namely that each entity nests within a larger entity, as the liver in a vertebrate body, a planet in a solar system, an electron in an atom. Such a discovery will spell out the details of Jung's psychoid field, just as modern evolutionary biology, neuroscience, archaeology and ethology have clarified the hypothesis of the archetypes. A field so specified would then be testable with experiments rather more sophisticated than those Rupert Sheldrake has proposed in *Seven Experiments that Could Change the World* (2002).

While we wait for a unifying model to emerge, however, we can look at the history of parapsychological investigations and the variety of roles they have played in Western societies. Their status today is still unclear. In some laboratories statistical verification of non-ordinary phenomena has grown steadily stronger. In others, some with financial support from government agencies, a strong case has been made that ESP is a normal human capability that can be developed and refined with training. This chapter and the next two provide an overview of the contemporary field of parapsychology. After that, we will take up some proposals that might lead to a useful hypothesis.

Parapsychology in the eighteenth and nineteenth centuries

Parapsychology has never been a neutral, merely factual realm of experimentation and study. From the beginning its significance has been entangled with issues of social status and manipulation. Demonstrations of psychic powers have functioned as symbolic claims to authority on the basis of class, or as a means to undermine those claims. Battles over who should be in charge of demonstrations and where they should take place have had much to do with the ambitions of the scientific and medical establishments to claim territory, expertise and financial advancement. Struggles over the validity of psychics' claims have to be seen in the light of social turmoil. Bertrand Méheust, Professor of Philosophy at the University of Picardie, has published a huge two-volume study (1999) of "Somnambulism and Mediumship" in France from the eighteenth through the twentieth centuries as well as a later more accessible study (Méheust 2003) of a single psychic, Alexis Didier (1826–86) based on an exhaustive study of every available contemporary document concerning this "prodigious seer." On the other side of the Channel, the role played by Mesmerism in the dynamics of Victorian society has been described by Alison Winter (1998), Associate Professor of History in the Division of Humanities and Social Sciences of the California Institute of Technology.

Mediumship in France

Rumors of psychic powers suggesting "the hidden secrets of nature" began to invade Europe in the seventeenth century, when the first reports of shamanism in Siberia were published. Fears that the Church would retaliate with accusations of witchcraft and the devil, however, forced serious investigators to "adulterate their findings," resulting in a hodge-podge of fact and fiction (Flaherty 1992: 21). A century later, Anton Mesmer's discovery of "magnetic sleep" brought experimentation with altered states of consciousness into public awareness in a brand new and acceptable context. Mesmerism claimed to be a benevolent healing process based on the science of magnetism. This shrewdly removed the phenomena of healing through altered states of consciousness out from the domain of ecclesiastical control. In the course of his first two years of experimentation (1774–76), however, Mesmer eased away from the high prestige he had hoped for from an alliance with the physical sciences as he began to suspect that the mysterious agent of change in "animal magnetism" emanated not from magnetized iron but from his own body (Crabtree 1993: 3–10). This discovery that hypnosis was in some mysterious way based in human relationship set the stage for its multifarious roles in social experimentation. Psychics and their animal magnetizers became celebrity-pairs.

   The age of the celebrity psychic began in 1784 when the Marquis de Puységur began experimenting with Mesmerism to occupy himself and entertain his troops. Victor Race, a young peasant suffering from an inflammation of the chest, entered into a trance where an alter ego could foresee the future course of his illness. Puységur found other subjects who responded similarly when they entered an altered state he called "artificial somnambulism." Within a year he had enough data to publish a book on his experiments that had the "effect of a bomb-shell" (Méheust 2003: 23). It started a fad of hypnotic experimentation and psychic celebrity in which aristocrats assumed the role of scientific demonstrators. No money exchanged hands, and the demonstrations took place before invited guests in the drawing rooms of the "investigators." The aristocratic "magnetizer" did not impose his will on his talented subject to work him like a marionette. Rather he gallantly "inspired" a state of "magnetic lucidity" in an individual of lesser social status (Méheust 2003: 170–7). The ability to magnetize their servants demonstrated the superiority of aristocrats and seemed to validate them as a superior class, conducting scientific experiments as they dispensed magical powers. Writers who reported on the séances were exploring nature "in a romantic-progressive spirit"; and Catholics believed they were witnessing "the recovery of human powers that had belonged to the Garden of Eden" (Méheust 2003: 232f).

With the onset of the French Revolution little more than a decade later, these aristocratic demonstrations fell out of favor, and the whole matter was forgotten for twenty or thirty years. In 1831, as "animal magnetizers" and their talented psychics began to reappear—this time with a more explicit claim to scientific experimentation—a Commission of Inquiry was appointed by the French Academy of Science. Although it declared the majority of the claims valid, it provoked such incoherent debates over matters of procedure and what might count as experimental success that the Academy closed the door to all discussion of hypnosis in 1842.

When scientists withdrew from the field, entrepreneurs hungry for fame and money, as well as writers, philosophers and artists, found themselves free to explore the phenomena unhindered by restraints of method. The new magnetizers assumed pseudo-aristocratic power by ostentatiously dominating their lower-class clairvoyants. Many of the entranced, however, found hypnosis to be a wonderful tool for overturning the power structure, and "in a state of magnetic lucidity took ascendancy over their masters" (Méheust 2003: 173). Thus experiments in parapsychology departed more and more from the ideals of science as they became subsumed to the political hopes and confusions of the day.

In the sixteen-year period (1842–58) between the fall of the French Monarchy and the start of the Second Empire, Alexis Didier, a true "hero of magnetic lucidity," enjoyed his public career. Méheust presents Didier as "an Icaros of the spirit who beats his wings and wants to break free of the human condition," the most complete and subtle somnambulist as well as the best documented. A famous picture from 1847 shows Alexis with his "magnetizer," Jean-Bon Marcillet, a formidable old officer of the Guard, haughtily dispensing "magnetic fluid" upon a frail, blindfolded youth reading from a closed book held before his shrouded face (Méheust 2003: 21–3).

At the same time that Alexis Didier was both victim and hero of the civic chaos surging around him, his public séances threatened a fledgling science only beginning to establish its goals and methods. Animal magnetism, now rather removed from the realm of physics, borrowed instead from the imagery of the latest technology: the telegraph's communication over great distances (telepathy) and the daguerreotype's optical precision (clairvoyance). With a hood over his head to assure witnesses that he was not using his eyes to gather subtle cues, Alexis would describe the contents of sealed envelopes, and read from a book he had never seen before, opened to a random page by his interrogator. The latter would be a third person on the stage alongside Alexis and Marcillet, often the individual who had requested the séance. Sometimes the performance would open by introducing the interrogator, a complete stranger, to Alexis. Entering hypnotic trance, Alexis frequently described the interrogator's home or a favorite painting hanging in it. Sometimes he identified the location of lost objects. Méheust carefully analyzes every document left by contemporary observers and commentators on the séances, and concludes, "It is very probable that Alexis had, at least in part, at certain moments, the powers he claimed to have" (Méheust 2003: 418).

Alexis Didier's stage career ended when the scientific community reclaimed the practice of hypnosis as a diagnostic and healing tool. In 1882 Jean Martin Charcot used his prestige as one of the world's foremost neurologists to reopen the Academy of Science to hypnotic explorations, by painting the altered states of somnambulism as pathological and related to hysteria. What resulted from this new, more medical excitement was the psychology of dissociation that Jung calls the "French School" as well as parlor experiments in table turning, communicating with spirits, clairvoyance, telepathy, and psychokinesis.

For Méheust,

> The singularity of Alexis' "magnetic" clairvoyance resides in the fact that a fugitive equilibrium was realized between tendencies about to go their separate ways, between factual demonstration and a spiritualist approach to the world, between a reality that is human and one that has been purified and constructed in the laboratory.
>
> (Méheust 2003: 195)

Méheust takes the view that spontaneous manifestations of ESP are far more significant and revealing than those produced by the likes of J. B. Rhine. At the same time, pathologizing them in the spirit of Charcot amounts to the denial of a significant human capability. Méheust gives us a phenomenology of magnetic lucidity and takes to task the philosophers, anthropologists and others who refuse to investigate

> one of the greatest taboos in modern times; it has withstood the hunt for taboos that has been an essential part of the second half of the twentieth century, and is today stronger than ever. . . .
>
> If, indeed, *métagnomie* [the super-knowledge of lucid trance] exists, we Westerners do not escape from illusion in rejecting it. . . . [It] would allow us to escape from our cultural dead end and envisage a richer and very different [psyche and world].
>
> (Méheust 2003: 460, 472–3)

Mesmerism in Victorian society

Alison Winter (1998) takes an entirely different approach to the history of Mesmerism and somnambulism from that taken by Méheust. She does not concern herself with the trance states themselves or their truth value but rather with what Victorians thought Mesmerism revealed about who they were or might become. In her hands, it becomes a series of experiments that Victorians were doing on their own society, working out for themselves the nature of influence and authority. In the process, the nature of hypnotism and the human mind became confused and contaminated with a series of social prejudices.

John Elliotson, Professor of Medicine at University College Hospital, London, in the late 1830s tried to show that Mesmerism was a physical reality in which the brain was influenced by an invisible fluid; but his pretensions of scientific objectivity ended in disgrace when his subjects, "a number of sickly, impoverished young girls" made a laughing stock of him (Winter 1998: 59). Powers that had seemed to be firmly in the hands of the medical practitioner went out of control, as entranced, lower-class subjects—rather in the style of contemporary blackface entertainers—straddled the domestic and the exotic, the authentic and the fraudulent (Winter 1998: 90). Thomas Wakley, founder and editor of the *Lancet*, warned by such disgraceful episodes, managed to establish the hospital and the laboratory as the proper places for the medical profession to pursue its expertise and guard its authority.

Mesmerism influenced theology, literature, orchestral performances, and politics: both Charles Dickens (1812–70) and Richard Wagner (1813–83) studied Mesmerism in order to be able to "orchestrate" the responses of their readers or hearers (Winter 1998: 314–30). But its biggest influence was always in medicine. In 1843 when James Braid (1795–1860) published his magnum opus, *Neurypnology; or the Rationale of Nervous Sleep Considered in Relation to Animal Magnetism*, Mesmerism had still not shaken its popular reputation as a demonic force (Winter 1998: 275). Determined to assimilate the field for science and medicine, Braid made three important changes: he removed all reference to those fanciful "magnetic fluids" that had been talked about since the days of Mesmer; he dispensed with the "magnetic passes" (and their sexual overtones) that supposedly had been essential to induce hypnotic states; finally he removed references to the notion that one person's will was imposed upon and came to dominate that of another (Winter 1998: 185). His work was a great success. Within a very few years Mesmeric societies had been formed in all the major towns of England, and a few specialist journals had been founded. Meanwhile, an opposite effect was occurring due to the popular enthusiasm fueling the rise of spiritualism and psychic research. As a result, the infirmaries declined between 1850 and 1870 (Winter 1998: 156). The field was splitting between those who treated it as a secular religion and those who were appropriating it for science.

Even in its medical applications, class issues persisted. In a chapter on the history of anesthesiology, Winter (1998) shows that the administration of ether, which was nearly as difficult to use as Mesmerism and far more dangerous, succeeded in becoming the treatment of choice in surgery—not through superior efficacy, but because its usage was considerably less public and therefore remained under the control of the medical profession. Due to the single-minded efforts of

James Esdaile in the late 1840s, Mesmeric anesthesia did succeed, but only for a time, only in India, and only with lower-class Indian patients. In his Calcutta hospital, Esdaile was able to train a small army of Mesmerizers to prepare his patients for surgery. Eventually, however, the low class of his patients and the "oriental" nature of his activities lost favor with the colonial administration and the practice was halted (Winter 1998: 163–86). Today in the West the same prejudice attends ASCs, hypnosis, and ESP: the idea that only the intellectually lower class is gullible enough to take them seriously.

Throughout this history, the issues revolve around who has the power: the upper class, the specialist, the Westerner, and the man; or the patient, the educated commoner, the "oriental," and the woman. The influential writer Harriet Martineau, ill with a malignant uterine tumor, described the invalid as "a seraph outside the 'real' world and looking on," able to see whole truths undistorted (Winter 1998: 219). She claimed to have discovered the highest truths while in Mesmeric trance. Meanwhile, Elizabeth Barrett feared her very self would be obliterated through the penetration of the Mesmerizer's will—at least until she fell in love with Robert Browning and found the language and imagery of Mesmerism aptly describing the blending of two people in love (Winter 1998: 240).

By the end of the century, Mesmerism had not so much declined in importance as been absorbed into other fields: psychic research (the SPR), physiology (Charcot), dissociation psychology (the "French School"), and psychoanalysis. "Modern science . . . [as a set of] clearly demarcated disciplines . . . arguably did not exist before there was a means of training individuals to ask similar questions and pursue similar lines of investigation" (Winter 1998: 300). Issues of authority and methodology raised by the disputes over Mesmerism played a central role in such demarcation. Although Winter (1998) limits herself primarily to the years between 1835 and 1860, she makes it clear that the question of whether psychic claims were true was rarely as important as what they meant for social status and professional prestige.

In the end, parapsychology operates under a very subtle taboo. It is deemed to be the province of the uneducated, the gullible and the emotionally labile. It has trouble shaking its famous association with spirits and ghosts. Because it inevitably involves what appears to be some sort of action-at-a-distance (psychokinesis), seeing-at-a-distance (clairvoyance), or feeling-at-a-distance (telepathy), it is as easy to overlook or dismiss as were gravity and magnetism in earlier centuries. Newton's and Faraday's inexplicable forms of action-at-a-distance at least obeyed mathematical laws. Phenomena associated with the psyche are not so compliant. They show only statistical regularities, rather like the evanescent particles of quantum theory.

Parapsychology in the laboratory

It has often been said that "new ideas" go through a predictable course on their way to acceptance. First, they are declared to be impossible. Parapsychology is said to be impossible because it "violates the laws of science." Later, as more evidence comes in, it is said that the new idea may have some merit, but it is trivial. For parapsychology, this means that results may show performance to be better than chance but only marginally so. General opinion today oscillates between these first two positions. We will shortly see that results have *not* been trivial. Nevertheless, it is clear that the Western world is not ready for the third stage in accepting parapsychology: that it is important and that its effects are stronger and more pervasive than formerly believed. When our world gets there, however, it will not be long before it moves to the fourth and final position: we have known about parapsychology all along and it is not interesting.

Dean Radin, Director of the Consciousness Research Laboratory at the University of Nevada, Las Vegas, says in his 1997 survey of the field that most researchers in parapsychology today are already at the third stage. They are so confident of the evidence for the basic phenomena that they are no longer trying to prove merely that ESP happens; they have moved on to trying to figure out *how* it does so. Nevertheless, the larger climate is still hostile. For example, in 1984 the US Army Research Institute asked the National Academy of Sciences to evaluate some of its training techniques in the areas of parapsychology, sleep learning, biofeedback and the like. After three years of study the National Research Council held a press conference to declare its most dependable finding, that there has been "no scientific justification for research conducted over a period of 130 years on the existence of parapsychological phenomena" (Radin 1997: 215).

Why were the results so bad? It turns out that the two principal investigators had had a long history of publications declaring that parapsychology is not a legitimate science. There were no parapsychologists on the panel. Despite this imbalance, however, their report admits that phenomena exist for which the investigators could find no alternative explanation. In effect they had ignored studies that contradicted their conclusions. When asked why they failed to mention this, they said that they wanted to avoiding sending out "mixed signals" (Radin 1997: 216). This is the sort of behavior that makes Bernard Méheust so angry about "a reality that has been purified and constructed in the laboratory." In his two-volume history that deals in large part with nineteenth century battles over parapsychology in France, he provides many details of how prominent scientists sitting on officially sanctioned committees sabotaged demonstrations of parapsychology so that they would not have to admit that they had seen something they could not explain (Méheust 1999). There truly has been and still is a conspiracy of silence.

Research standards

Due to the general disinterest or hostility experienced by parapsychology, the field today holds itself to much higher standards than those of mainstream science. Rupert Sheldrake (2002: 170ff) devotes several pages to these sorts of disparities. Dean Radin reports that parapsychology generally considers its results significant when an experiment beats the odds against chance by at least 20:1. Even so, the probability of *repeating* those results with a fresh group of subjects under the same conditions and following the same procedure is only about 50 percent, "because experiments involving human beings never turn out the same way twice" (Radin 1997: 47).

The journals in most of the sciences do not regularly publish so-called "negative results," what happens when experiments fail to support the hypothesis they were designed to explore. Consequently, failed studies end up in file drawers—what Radin (1997) calls the "file-drawer effect." Because of the skepticism its work arouses, however, parapsychology cannot afford to keep file drawers full of undeclared failed experiments. For this reason, the Parapsychological Association has since 1975 required that every study be published, regardless of outcome. Furthermore, "because it is possible there may still be unreported studies," Radin's practice is "to calculate how many unreported studies would be required to nullify the results in the known studies" (1997: 80). When that number of hypothetical "file-drawer" studies gets to be huge, the researcher can be quite confident that he is on to something.

Studies in physics have not been so scrupulous. Radin (1997) describes the procedure of the Particle Data Group of the American Physical Society. These are the people who evaluate experimental data regarding subatomic particles. Standard procedure for the Particle Data Group is to discard the data they deem unreliable, usually because the numbers lie too far outside a central cluster of results. In doing so, they may discard as much as 45 percent of the data (Radin 1997: 57f). In an extreme case, "the omega-minus particle was considered to be 'found' on the basis of only *two events* out of a total of nearly 200,000 experimental trials" (Radin 1997: 49). Rupert Sheldrake adds that in the fields he is personally acquainted with—biochemistry, developmental biology, plant physiology, and agriculture—"only about 5–20 percent of the empirical data are selected for publication." He has questioned researchers in other fields, and they report about the same level of file-drawer effect (Sheldrake 2002: 170).

Meta-analysis

Parapsychology encounters three natural obstacles in getting dependable results: first, the problem of repeating an experiment with a fresh group of human subjects ("practically no one bothers," Radin 1997: 38), second, the "decline effect" (Rhine's discovery that the level of performance falls off as boredom increases), and third, the fact that for practical reasons, including the decline effect, the number of subjects or trials in any given experiment is necessarily small.

The number of trials or subjects undergoing a trial is the heart of the problem, and on account of the three obstacles just described, that number is always low. To get an idea of what this means, let us take the example of a baseball player's "batting average"—how many hits he gets for every "at bat" opportunity. At the beginning of the season, he may get eight hits in his first ten "at bats," giving him a batting average of 0.800. We will have little confidence in this statistic as a prediction of his future performance. For not only is it extremely rare for a player to have an average above 0.400, but also the number of trials is tiny. Perhaps he will strike out in his next five opportunities and see his average fall to 0.533. This would still be a very high average with a very low confidence factor. But when he has batted 0.300 over the course of two or three seasons and had more than 1000 "at bats," we can have confidence that he is an excellent hitter.

The same issue of confidence attends statistical studies in the parapsychology laboratory. Suppose we have a hundred independent studies of a certain type of ESP performance, each with only twenty-five trials. Even if each study shows a high level of success—say 60 percent of the time the subject comes up with the right answer, when chance would expect 50 percent—none of the experiments will inspire a great deal of confidence. But when we combine those hundred studies and consider them as a single study of a particular ESP-type performance, we wind up with a population of 2500 trials. Now the 60 percent rate inspires confidence.

This is what Radin has been up to, using a procedure he calls "meta-analysis." He begins by collecting all the published studies he can find that address a certain parapsychological phenomenon. After careful inspection of experimental and statistical procedures used in those studies, the types of control and so forth, he determines which studies are compatible for combination. His results are quite impressive.

To illustrate, skeptical British psychologist Mark Hansel (1980) has offered a stiff challenge to the field of parapsychology, one he probably thought would never be met: *Parapsychology will inspire confidence when an experiment can be repeated three times and beat the odds against chance by 100:1* (Hansel 1980: 298). Radin's meta-analysis enables parapsychology to meet this challenge. The method takes the third, fourth, etc. experiments on the same hypothesis by different experimenters as "repetitions of the experiment," as they certainly are. And the results are encouraging:

> Hansel would be pleased to know that this has been achieved dozens of times, in numerous categories of psi experiments. This is why informed skeptics today agree that chance is no longer a viable explanation for the results obtained in psi experiments.
>
> (Radin 1997: 50)

Spontaneous psychics: commonalities

Stephen E. Braude, Professor of Philosophy at the University of Maryland Baltimore County, entered the field of parapsychology for reasons similar to Jung's. He thought it necessary for a complete philosophy of mind, much as Jung thought it necessary for a complete science of the psyche. Although Braude was cautious enough to wait until after he had tenure to enter the field, he was still surprised at what he found:

> Since dipping into the data of parapsychology, I have encountered more examples of intellectual dishonesty than I had previously thought possible. . . . I have seen how scientists are not objective, how philosophers are not wise, how psychologists are not perceptive, how historians lack perspective—not to mention how physicians are not healers, and how attorneys are not committed to justice.
>
> (Braude 1986: ix)

Braude, in short, is as outraged as Méheust, and like his French counterpart prefers non-experimental or spontaneous evidence of ESP over that produced in the laboratory. He declares that "Rhine's so-called revolution has failed" because the fence-sitters will always find some reason to resist the evidence; and even if all the skeptics were to accept the existence of psi phenomena, "it is doubtful that further laboratory experiments would yield much enlightenment" (Braude 1986: 5f). Laboratory experiments are contrived events that have little to do with real life experience and little if any transformative value. In short, Braude is convinced that psychic experiences really do occur, and he would like to go on from there and try to find out what sort of talent ESP might be and what it tells us about ourselves.

He wonders to what we might liken ESP. He notes that parapsychologists often seem to assume that the talent for psi is as unremarkable as digesting food or pronouncing words, while it surely must be more like making clever retorts or being able to empathize (Braude 1986: 56). Its occurrence probably always has to do with a person's physical or psychological needs. It might be compared with athletic prowess, in that some people seem to be better at it than others, but even the stars need to be in the right frame of mind to perform well. "Analogously, while some people can arouse themselves sexually under almost any conditions, few can do so under laboratory conditions" (Braude 1986: 10).

Where the mediums are

Unfortunately, it is not easy to find mediums like Alexis Didier today. Braude (1986: 65) says, "The overall psychic climate has changed so profoundly since the turn of the [twentieth] century that few today even try to discover whether they have mediumistic abilities." In this context, a "medium" would be an individual who enters an altered state in order to produce non-ordinary phenomena. In the language of the nineteenth century, that would mean a somnambulist, an individual with two or more subpersonalities. The historical record shows clearly that different subpersonalities from the same individual may manifest different physiological states, "including measurable differences in autonomic nervous system functioning, visual acuity, spontaneous brain waves, and brain-wave evoked potentials" (Radin 1997: 149).

Although a hundred and more years ago mediums were fascinated with the idea of communicating with the dead, and dissociated subpersonalities were taken as evidence for it, the hypothesis of ghosts and spirits is not necessary for medi-umship. Today's participant-observer anthropologists have come to a similar con-clusion regarding the spirit claims of pre-literate peoples. Although the natives may insist that spirits are in play, the anthropologist can accept the non-ordinary result without accepting the native hypothesis: "What we have called an extra-ordinary experience probably is not the result of experiencing something from another dimension, but an experience which occurs when one opens oneself to aspects of experience that previously had been ignored or repressed" (D. E. Young and Goulet 1998: 9). This is what studies in parapsychology propose to us: that we consider aspects of experience we have been systematically ignoring.

While today's anthropologists struggle to find appropriate words to designate their non-ordinary experiences, nineteenth-century investigators described somn-ambulism with fine differentiation. By my count, Méheust (1999) identifies at least eleven types of somnambulistic talent: hyperesthesias (greatly enhanced sensory acuity); synesthesias (hearing colors, tasting shapes, etc.); the ability to see inside one's own body or inside the body of another; spontaneously feeling anoth-er's pain or emotion; deliberately feeling another's pain or emotion; clairvoyance; clairaudience; traveling out of body; reading another's thoughts; and seeing the future. Shamdasani (2003: 110) provides a list from 1826 that adds another four or five talents: the ability to estimate time, insensibility to exterior sensations, exalta-tion of the imagination or memory, and hyperdevelopment of the intellectual faculties.

Although many of these talents do occur today, the most spectacular "pack-ages" of mediumistic abilities are to be found in the historical record. This is hardly a reason for the phenomenologist of mediumship to despair, however, for the data are dependable. The most famous psychics were repeatedly tested by some of the best informed and most skeptical observers of their day, and they left detailed written records. The Society for Psychical Research was extremely strict in its standards—perhaps overly so. Their policy was to eliminate any medium ever found cheating. By all accounts, however, some of the genuine ones *did* cheat when they were having a bad day. Eusapia Palladino was famous for it, but eventually did get a second and third look from the SPR. The most active inves-tigators for the SPR were people who had come from very religious families but, in the face of science, were no longer able to believe traditional doctrines. They came to hope that parapsychology would convince them of the reality of a soul that survives bodily death. What made them hard-headed skeptics, however, was their determination not to be fooled again (Gauld 1968: 263). The ASPR, the American branch of the SPR, turned away so many interested supporters for being insufficiently skeptical that the organization failed to survive (Blum 2006: 263). The literature on the great mediums of the past is extensive and reliable.

Even the best of the nineteenth-century psychics, however, manifested behav-ior that seemed to border on the pathological. Great psychics like Alexis Didier and Rudi Schneider were often subject to so many demands for performance—sometimes several in a single day—that they easily became exhausted, began to show symptoms of breakdown, and found their psychic powers diminished. William James was familiar with the problem: "Their abilities if genuine were unreliable and erratic. Even the good ones eventually tended to suffer from the decline effect. The weirdness of their profession often produced mental problems, if those didn't already exist" (Blum 2006: 155).

ESP and non-ordinary states

It seems clear that the altered states of consciousness we studied in connection with ritual, shamanism, ayahuasca ingestion, meditation, and the like, have much in common with those of the nineteenth-century mediums. Back then, the most common method of inducing states of psychic receptivity was hypnosis, for the entire somnambulism phenomenon was an outgrowth of Mesmerism. Mesmer himself reported evidence for a "sixth sense" in some of his subjects (Mesmer 1980: 135). But, as we shall see, some mediums have also employed what appears to be self-taught breathing techniques and the ingestion of alcohol. Furthermore, about half of all spontaneous psi experiences occur when we are in the most common of ASCs, the dream state (Radin 1997: 68). Because synchronistic dreams are quite common, it is likely that few of us are entirely innocent of ESP.

All of this implies that our ordinary state of consciousness, although an inconstant thing itself, is the primary obstacle to our experiencing ESP, or recognizing parapsychological experiences when they occur. This Western prejudice is certainly the reason ESP is far less common in the West than elsewhere. Our cultural expectations reinforce the beta brain-wave state that we take to be ordinary, and reject the others as absurd or pathological. Jung recognized this reality in 1919: "If a European had to go through the same experiences and ceremonies which the medicine man performs in order to make spirits visible, he would have the same experiences" (*CW8*: ¶303).

Jung's idea is supported by anthropologist Jean-Guy Goulet. He was in Alaska in July 1984, participating in a pre-ceremony discussion with natives and others, when the teepee they were sitting in filled with smoke. Before his smarting eyes, Goulet saw "a detailed life-size image of myself . . . wearing the same clothes I was wearing, kneeling by the fire, fanning the flames with my hat." Then another non-native got up and began blowing on the fire, whereupon an Elder immediately instructed him to fan it with his hat lest he offend spiritual entities who might cause a violent wind in camp. Goulet was shocked at his apparent telepathic foreknowledge. "Up to that time, I knew neither the right nor the wrong way of fanning a fire, nor the rationale" (Goulet 1998: 30).

ESP in pre-literate cultures

Australian lay researcher Ronald Rose attempted in the 1950s to test the hypothesis that non-Westerners would be more familiar with and more adept in psychic experiences. He and his wife conducted a lengthy investigation of Aborigines who had had minimal contact with Whites. His use of J. B. Rhine's laboratory procedures, the Zener cards and dice, provided only very limited support for his hypothesis. Only one of the Aborigines did well with the cards, an elderly woman called "Granny," who had expressed doubt about her competence. All the others worked hard, trying to prove that they could succeed, but failed (Rose 1956: 221f). It looks as though these latter took it for a Western task that required ego-directed thinking, whereas "Granny" retained her native way of thought.

Evidence that ESP belongs to the everyday experience of Aborigines is abundant in Rose's book. For instance, he learned that telepathy is essential for sending "smoke signals." While Westerners tend to assume that Aborigines and Native Americans communicate across canyons with puffs of smoke, like a sort of Morse code, Rose learned that the fire indicates merely that there is a message to be sent. The message itself travels telepathically. Tjalkalieri, Rose's informant, says:

> I would make the smoke so that a man could see it—a good big fire with green boughs that makes good smoke. When he sees it, he knows it is not a camp fire and he gets to thinking. And I am thinking, too, so that he thinks my thoughts.

> (Rose 1956: 54)

Trained anthropologists report that telepathy is ubiquitous in the pre-literate world. Reichel-Dolmatoff (1997) found that the Tukano hunters of the Amazonian rain forest say one must never think of the animal one is hunting: "If we think of [the tapir], then she sees us in her thoughts . . . If we want to kill her we must think of other things" (Reichel-Dolmatoff 1997: 115). Similar advice was given to Marie-Françoise Guédon during her work with the Dene speakers of Alaska. For example, "Don't think about the 'big one' [the bear] when walking alone in the woods." At first the advice confused her, but after ten years, "I finally grasped: Thought is communication with other thinking entities and therefore has consequences" (Guédon 1998: 55).

Rupert Sheldrake (2003) gives an example from naturalist J. Allen Boone, studying monkey behavior in the wild. One day after observing a band of monkeys playing in a clearing and then, with sudden purpose, disappear, he waited to see why they had gone. After three hours, two hunters appeared with rifles. Boone learned, "At the precise moment those two hunters had picked up their rifles and headed for the clearing, three-hours' walking distance away, every monkey in the clearing had fled from the place" (Sheldrake 2003: 153).

Psychic contagion

The presence of other people can have a noticeable effect on psychic performance. At an ayahuasca ceremony, for instance, a vegetalista announced that he would like to sit beside Luis Eduardo Luna, "because you have beautiful visions." Luna says it is common for vegetalistas to "join their visions . . . so as to see better and perform a shamanic task" (Luna 1986: 151). Similarly, during the Victorian rage for table-tipping, "People said that when a gifted psychic joined in, tables did more than tilt and wobble. They hopped, crackled, hummed like a vibrating string. Some rose into the air, as if being tugged by invisible hands" (Blum 2006: 20).

Such contagion can also work the other way, when the presence of skeptics interferes with a psychic's performance. Regarding Alexis Didier, Méheust says that there was evidently some interference when skeptics were present, but not every time and it was never complete. Sometimes Alexis "could evade the effects of incredulity by having another person in the group, preferably a woman, hold the object" whose contents he was to describe (Méheust 2003: 448f).

Even physicists are cognizant of such phenomena. In a 1959 article in *Scientific American*, the great theoretical physicist George Gamow described what he called the "Pauli Effect":

> The standing of a theoretical physicist is said to be measurable in terms of his ability to break delicate devices merely by touching them. By this standard Wolfgang Pauli was a very good theoretical physicist; apparatus would fall, break, shatter or burn when he merely walked into a laboratory.
>
> (Radin 1997: 131)

Chapter 9

Seeing at a distance and its mastery

There are two categories of parapsychological phenomena, which can be roughly distinguished as, first, seeing or otherwise knowing facts that are inaccessible to the sense organs, either because they are distant in space and time or because they are the contents of other people's minds, and second, causing empirical changes in the material world through one's own mental activity, alone. For convenience, we shall call them "seeing (or knowing) at a distance" and "psychokinesis." Psychokinesis will be the topic of Chapter 10.

This chapter considers only the first type of "psi" event, the "wholly mental" sort, including clairvoyance, clairaudience, telepathy and the like. Such "non-ordinary knowing" is the easier category of parapsychology to accept, and we shall find that in many ways its operation resembles what we have already learned about altered states of consciousness. Telepathy and clairvoyance are talents that can be developed and refined by those who train themselves in the receptivity of the "meditation complex" or "transcendental ego" and then learn to steer their attention by dropping auto-suggestions into the warps of their own conscious states.

Two levels of activity

According to our culture's mainstream view, shamans, if they are taken seriously at all, are able to gain access only to their own unconscious networks—even when they are able to generate extraordinarily unified brain-states. This perspective suits our usual linear, "scientific" way of understanding things—i.e. by identifying a chain of specifiable causes. In taking up parapsychological claims, however, we are beginning to challenge the assumption that everything "real" can be explained by chains of causal interactions.

In parapsychology it seems that the psyche is able to gain information that cannot have come through the sense organs and cannot be accounted for as something the brain can have acquired by any known means. Seeing and knowing at a distance require us to consider the "border-zone" possibility that psyche sometime acts independently of the brain. The crucial piece in knowing "the impossible" is that no chain of causes can be found to connect the verifiable but distant outer event and our subjective knowing it. The situation is analogous to the so-called "non-locality" provision in quantum mechanics (Bell's Theorem). Even when a pair of electrons are widely separated from one another, they will simultaneously undergo precisely the same changes in momentum or spin, just as though they were able to communicate with one another. It looks as though a message to change has been sent through space at a velocity greater than the speed of light. Because such speeds are physically impossible, quantum mechanics says that each member of the electron pair influences the other "acausally" (no chain of causes) and "non-locally" (across distance).

Similarly, when Jung wakes up in a German hotel room and finds himself experiencing the suicidal despair of a patient back in Switzerland, the psyches of Jung and the patient have simultaneously entered the same state of despair, acausally and non-locally. Jung's whole organism has undergone a change in state, bringing it into sympathetic resonance with the whole organism of his patient. This is the synchronistic dimension of the event. When Jung becomes conscious, however, that this is not his own despair he is feeling but that of his patient and subsequently feels the shadow of a bullet passing through his head, his brain has become active and is interpreting for him the meaning of the change of state in his body-and-mind.

In what follows in this chapter and the succeeding one, we will be able to say a great deal about how our organism interprets and misinterprets its states of consciousness. But how that consciousness has been changed in the first place, namely how a telepath or a clairvoyant has "received an impossible message" will be allowed to remain unexplained. We will simply say that this change has occurred "synchronistically." Discussion of what it means that an event is synchronistic will be saved to subsequent chapters.

Studies in telepathy

It is often difficult to decide whether a parapsychological event should be categorized as telepathy or clairvoyance. For example, when Alexis Didier accurately described his interrogator's living room hundreds of miles distant from his stage in Paris, was his psyche "visiting" that living room directly or was Alexis reading the mind of his interrogator? Either hypothesis is equally likely. In this section, we select evidence for incidents that unmistakably involve telepathy and find that they are extremely common. It is instructive not only to consider the evidence that telepathy really occurs but also to see how it fails and what its failures have to tell us.

The feeling of being stared at

In his project to convince the world that we need an organismic theory to account for everyday phenomena in biology and consciousness, biochemist, cell biologist and philosopher of science Rupert Sheldrake has been working to reveal how common so-called impossible occurrences are. We have a "taboo," for instance, against investigating whether and how it may be that when someone stares at the back of our head we regularly turn around and look back. Our Western metaphysics tells us that eyes are organs for receiving photons and that they do not send out perceptible rays. Yet we act as if they do. Then we deny it. We say it is only a superstition; or that we have responded not to telepathy but to some very ordinary subliminal cues; or that it was just blind chance that we looked back when we did; or that we selectively remember our successes and forget our failures (Sheldrake 2003: 137). Thus do we talk ourselves back to respectability.

Certain professions, however, do not allow us piously to debunk the feeling of being stared at. Sheldrake has found that surveillance personnel "generally agree that when people are being watched or followed, it is important to look directly at them as little as possible" (Sheldrake 2003: 141). Similarly, during the Second World War, RAF pilots were instructed "not to stare at an enemy pilot when preparing to shoot him down" (Ibid.: 125).

Sheldrake was able to assemble 13,900 being-stared-at trials as a result of publicity gained from his book, *Seven Experiments that Could Change the World*, a program on the Discovery Channel, and an article in *New Scientist*. He found that staring was detected 55 percent of the time, giving an odds against chance of 10^{20}:1. In a similar experiment conducted in Amsterdam in 1995, subjects scored above chance at 10^{376}:1 (Sheldrake 2003: 171, 176f). In a 1980 version of the experiment, closed circuit television was used, with one person staring at a monitor in the room next door to the test subject, who sat in range of a television camera. This time, the subject was not asked to identify when she was the object of staring, rather her skin was tested for the galvanic response. It turns out that we register an emotional disturbance ("the feeling of being stared at") unconsciously in our bodies, even when we are not aware of the fact (Sheldrake 2003: 183).

Sheldrake (2003) has also gathered information about animals similar to what we have already seen concerning pre-literate hunters trying not to think about their prey. There is overwhelming evidence that dogs and cats at home know when their owners have decided to return from wherever they have been, and he has accumulated 106 accounts of dogs who responded with distress at the time that a person they were attached to died at some distance from home. The dogs apparently knew about the death long before the news arrived by telephone call or telegram (Sheldrake 2003: 78).

A survey of sixty-five London veterinary clinics revealed that all but one were plagued by frequent cancellations of cat appointments because the cat had suddenly disappeared. The sixty-fifth clinic had ceased making appointments for cats for just this reason. Their new policy was that cat owners could bring their animals in without first making an appointment, but spontaneously whenever it was convenient (Sheldrake 2003: 20). Sheldrake includes a related report from American naturalist William Long who watched a family of foxes over a long period of time. The young kits were allowed to caper about in the vicinity of the den. When one of them strayed too far, the vixen would silently and intently stare at it. At that point, the kit "suddenly checks himself and turns as if he had heard a command."

Only then does he see her intent look and return "like a trained dog to a whistle" (Sheldrake 2003: 165).

Mental radio

In 1930 Upton Sinclair published a book that he wrote under the direction of his wife, entitled *Mental Radio*. It described telepathy experiments she had made. Sinclair says his wife of fifty years, Mary Craig Kimbrough, called "Craig" throughout the book, had shown evidence of powerful intuition and psychic gifts for ESP from her childhood. At the age of forty she suffered a breakdown in health that led her to an intensive study of "what the mind really is" (Sinclair 1930: 17). In 1927 she witnessed a stage demonstration of telepathy and decided she had to learn how to "read minds." She hired the young man who had given the demonstration and asked him to hypnotize her; but instead of falling under his power, she began to give *him* mental commands (Sinclair 1930: 20f). She realized hypnosis would be no shortcut to her goal and that she would have to devise her own method of telepathy.

Most of Craig's experiments were done with the help of her husband. Sinclair would make a set of drawings, wrap each individually to make it opaque, and seal it inside a plain envelope. He would give Craig a pile of six or eight envelopes, and she would choose one at random, lie down on a couch, placing the envelope over her solar plexus. When she got what she felt was a convincing image, she would draw it. In this way she would work through the whole pile, and later on the two of them would compare the originals with the telepathically received images. The results of the experiments are fairly impressive: out of 290 drawings, she had 65 complete successes, 155 partial successes and 70 failures (Sinclair 1930: 14). She had some degree of success, therefore, in 76 percent of the trials.

Much of the book is taken up with discussing each pair of drawings, the original and Craig's telepathic copy. Here are a few of the more interesting observations. Once Sinclair chose a page from the Sunday newspaper supplement as a target, wrapped and sealed it, and put it in the pile for Craig's exercise. What she drew, however, corresponded to the picture on the *backside* of the newspaper page (Sinclair 1930: 73). This seems hardly a chance event, and one is left to wonder whether Sinclair had taken subliminal notice of the picture on the reverse or whether that second picture was dimly visible through the page while he contemplated the intended image. Alternately, it may be that Craig was clairvoyantly viewing the contents of the envelope directly rather than telepathically reading her husband's mind.

On another occasion, Sinclair drew an obelisk for the target, and Craig responded with three nearly parallel lines, meeting at the top, pretty similar to Sinclair's obelisk; but then instead of drawing a base for the monument, she drew little circles at the bottom end of each of the three lines. Sinclair (1930: 92) says, "Why should an obelisk go on a jag, and have little circles at its base? The answer seems to be: it inherited the curves from the previous [drawing of a] fish hook, and [picked up] the little circles from the next drawing." This contagion from one trial to the next is precisely what Jung described in doing the Word Association Test some quarter century earlier. He noticed that when a complex was touched with one word, the emotional effects would carry over and influence the responses to one or several succeeding words. In this way, we see that telepathy is not a wholly new capacity. We use the same associations and limbic-system connections in telepathy as in other life tasks.

Again, Sinclair gave his wife a set of eight drawings and went outside for a walk along the ocean where they lived in Long Beach, California, while she struggled to discern the contents of the sealed envelopes. This time she did not get a single drawing right. Instead of reproducing the drawings, she sketched the thoughts Sinclair was entertaining on his walk (Sinclair 1930: 100). Here, it seems that a spontaneous form of telepathy triumphed over the laboratory variety, and it is to be noted that the telepath cannot discern the difference any more than she can tell whether her image derives from telepathy or clairvoyance.

How to mind-read

In the beginning Craig thought she might succeed by tensing up and concentrating on her tightly closed eyes, as though to bore through the darkness to a vision. She got nothing but headaches and learned that she could not succeed unless she relaxed her eyes (Sinclair 1930: 140). When she did so, she learned that what appears is anything but dependable: "Imagination is a far more active function than the average person realizes. This conscious-subconscious mind is 'a liar,' a weaver of fictions. It is the dream-mind, and also it is the mind of memory-trains" (Sinclair 1930: 131). One thinks immediately of Taussig's (1987) informant: "Yagé [ayahuasca] lies."

In the end, Craig learned she had to deal with this lying dream-mind because it was the only tool she had. What she discovered about it is very much what Jung discovered about active imagination and Husserl about the transcendental ego. She urges the reader not to try to will the image into appearing but rather to work on developing the field of consciousness within which it may appear. She calls the goal "undivided attention," and the "trick" to managing it is: "Putting the attention on *one* object, or one *uncomplicated* thought, such as joy, or peace, and holding it there steadily. It isn't thinking; it is the inhibition of thought, except for one thought, or one object in thought."

She urges the would-be mind-reader to learn to relax and simply observe what happens within the conscious field. Avoid falling asleep on the one side or being carried away by "a train of subconscious daydreams" on the other. All the while, she learned to hold the envelope "easily without clutching it." In that mentally alert and physically relaxed state, the mind-reader must "give the mental order to the unconscious mind to tell you what is on the paper."

Now she moves on to describe what will happen. Fragments of images will begin to appear faintly, and "notions" will occur to you about what the image might be. Take those notions seriously and make a mental note of them, but do not jump to conclusions. Make the mind blank again. Return to your uncomplicated single thought of joy or peace and give the order again to present the image. Repeat this process two or three times. If a single image persists, accept it and draw it (Sinclair 1930: 124–31).

Toward a mind-to-mind theory

A much more systematic approach to telepathy was taken in the second decade of the twentieth century in France by René Warcollier. Trained as a chemical engineer, Warcollier made a fortune early in his life by coming up with a procedure to manufacture jewelry from the scales of fish. His livelihood taken care of, he began experimenting with telepathy in 1910, and by 1922 had set up "telepathic posts" in several European countries.[1] Warcollier himself uses the definition of telepathy that was coined in 1882 by SPR investigator F. W. H. Myers. It is a transmission from one individual to another without the help of the senses or of anything mental, including emotions, ideas, mental images, sensations, or words (Warcollier 1948/2001: 1).

Warcollier takes the very sensible position that in telepathy one unconscious "meta-mind" is in communication with another. Because the essence of the process is unconscious, far more of such communication takes place than we know. He estimates, in fact, that probably no more than a quarter of this meta-communication actually enters consciousness. Telepathy is, therefore, not at all limited to humans, but is a primitive process—common, he thinks, especially with herd animals and insects.[2] Probably flocks of birds and schools of fish are also in constant communication at this very basic level. Because it is so primitive, emotion plays a larger role than generally thought, and in the transition from unconscious to conscious, the impulse takes the form of dream-images and may be distorted or turned into symbols.[3] Thus Warcollier's views are closely harmonious with those of Sinclair's wife and C. G. Jung.

Warcollier gives us several observations that help identify the process. He notes that in *spontaneous* telepathy a "signal *forces itself* on the subject." The spontaneous subject is surprised by a signal strong enough to break through the barrier of his ordinary consciousness. This is probably why the whole message comes through. The experimental subject, by contrast, does not just receive; she has to "reach out for the signal"; as a result her attention wavers toward and away from the target and is more likely to come up with disconnected elements of the image (Warcollier 1948/2001: 16).

He notes that it is not the details of the message but its deep significance at the level of "meta-mind" that has effect. He illustrates this principle with an example of a clairvoyante who was able correctly to answer questions put to her in languages she did not understand, giving her answers in French. On one occasion, a man tested her with a question formulated in Hebrew. She responded that she was unable to answer the question because the man who asked it did not understand what he had asked. The questioner admitted the truth: he had had the question written out for him phonetically by a Hebrew speaker, and he had learned to pronounce the syllables without understanding what they meant (Warcollier 1948/2001: 50).

Warcollier's technique for receiving telepathic messages is virtually identical with that of Mrs. Sinclair. The "percipient" and the "agent" would agree in advance on a time for the experiment. At the appointed moment, the agent would spontaneously choose an image and draw it. Meanwhile, the percipient would focus his attention on the agent, "clear his mind of all thoughts, and note the mental images appearing in consciousness" (Warcollier 1948/2001: 2).

Warcollier's short book (less than 100 pages) is largely taken up with analyses of telepathic hits and misses, intelligently categorized according to type. For example, he speaks of a message sent and received as a "psychic molecule" that is made up of both intellectual and emotional components. We would call it an altered state of consciousness. The psychic molecules received, therefore, will interact with the expectations, conscious and unconscious, of the percipient's own psyche. Needs and associations based in past experience will draw the psychic molecule into agreement with them. The point could not be made more clearly that the reception of telepathic information is subject to distortion by the percipient's own complexes, by neural pathways long established in the percipient's limbic system (Warcollier 1948/2001: 29).

The French investigator's main area of interest is in the fragmentary nature of most of the percipients' drawings. His observations are very suggestive for those who have familiarized themselves with recent studies in neuropsychology and ethology. He says the percipient responds "like a child," because when the image appears "the first thing he observes is movement" (Warcollier 1948/2001: 22). Not only like a child, we would say, but also like a vertebrate. For evolution has established the most sensitive defense insuring our survival in the wild in the form of alertness to movement that might suggest either a lurking predator or a convenient meal. The same instincts are mobilized in telepathy as function in every other life-situation.

He speaks, too, of "the irrationally mechanical decomposition of the target [image] into elements," which he says reveals the primitive nature of "the latent model in the unconscious." For example, the percipient rarely sees closed, static structures like circles and squares but rather the disconnected angles and arcs that comprise them or sometimes only the pattern of relations between the parts of the image, while leaving out the parts themselves (Warcollier 1948/2001: 10, 3, 18).

All of these observations suggest that several visual cortex areas of the percipient's brain are at work in response to the "psychic molecule" received. The problem is that the "binding" action which organizes our sensory world into a unitary reality for us remains for some reason unengaged, probably because emotion is lacking, leaving us with the fragmentary elements of edges, angles and relationships. This suggests Warcollier's first reason why experimental telepathy is inferior to the spontaneous variety, for spontaneous images are "bound" into emotional/sensory/intellectual wholes. Something alive and numinous in the agent comes through as a whole to the percipient. Telepathy is more likely—synchronicities are noticed—when archetypes are engaged.

Causal and synchronistic elements in telepathy

Warcollier's astute phenomenology of experimental telepathy reveals that both causal and acausal elements are involved. The neurobiological processes that occur to bring angles, arcs and relational patterns to consciousness belong to the field of *causality*, where one entity (neuron, molecule) interacts physically with another at a discrete moment and location. The "meta-mind" of the percipient, however, is not in physical contact with or within sensory range of the agent's meta-mind. This is where the *synchronistic* field, characterized by non-locality and acausality, plays a role. In this section, we consider the physiological mechanisms that bring messages up from the deeply unconscious psychoid functioning of the human organism to the point that we can become conscious of the message content. The mammalian organism is *designed* for communication—for sending, receiving, and interpreting information from relatives, from species members and even from members of other species. And the capacity for deep communication increases and becomes more differentiated among more recently evolved mammals, particularly among primates.

The role of ASCs

All of the experimental telepaths describe cultivating a non-ordinary state of consciousness similar to what is familiar to us from Jung's active imagination and Husserl's transcendental ego. More spectacular experiences of telepathy occur when the conscious state is further removed from the range of our everyday awareness. Thus Benny Shanon, the Israeli cognitive psychologist, reports that "practically everybody" who has had some minimal exposure to ayahuasca reports having had telepathic experiences: some involuntary, and others deliberately sent or received. Furthermore, ayahuasqueros are familiar with direct insight into the personality of others, of having "special access to their mental states and inner feelings" (Shanon 2002: 256f). For example, he reports an incident in which he and several others "saw" a woman lose her soul:

> Yes, I saw it. And apparently other people saw this as well. The dancing and chanting stopped. Assisted by another woman, the *madrinha* held the troubled woman. They sustained her, and at the same time sang. Over a period that I would estimate to be about twenty minutes, the woman's soul came back and was lost again. Eventually, the woman regained her soul and her normal self. She then appeared tranquil, clean and visibly younger than she had looked before the session started.
>
> (Shanon 2002: 71)

How they saw and knew so much, as we shall see, no doubt had much to do with perfectly explicable causal processes belonging to the physiology of the human organism. But these things almost never come so vividly to consciousness without the help of an alteration in brain state. We have to get out of our left-brain rational habits, at least; and very likely we have to induce a unitary brain state of a shamanic sort before such visions become common.

Telepathy of every variety involves some degree of empathy, of "feeling-into" the mental state of another, whether voluntarily or not. Walter Freeman, who describes the brain states that arise as AM waves fall into their basins of attraction, says that empathy is possible only when we leave the everyday mode of brain-function. "You have to learn to understand and unlearn to empathize"[4] (Freeman 2000: 154). "Unlearning" is brought about by the release of neuro-modulators in the brain, resulting in a loosening of "the synaptic fabric of the neuropil," thereby loosening old beliefs and making it possible for new ones to be adopted. Such neuromodulators account for the sense of numinosity that accompanies religious and political conversions, as well as falling in love. These alterations occur every night during sleep and have to do with the influence dreams may have on our conscious attitude (Freeman 2000: 151, 153).

> It seems to me that humans discovered how to control unlearning through trance states, using techniques of behavioral modification for [interpersonal] bonding far beyond the range of the nuclear family and the tribe. These practices have been elaborated through cultural evolution and are pervasive in modern society, although their social significance goes largely unnoticed and their neurochemical bases are largely undocumented.
>
> (Freeman 2000: 153)

Thus the "dysregulation" of the condition we think of as "ordinary consciousness" is essential if we humans are to communicate deeply with one another, form attachments, and communicate the most important things.

Mirror neurons

A good deal of excitement has attended the discovery by Giacomo Rizzolatti of the University of Parma and Michael Arbib of the University of Southern California that there is a small batch of neurons located in pre-motor tissue in the region where Broca's speech-motor area is located in humans (Mithen 2006: 130f). They have been called "mirror neurons" because they respond to the sight of a species member performing an action, and their firing results in the activation in the observer of the same brain areas that are involved in carrying out the observed action. They link Broca's area solidly to communication and motor activation, again reminding us that speech in humans is an adaptation of the communication behaviors of lower primates. Mirror neurons assist in discerning the intentions of the other through observing how she behaves (*Science News 167*, April 30, 2005:

278). They are responsible for visual-motor coordination (Allman 1999: 152), but most importantly for understanding.

Although we have not used the expression "mirror neurons" earlier in this book, the idea behind them has been fundamental to the top-to-bottom structure of the archetype. At the "top" of the structure, the animal recognizes a species pattern or a trigger for that pattern or perhaps just imagines or dreams that pattern. Such recognitions and projections, however, never take place in isolation; they involve cortical networks, limbic associations, typical forms of autonomic nervous system balance, altered hormone levels, and more. Years before the discovery of mirror neurons, philosopher Harvey B. Sarles (1985) discussed the report that the pulse rate of a person who has just been jogging will be "pulled down" through eye contact made with a non-jogger. "This suggests that interaction involves shared rhythms, that heart/pulse rates are susceptible of being shared, and that eye contact is sufficient to set up shared rhythmicity" (Sarles 1985: 234).

Douglas T. Kenrick (2006) of Arizona State University refers to the same dynamic, employing the expression "inherited decision biases." He calls them "cold, hard economic rules designed to serve selfish genetic interests. Yet they are accompanied by affective states that may be warm and fuzzy or even hot and steamy." They facilitate coalition formation, status, self-protection, winning mates, retaining mates, familial care, and more. Dynamic interaction between conspecifics inevitably activates these decision biases and produces "reliable social dynamics." Because such communications produce changes in autonomic nervous system balance, hormones must be involved (Kenrick 2006: 21–6).

Limbic communication

In the West we tend to undervalue such things and need our laboratories to discover them because we rely so heavily in everyday life on the left hemisphere, which "appears to be inept at reading non-verbal social or emotional cues from others" (D. J. Siegel 1999: 185). Here is one of the most glaring examples of how we can overrule an evolutionary asset that is fundamental to all birds and mammals, the limbic system—despite the fact that each of us has been almost completely dependent on it during infancy and that we use it constantly as adults, albeit unconsciously.

The limbic brain is not limited to the complex reactions we discussed in Volume 1. It gathers emotional significance from the facial expression, pupil size, body posture, gait and scent of another and determines immediately whether the other individual is careless, aggressive, friendly, sexual, submissive, and so forth (Lewis *et al.* 2000: 53). Infants scan their mother's face to determine the emotional significance of a situation by discerning what is on mother's mind. Is this unfamiliar situation safe or dangerous? Through the limbic system, mothers and babies share an inborn common language in the form of real-time feedback. Watching a mere videotape of mother's face will soon provoke distress in an infant because the signals she is giving have no emotional connection with the baby's present situation (Lewis *et al.* 2000: 61f). Similarly, experiments show that if one monkey hears a tone signaling that a shock is coming, his facial expression is enough to prompt a second monkey to press a lever to prevent the shock (Goleman 1995: 103).

The limbic system is essential to all social consciousness. Because it receives whole messages, wordlessly and without effort, it stands as the best candidate to play the role of Warcollier's meta-mind. It must be the essential piece in the sending and receiving of telepathic messages. It creates emotional resonance between individuals, whereby we become attuned to one another's internal states (Goleman 1995: 86). For infants this means that they are regulated by their parents' demeanor and behavior; but we adults, too, stabilize one another by alternately aligning ourselves and breaking away to re-establish our autonomy (D. J. Siegel 1999: 71). All of our social life is a dance of emotional connections, where limbic states "leap between minds [and] feelings are contagious" (Lewis *et al.* 2000: 64). We lure one another into our own emotional space, revising one another by emotional entrainment, not unlike the way that laughter and yawning are contagious.

Once we are drawn into the emotional space of another, our own top-to-bottom archetypal structures become activated, hormones dispatched, memories and images evoked, inherited decision biases tapped. This is the causal, body-centered chain of events that is opened up by communication between limbic systems, and it is the organic computer that deciphers the information coming from another's meta-mind. It is the explanation for the idiosyncratic failures of telepathic messages received under experimental conditions—the fact that images degenerate into angles and arcs as the percipient's cortex struggles to reconstruct the source of a limbic impulse.

It is also the explanation for why spontaneous telepathic experiences can be so vividly accurate. When Jung awoke in his hotel room feeling his patient's despair, it was a limbic resonance he knew very well, for he had sat with that man over the course of many hours, cultivating an empathic connection. When he felt the shadow of a bullet pass through his skull, the patient's vivid obsession coincided with a strong, sharp sensation, the culmination of that suicidal limbic state of mind. Nothing is more numinous than matters of life and death. The *causal* sequence in the telepathic reception is easily explicable. All we can say about the *synchronistic* dimension of that moment is that these things really do happen. It really looks as though the psyche is non-local in its functioning.

Remote viewing: scientific pretensions

In the 1970s under the influence of the Cold War and publicity gained by a popular book entitled *Psychic Discoveries Behind the Iron Curtain* (Ostrander and Schroeder 1970), the CIA and other government agencies put some effort into researching opportunities ESP might provide in their standoff with the Soviet Union. Their primary interest was clairvoyance and the possibility of spying on the enemy without having to be physically present. But being leery of the less than respectable reputation of the term *clairvoyance*, they preferred to describe their activities as "remote viewing," sometimes further dignified as "scientific remote viewing," abbreviated RV and SRV. In general, they did not distinguish between clairvoyance (psyche's contact with physical facts) and telepathy (psyche's contact with psychic facts in the mind of a second person). In this section, we are concerned with the methods and refinements these scientifically inclined researchers developed.

The Army's Intelligence and Security Command (INSCOM) at Ft. Meade, Maryland, explored the capabilities of some individuals known for their psychic skills (Schnabel 1997). Mel Riley, a staff sergeant who had been a photo interpreter for INSCOM and was known to have a sixth sense, employed a series of visualization techniques for reaching a reliably receptive state of mind. First, lying on his back and breathing slowly and steadily, he visualized his anxieties and distractions as a heap of clothing that he would gather piece by piece and by the armload to stuff into an oversized suitcase, which he would then lock and place behind himself. Then he imagined donning scuba gear and diving into a limpid, tropical pool fifty feet deep. The goal was to hold himself motionless about ten feet off the bottom, where lying on the bottom represented falling asleep. In that deep and stable psychic space, he would accept a folder that symbolized the remote target he was to view in his imagination, but with the same critical intelligence he had been using with actual photos. He allowed the images from the destination symbolized by the folder to enter his consciousness in much the same manner as Jung, Husserl, and Craig Sinclair.

Evidence for the sort of altered state Riley cultivated in this exercise may be gathered from his description of how he felt after finishing the remote viewing experiment: "When you get done, you have a tingling throughout your body. It's like a high, only it's a natural high" (Schnabel 1997: 73). This is clear evidence of ANS tuning. The meditative quiet suggests elevated parasympathetic activity, while the tingling sensations imply elevation of the sympathetic system. Probably both were elevated at the same time, promoting a brain state characterized by some degree of integration. Riley added that after remote viewing, the sky was bluer, two birds on a wire sang like a rainforest full of toucans, Huxley's "doors of perception" had opened wider, and he could feel the adrenaline pumping through his system (Schnabel 1997: 74f).

One of the leaders of the team at Ft. Meade, Lt. "Skip" Atwater, had been able to travel out-of-body at will when he was a teenager (Schnabel 1997: 12). Another of the psychic stars there, Joe McMoneagle, had a knack for remotely viewed visions characterized by great realism, detail and narrative consistency. Some years earlier, he had suffered a near-death experience that taught him how to remain alert while descending into a dream-like state of consciousness (Schnabel 1997: 65ff).

Out-of-body journeys and near-death experiences are similar in that one seems to have left one's body behind and gained vivid, realistic imagery, as well as the numinous sense that one is encountering profound truths. Furthermore, their capacity to combine deep bodily relaxation with high emotional arousal, often terror, again implies elevation of both halves of the autonomic nervous system and therefore of integrated brain-states. The great master of out-of-body journeying, Robert A. Monroe, explains in the first of his three books on the topic that the secret to generating the experience of "leaving the body" is to learn to remain aware and focused while the body falls asleep. Then one simply "rolls out of the body" while it lies insensible (Monroe 1977).[5] Thus McMoneagle learned the same lesson from his near-death experience that Monroe learned from his out-of-body journeys: how to combine deep relaxation with alertness.

The Stanford Research Institute

While remote viewing at Ft. Meade on the US East coast relied on individuals gifted at attaining unitive/transformative states of consciousness and who were aware of how they did so, another group of researchers on the West coast, at the Stanford Research Institute (SRI), began working in 1972 on the hypothesis that every human being has the capacity for remote viewing (Targ and Puthoff 2005: 69). Physicist Russell Targ and engineer Harold "Hal" Puthoff, who led the SRI team, both had belonged to Scientology briefly in the 1960s and took seriously its belief that psychic abilities are natural to the human condition (Schnabel 1997: 198ff). "Our laboratory experiments suggest to us that anyone who feels comfortable with the idea of having paranormal ability can have it" (Targ and Puthoff 2005: 4).

Despite the hypothesis, however, Targ and Puthoff managed to find some individuals with psychic gifts, and it is the results from these individuals that are the most discussed. Their first promising psychic was a New York artist named Ingo Swann. On his initial test, he was given the geographic coordinates of a target, and came up with a description that was "correct in every detail, even the relative distances on his map were to scale" (Targ and Puthoff 2005: 4). The real star of the SRI, however, was Pat Price, the president of a West Virginia coal company who had formerly been the police commissioner of Burbank, California. While Ingo Swann eventually developed a "method" to discipline his less spectacular psychic gifts, Pat Price said he would "just decide" to view a remote target. He thought that as long as he believed in himself he would succeed, there was nothing special to do (Targ and Puthoff 2005: 56).

In his first test, Price was given the same target Swann was working on at the time, the Hoover Tower at Stanford University. Targ received in the mail from Price, who was still in West Virginia, a five-page commentary, starting from the correct altitude of the tower and ending with a tour of the building's interior, including accurate descriptions of the equipment inside. He also listed the labels on a dozen file folders inside a locked cabinet (Targ and Puthoff 2005: 47f). When compared with the SRI's less fabulously gifted psychics, Price's results showed more detail and more "first place" matches. But he also had more clear misses and more erroneous interpretations of the data. In defense of the less gifted psychics, they worked harder and doubted themselves more, but they also failed less spectacularly when they did fail.

Standard procedure at SRI for testing and training psychics mixed clairvoyance with telepathy. Hal Puthoff would take ten sealed envelopes, numbered zero to nine, with him in his car and begin aimlessly driving around for a prearranged length of time. Meanwhile, Russell Targ was settling down with the psychic in a "viewing room." At a specific time, Puthoff would generate a number between zero and nine on a random number generator and select the envelope with the corresponding number, open it and find inside the day's target destination. Then he would drive to that location and gaze upon the site for fifteen or twenty minutes. Back in the viewing room, Targ would alert the would-be psychic to the time-frame for receiving information about the site. The psychic would enter a receptive state and draw the impressions received with pencil and paper.

Favorable circumstances

Eventually, Targ and Puthoff arrived at a number of conclusions about how to achieve the best results. First, intelligent, agreeable people with whom heart-to-heart trust could be established made the best candidate psychics (Targ and Puthoff 2005: 70). Second, it was better not to impose a rigid experimental procedure on the subject but to allow her to do what she feels she is good at and to work in the way she feels most comfortable. Third, the candidate's seriousness of purpose being essential, the more challenging the task she is given, the better her chance of success. Fourth, a second person who is ignorant of the target should stay with the candidate to provide a comfortable, relaxed, structured environment. Fifth, one of the most important details is that the candidate should be given feedback on the success of her work as soon as possible after the test—even including a trip to the target site (Targ 2004: 94; Targ and Puthoff 2005: 10f). It is also important to have the psychic draw the images that arise during the procedure and to write down all impressions (Targ 2004: 43f). The common theme in all six of these conditions is finding and maintaining an upbeat and cooperative frame of mind.

Exceptionally good results were most likely in spontaneous situations that were life-threatening and required strength and courage (Targ and Puthoff 2005: 196). Possibly as an offshoot of this principle, Targ and his physician daughter began practicing psychic diagnosis around the year 2000. Targ says it is much easier to get good results with this practice than when remotely viewing "an object in a box," very likely because of the life-or-death meaningfulness and the human connection (Targ 2004: 33).

Certainly the emotional charge associated with a target makes a big difference in how easily and clearly it can be seen. This was also an early discovery for Robert A. Monroe as he experimented with clairvoyance. Going out-of-body to a friend's house to observe what was going on there, with the intention to verify his degree of success later, first required that he find his friend; and he did so by homing in on an emotionally charged picture of his friend. Sometimes, however, the emotion is not interpersonal. For example, when Pat Price was given the coordinates for a vacation cabin, what he drew and described was a National Security Administration facility located just over the hill from the cabin. When told about the nature of his "miss," Price explained, "The more you try to hide something [emotional valence], the more it shines like a beacon in psychic space" (Targ 2004: 36).

Probably this secrecy factor lies behind the SRI's greatest psychic triumph, Price's 1973 drawing for a CIA spy project to determine the nature of an unidentified research and development facility the Soviets ran in Semipalatinsk, Kazakhstan. He drew a huge crane mounted on four sets of railroad trucks rolling on tracks that ran alongside buildings. Other aspects of the site were no less accurately described, including their function. Price's results were verified years later by satellite photos (Targ and Puthoff 2005: Preface).

Back at Ft. Meade on the East coast, Joe McMoneagle had similar success with a set of classified US military secrets. Given a sealed envelope containing a black-and-white photo of an aircraft hanger at an undisclosed location, Joe did not draw the hanger, but the experimental tank it contained, a weapon whose existence had been a secret to McMoneagle. He produced an engineering-style drawing with cut-away views of the tank's laser targeting system, its ammunition storage and feeder, main gun assembly, special high-tech armor, and more (Schnabel 1997: 51).

Separating signal from noise

Unfortunately for the less gifted psychics, every task was not emotionally charged, a matter of life-or-death, or concerned with a closely guarded secret. To get accurate everyday readings out of a modestly gifted psychic like himself, Ingo Swann was convinced there had to be ways of refining his psychic techniques. His first proposal was to eliminate geographic coordinates from the assigned targets because they provoked too much involuntary, left-brain speculation. The coordinates 30°N/90°W, for instance, suggest immediately the environs of New Orleans; a fact that could well turn out to be an insurmountable distraction from the psychic task, which might have been targeted on a ship in the harbor or a drilling platform in the Gulf. Targ and Puthoff agreed to assign random four-digit numbers instead of coordinates.

Eventually Swann began to think of remote viewing as a matter of separating signal from noise. The "signal" would be the images and impressions actually received synchronistically (via clairvoyance or telepathy)—the crucial change in state of his whole organism. He had no doubt that there always was a signal. The problem was caused by his memory, his daydreaming imagination, and his compulsion to analyze and draw premature conclusions. All this semi-conscious, quasi-logical, left-brain activity that belongs to ordinary consciousness amounted to "mental noise," and it constantly threatened to "overlay" and even drown out the signal (Targ and Puthoff 2005: 37–42).

As he attended to the changes in his consciousness during a session of remote viewing, Swann was able to distinguish four typical phases. First came kinesthetic sensations and fragmentary images that could be sketched. Then he would become aware of emotional and aesthetic responses to the target, such as fear, loneliness, or beauty. In a third stage, the psychic becomes aware of the physical dimensions of the target, whether it is heavy, tall, or wide. Often a strong urge to sketch is felt and should be indulged. But at this point one is also strongly tempted to jump to conclusions. This is where ordinary memories and daydreams threaten to drown out the signal with their noise, what Swann calls "analytic overlay." The psychic may make a brief note of them, but they should be placed in their own sector of the note page and labeled as "AoI" (analytic overlay). Once the impressions from all three phases have been collected, the psychic should write out a detailed report on the target's appearance and function or purpose (Targ 2004: 55).

Social scientist Courtney Brown, who is Director of the Farsight Institute in Atlanta, has refined Swann's ideas into a "matrix" or spreadsheet format that amounts to a device for very subtly manipulating what the biogenetic structuralists call the "warps" in consciousness (Brown 1999). In this method, the novice psychic works with a guide who does the left-brain thinking and manipulations of the warps—very much as the master shaman guides the novice. A spreadsheet, like the example provided in Table 9.1, maps the psychic space of remote viewing. The guide directs the novice viewer's wordless (i.e. right-brain) attention by pointing to squares in the matrix.

In my translations of Brown's jargon, the columns in Table 9.1 are labeled with letters across the top of the page, each standing for a different characteristic of the target and the effect it may have on the psychic: (KS) kinesthetic sensations felt by the viewer; (GI) general impressions of the magnitude and layout of the target; (SF) subjective feelings aroused in the viewer; (EP) emotions picked up from people who might be in the region of the target; (PO) physical objects detected at the target; (Atm) the feeling atmosphere of the target (dangerous, peaceful, etc.); (GQ) conclusions about the target provoked by the guide's questions; and (VC) viewer's conclusions about the nature and function of the target. The last category at the right (AoI) stands for "analytic overlay." Each of Swann's stages of the remote-viewing session is represented by a different horizontal row on the spreadsheet. Consequently, each square on the page has a distinct meaning.

Table 9.1 A remote viewing "matrix".

	KS	GI	SF	EP	PO	Atm	GQ	VC	AoI
Initial impressions									
Emotional responses									
Dimensions of target									
Conclusions drawn									

Source: summarizing the argument of Brown (1999).

The guide directs the psychic to touch a square with the pencil point and word-lessly attend to the images, sensations, and feelings corresponding to that square on the matrix. Pointing wordlessly with the pencil maintains the viewer's right-brain dominance by avoiding language. Finally the viewer does employ words by making a note of his right-brain impressions in the designated square. Finishing this sub-task leaves an empty warp in the psychic's consciousness, and the guide immediately introduces a new right-brain suggestion by directing the psychic to touch a different square with the pencil.

Clearly what Swann and others have done amounts to a very subtle refinement of a practice closely resembling Jung's active imagination. By carefully separat-ing aspects of the remote viewing experience into internal sensations, kinesthetic sensations, feelings, emotions, intuitions, and thoughts, and by attending to each category individually, they learned to derive a great deal of information from what might first seem to be poor and indistinct impressions. They have devoted particular attention to managing the transcendental ego, the non-ordinary psychic space that is free of incessant chatter and our usual tendency to reduce everything that is new to old familiar assumptions. They develop a sense based in the quality of their consciousness for what is "signal" and what is "noise."

Cosmic visions

While Ingo Swann and his followers are rightly concerned with the noise of the limiting habits in our ordinary consciousness, Courtney Brown reveals a different sort of remote viewing error. Brown claims that anyone of average intelligence can be trained to do what he calls Scientific Remote Viewing, and that it does not involve altered states of consciousness (Brown 1999: 19). At the same time, however, he describes what he calls a "deeply settled mind" that appears to resem-ble very closely the transcendental ego we have been concerned with—certainly not an ordinary sort of consciousness. When we are in this deeply settled state, he says, our consciousness is open to receive information from "subspace mind," an expres-sion that seems to refer to what Warcollier called "meta-mind" (Brown 1999: 9f). It appears, therefore, that everyone agrees on the phenomenology of the process.

However, when Brown (1999) begins to describe how his method is practiced, we find two consciousness-changing preliminaries. First, one performs a brief bodily massage on oneself, beginning with the hands and arms up to the head, and then with the feet and legs up to the heart. This is followed by breathing exercises: ten seconds of "fast pranayama" and ten minutes of "slow pranayama."[6] This is then followed by the recitation of an "affirmation" of about 120 words in which one declares oneself a spiritual being capable of remote viewing and promising to use it only for the "growth" of oneself and others (Brown 1999: 30–3). Clearly, then, Brown works more aggressively at changing his consciousness than any of the others we have considered, including Mel Riley, with his three-stage scuba-visualizing technique.

Probably the most telling of his preparations for remote viewing is his dedica-tion to the well-being of humanity, for this has taken him beyond the confines of

Earth in his explorations. In the 1970s, Monroe also journeyed about in the solar system, out of curiosity to see the far side of the Moon and the surface of Mars. Later he discovered spiritual beings inhabiting a space he called Locale II, a non-material dimension of reality (Monroe 1977, 1985). Brown has been finding aliens living in caves beneath the surface of Mars, also an expeditionary force of Martians in caverns in New Mexico. His books are warnings to all Earthlings that we are caught in the middle of an intergalactic battle between two groups of aliens: Reptilians who want to interbreed with us and take over our planet by sowing tribal warfare, and the Galactic Federation which wants to promote peace on Earth and subtly to assist us in realizing our spiritual potential as humans.

Improbable as they may seem, it is not possible to disprove Brown's claims. But it does seem likely that Reptilians and the Galactic Federation are mythic realities, that Brown is not exploring the Milky Way but the collective unconscious. No doubt we Earthlings *are* faced with an upcoming battle between the forces of aggrandizing and tribal warfare on the one side and peaceful, spiritual aspirations on the other. Recent current events render such a prediction less than surprising. Given the dangers we face in global warming, the end of petroleum, the scarcity of fresh water, and our propensity to go to war over differences in ethnicity and religion, it does look as though we do not have much time to settle on the right approach.

These issues are mythic. They have to do with the myth we are unconsciously living right now and the one we may be conscious enough to choose to live in the near future. Discovering the myth we are already living without knowing it was Jung's original motive for exploring active imagination in 1913, when his dispute with Freud and his "creative illness" forced him to get to know his own myth. It looks as though Brown is on the same track but does not know it. He seems not to know that he is describing a myth for us all, and not literal outer-space armies.

Here, then, is the second way that remote viewing can go off course. Brown has not lost his way due to the noise of ordinary consciousness drowning out the signal of synchronistic receptivity. Rather, he has found his way to a deeper reality, one that is not "remote" in a physical sense. It is remote in a psychological sense. In all probability, Brown has not been listening in to literal intergalactic councils; he has been watching the archetypes of the collective unconscious as they are arraying themselves behind the scenes in our present worldwide condition of crisis and confusion.

Chapter 10

Psychokinesis

Mind and matter

The fact that Alexis Didier can describe the painting hanging in a stranger's living room or that Joe McMoneagle can produce an engineer's drawing of a prototype tank he had not known existed are "irrational" facts that "insult," as Jung puts it, our habitual certainties. Instances of remote viewing are hard enough to grasp, but psychokinesis (PK) presents us with an even greater challenge. Uri Geller's bent spoons, Victorian tables leaping and humming: these are the things that make us almost ashamed not to side with the skeptics. What happened when that rose chafer tapped on the window of Jung's office? Had the patient's "psyche cast a spell on it"?[1] It is harder to think that the rose chafer "bewitched her psyche," for that would have required the beetle to have played a role in initiating the dream of the golden scarab that the patient had had the night before. Jung advises us not to worry about causes. There are none we can demonstrate or believe in. It is simply an acausal but meaningful coincidence.

Yet psychokinesis happens, and there seems to be some invisible cause. Between 1850 and 1930 quite a few "physical mediums" plied a trade that seemed to make violins float about the room and play themselves and disembodied hands and arms materialize. Psyche was involved in these goings-on, but not necessarily "will." Philosopher Stephen Braude's (1986) survey of the field reveals that the agent's intention was only doubtfully related to PK events. Most poltergeist cases seem to have involved only random "flailings" by objects in the psychic's vicinity. Although mediums usually had some sense for when they were in the right state of consciousness to expect something, they often "had no idea, conscious or unconscious, of what phenomena were to occur." Still, undoubtedly "in some cases the ostensible agent seemed either to know which phenomena were to occur, or at least consciously *intended* certain phenomena to occur" (Braude 1986: 228).

When anthropologist Edith Turner saw a "spirit tooth" leave the back of an afflicted Ndembu woman, in the form of "a large gray blob about six inches across, opaque and something between solid and smoke" (E. Turner 1998: 83), some sort of event had been intended. Singleton, the shaman, had been pressing on the woman's back with his thumbs, and Turner had intended it, too, right along with the entire community. At the climax of the ceremony, she had suddenly felt powerless to help and then, in her confusion, she "learned how to clap." She immediately became one with the group. Remarkably, however, she had no sense of cause and effect:

> The time sense was not that of cause and effect; these things come as wholes. Either I was in the group or I wasn't. Such differences from Western ways of thinking are themselves interesting. I feel that my own experience of tension and its release was probably necessary for me to have partaken in the good outcome, just as Singleton and Fideli had previously come out with their "words" as well. How it was that the release happened to everyone simultaneously, including the patient, I do not know. That is how it was.
>
> (E. Turner 1998: 85)

In the end, she makes a plea for us to give up our blind reliance on Western certainties: "It is time that we recognize the ability to experience different levels of reality as one of the normal human abilities and place it where it belongs, central to the study of ritual" (E. Turner 1998: 94).

Micro-PK

When the parade of great physical mediums ended around 1930, parapsychology began to create its own psychokinesis experiments in the laboratory. Rhine's experimentation with dice was one example, but the favored type of experiment eventually centered on random number generators (RNG). Can the presence of a psychic maintaining a certain state of mind or intention bring about some non-random effect as an RNG machine spits out number after number? The effects can be very subtle, very small—more numbers between one and five, perhaps, than between six and ten, compared to what would be expected by chance. The tininess of the effects led to this sort of laboratory experiment being called "micro-PK."

Dean Radin (1997) reports that the reputation of micro-PK has greatly improved. In the 1950s it was nearly universally agreed that any effects at all were plainly impossible. Today, by contrast, "virtually no serious criticisms remain for the best RNG experiments. Informed skeptics agree that *something* is going on" (Radin 1997: 145). One of the reasons for this change has to do with the nature of random number generators. Positive results can be attained without having to cause a *single* event. One merely has to "influence the collective behavior of the entire system." Unusual things can happen without violating the overall behavior of the system as a whole (Radin 1997: 139).

In other words, micro-PK slips past the laws of physics without violating our Western sensitivities. In addition to that, some intriguing results have been obtained, suggesting that there may be lawful behavior at work. When more than one person is involved as agent in a micro-PK experiment, the results improve. On average, pairs of agents do better than single individuals. But when pairs are of the same sex, results decline, and when of opposite sex they double. Most impressively, bonded couples or close family members produce effects greater than four times that of individuals (Radin 1997: 143). One thinks of Edith Turner's report about the cure being effected just at the moment the community came fully together, of Rhine's results suggesting that interest and emotion are crucial to positive results in any form of ESP, and of Targ's observation that the best candidate psychics are those who are upbeat and can establish a trusting relationship.

All of these findings are intriguing with reference to Jung's theory that a psychoid principle may act to influence processes in a sort of organismic fashion. For organisms exert a holistic influence over all of their components. Consider how the neuron governs its component molecules on the one hand, and is governed within its neural networks on the other. Micro-PK might easily be an instance of this sort of thing.

The first test of his psychic abilities that Ingo Swann was subjected to at the Stanford Research Institute involved micro-PK. He was taken to Stanford's Varian Physics Building, where a quark detector was operating in the basement. The detector consists of a small magnetic probe surrounded by several levels of shielding, including a superconducting shield. It had been operating smoothly without irregularities for about an hour before Swann arrived. Having been asked to try to influence the frequency of the detector's oscillations, Swann, standing on the floor above, "focused his attention" on the magnetometer, and after five seconds the frequency doubled and remained at that speed for about thirty seconds. In a second test, he managed to hold the higher frequency for forty-five seconds. Swann described "focusing" as visualizing the inside of the apparatus. While he made a sketch of what he had visualized, more perturbations were recorded in the quark detector's oscillations (Targ and Puthoff 2005: 20–5).

Targ offers four working hypotheses for these results. One that he leaves unexplained is "weak quantum effects." The other three boil down to synchronicity. In one of them he names "goal-ordered synchronicity." In another he speculates that the mind may "involve control over noise signals . . . [and] bring order out of chaos," which is exactly how Jung describes the psychoid effect of the archetype. In the last hypothesis, Targ cites "interfering observer effects," which looks very much like the quantum discovery that the observer affects what is observed—i.e. one of Jung's starting points in coming up with the theory of synchronicity (Targ and Puthoff 2005: 61).

Bio-micro-PK

Holistic physician Larry Dossey mentions a number of intriguing experiments that really ought to be called bio-micro-PK. Dossey (1999) describes experiments done at McGill University by Bernard Grad in the 1960s. Barley seeds were watered (a) in the ordinary way and (b) with water in a sealed bottle that had first been held by an interested human for thirty minutes. An upbeat man with a green thumb found that his seeds grew significantly faster than those of the control, but Grad's expectations were surprised when a depressed woman's bottle of water produced even better results than those of the man. It had been thought that her depression would dampen the positive effects of her holding the bottle, but it seems the experiment had altered the woman's mood. She became intensely interested and began asking relevant questions (Dossey 1999: 40–2).

In other experiments, Grad found that the growth-retardant effects of watering plants with a saline solution would be diminished when the bottle of water was first held in the hands for thirty minutes. Also the growth of goiters in mice, produced by withholding iodine from their diet, was retarded when the box containing the mouse was held in a person's hands. Controls were (a) mice in untouched boxes and (b) mice in boxes artificially warmed to the temperature of a human hand (Dossey 1999: 42f). In a similar experiment at the Mt. Sinai School of Medicine, Qigong masters concentrated on test-tubes in which a slowly moving chain of biochemical reactions was taking place. The reaction speed increased by an average of fifteen percent when the masters were focusing (Dossey 1999: 52f).

In all of these bio-micro-PK experiments, organism is very much at the center of the effects. The processes affected are self-evidently organismic—growing seeds, growing goiters and the processes of biochemical reactions. The presumed source of the effects are also organismic—human bodies and the focus of human consciousness.

Macro-PK: the challenge of ectoplasm

As intriguing as these data from micro-PK and bio-micro-PK may be with respect to the theory of a universal psychoid field, philosopher Stephen Braude brushes them impatiently aside: "No amount of fiddling with random event generators promises the insights that could be gleaned from a medium the caliber of [Daniel Dunglas] Home and [Eusapia] Palladino" (Braude 1986: 65). Micro-PK is preferred in the laboratory because it is easy to do, demonstrates that these things do happen, and implies a theory whereby all sorts of mind-over-matter phenomena might be possible. But the slight, unthreatening magnitude of its effects renders it easy to dismiss. Furthermore, Braude (1986: 224) points out, trying to understand the broad variety of PK phenomena by studying a single type, like RNG effects, resembles an effort to understand the nature of humor by restricting oneself to slapstick. We will follow Braude's advice and consider PK phenomena documented to have occurred under the influence of four well-known physical mediums, beginning with Eusapia Palladino.

Ectoplasm

Many of the Victorian physical mediums were famous for their ability to produce a white or grayish fluidic substance, called ectoplasm, that usually was said to be extruded in some manner from the medium's own body while she was in a trance state. It was sometimes said to have a distinctive odor and to take on definite forms. Because ectoplasm was believed susceptible to destruction by light, the possibility that ectoplasm might appear became a reason for making sure that Victorian séances took place in near darkness. Poor lighting conditions also became an opportunity for fraud, particularly as faux ectoplasm was easy to make with a mixture of soap, gelatin and egg white, or perhaps merely well-placed muslin (Guiley 1991). Ectoplasm seems a most unlikely substance; and since it was often faked, many of the Victorian claims have produced unwarranted skepticism. It may therefore be useful to prepare for future objections by devoting a few words to the subject here.

Ectoplasm may be a Victorian word, but the phenomenon of its appearance is not limited to the Victorian period or even to Europe. Edith Turner's (1998) account of the shamanic extraction of a "spirit tooth" from the Ndembu woman comes to a climax with the extrusion from the patient's back of "a large gray blob ... somewhere between solid and smoke." In Chapter 4 of this volume, we encountered an extraordinary sort of "phlegm" that the ayahuasquero is said to produce from his mouth and that contains the "darts" with which he can inflict disease on others or absorb another shaman's darts while healing a patient. The case for the ayahuasquero's phlegm as a variation on an ectoplasm "archetype" is strengthened by the fact that on the other side of the world, another pre-literate culture's shamans produce a magic substance from their mouths. Explorer Ronald Rose (1956) reports Aboriginal stories about "clever men" who could produce a "magic cord" or "rope." Rose likens it to ectoplasm and learned that the cord can sometimes leave the clever man's mouth and crawl about on the ground like a snake—another parallel with Amazonian phlegm. Rose witnessed some demonstrations of magic cord extrusion but was himself never able to see more than a string of saliva, while the natives present became very excited and claimed to see it clearly (Rose 1956: 102–13).

Learning how

It may be necessary for the witness also to be in an altered state of consciousness before being able to see ectoplasm. Surely that was the case with Edith Turner, who felt powerless and isolated one moment and then became part of the clapping community the next, just in time to see the ectoplasm extruded. Rose (1956) makes clear the excitement of the Aborigines who swore they saw the magic cord, and most of those who have witnessed the Amazonian phlegm were also partakers of the brew. Indeed, since such things are "impossible" for Western ordinary consciousness, it would seem that seeing ectoplasm would be proof that the state of one's mind had changed.

Possibly this is the sort of change in consciousness that Ingo Swann believes we can all attain, and it is something we can train ourselves to do. There is an incident in Swann's life that suggests that this may be true. In 1992 he participated in an experiment with a one-legged man, named Casimir Bernard, who had a vivid sense of his phantom limb. If it were really there, Swann wanted to feel it, too. So they sat in chairs, face-to-face, a few feet apart. Swann was hooded so that he could derive no visual information. Bernard would lift his phantom leg or leave it bent with his phantom foot on the floor, while Swann's job was to determine whether the leg were up or down. To ascertain whether it might be up, Swann waved his arm through the space where he thought it should be. In his first 133 trials, Swann performed no better than chance at guessing whether the leg were raised. But then he suddenly said that he had learned what the phantom leg "felt like," and from then on his performance at guessing the position of the leg greatly improved (Sheldrake 2002: 147ff).

What this exercise suggests is that just as one has to learn to use the transcendental ego with the right sort of subtlety if one is to become clairvoyant, so also one may have to learn about the subtleties of psychic materialization before these phenomena become dependably (but subjectively) real.

Expert testimony

Charles Richet was one of the leaders of the "French School" of somnambulism studies and a very careful observer of psychics who often collaborated with the English SPR and shared their healthy skepticism. He made a number of observations on ectoplasm that leave little doubt that he found some of the phenomena both not fraudulent and impossible to explain. Regarding the Belfast medium Kathleen Goligher, for instance, he reported that ectoplasmic forms issued "usually from her navel or vagina and often raised upward like a cantilever to lift the table in front of her" (Braude 1986: 155). A psychosexual energy like the Hindu kundalini may have been involved, since Richet's vague reference to navel or vagina suggests the Svadhishthana chakra, which Jung associates with the opening of a world that is unthinkable from the everyday point of view (*Sem32*: 13–22) and may be familiar to many people as the location where danger and sexual challenge may be felt as a bodily disturbance.[2]

Another medium, Eva C., produced ectoplasm that was even more astounding. Eva's ectoplasm, like that of the ayahuasqueros and clever men, emerged from her mouth. In her case it slowly descended to her knees, alternately spreading out and retracting, like a living, growing thing. Richet said it formed pseudopodia as though it were a giant amoeba, and sometimes the ends of the pseudopodia took on the form of fingers and then were reabsorbed. On one occasion he was invited to touch the extrusion and says he found himself holding a "perfectly modeled hand . . . [that has] the feeling of a normal hand; I feel the bones and fingernails. Then it retreats, diminishes in size and disappears in the end of a cord" (Braude 1986: 154). The famous German student of the French School and parapsychologist, Baron von Schrenck-Notzing, said of the same medium that the flowing white substance that emerged from her mouth was about twenty inches long and eight inches wide (Braude 1986: 151).

Most astounding is a plaster cast of ectoplasmic hands, with fingers folded in an interlocked position, made by Gustav Geley in 1924. The medium's pseudopodia had not only formed themselves into two well-formed hands, but also interlaced the fingers as we might do with our fleshly hands while in the waiting room of the dentist's office. The ectoplasmic hands had remained stable long enough for Geley to pour molten wax over them to make a mold. When the wax had hardened and the hands had dematerialized, he filled the wax mold with plaster. When the plaster dried, he melted the wax away, leaving behind a perfect plaster model of clasped hands. Because the fingers of the model were interlaced, there would be no way for fleshly hands to be extracted from the wax without destroying it. Dematerialization was the only way they could have escaped the wax. Engineer, philosopher and parapsychologist Arthur M. Young (1976) recounts this story of the folded ectoplasmic hands to demonstrate our Western intransigence in the face of challenges to our metaphysical assumptions. He says:

> All necessary precautions against fraud were taken, and some of Geley's experiments were witnessed and testified to by a panel of thirty-four scientists and officials.
>
> More empirical proof could hardly be imagined, yet this work has been totally ignored. Why? Because *there is no theory to account for it*, and existing theories apparently rule out its reality.
>
> (A. M. Young 1976: 134)

Eusapia Palladino

Eusapia Palladino (1854–1918) is one of the most famous and notorious physical mediums. Volumes have been written about her, but we shall restrict ourselves to a few facts that give us a sense for what Braude calls the wide variety of spontaneous PK phenomena. Born to a lower-class family in Naples, Eusapia was found to be "vulgar, earthy, and addicted to bad company," and there are hints that she stole valuables from people who sat in on her séances (Gauld 1968: 224). Her psychic gifts were discovered in 1872, when she was eighteen. Having been orphaned at that age, she was taken in as a servant by a wealthy family given to spiritualistic practices (Feilding 1963: 22).

She may have been the most extensively examined medium in Europe. Some of the high points include a first examination in Turin by Professor Cesare Lombroso, who declared in 1891 that she produced her phenomena without fraud. In 1892, she was examined in Milan, where a group of scientists generally agreed that her phenomena were genuine. One of them, Charles Richet, declared they had no indisputable proof for that claim. Pretty much the same conclusions were arrived at in Warsaw in 1893–4 by psychologist Julien Ochorowicz, who collaborated later with the English SPR, which also examined her in 1894 and 1895. The members were split on the question of fraud in some cases but convinced they had found it in others (Feilding 1963: 22–5).

Eusapia's most dedicated examiner was Everard Feilding of the SPR. He was a non-practicing lawyer from a wealthy family. When he was twenty-eight, a sister died creating for him a crisis of faith and driving him to become an *active* member of the investigating core of the society, dedicated to finding evidence that the soul survives bodily death. Eleven years later, he lost a brother in a boating accident and became more persuasive than ever in the SPR for investigating psychokinesis. A visit to Eusapia in Naples convinced him that physical phenomena had occurred (Feilding 1963: v–xx). E. J. Dingwall assembled and reprinted some of Feilding's investigatory work as *Sittings with Eusapia Palladino and Other Studies* (Feilding 1963). The Palladino studies comprise 267 of the 316 pages, and they are cleverly sandwiched between four brief studies in which Feilding humorously unmasks frauds—one of them the same Carancini who Jung and Flournoy found wanting. In the end Feilding (1963: 63) was convinced that the evidence for Eusapia Palladino and Daniel Dunglas Home was sufficient to establish that some humans do have a supernormal faculty for PK.

Eusapia's altered states

Feilding (1963) reports that Eusapia's sessions generally proceeded through three fairly well-marked stages of consciousness change. She would begin sitting at the conference table gossiping with the sitters. Feilding says she seemed to be in a normal state of consciousness at this time, but she was apparently tiring herself out or waiting to feel premonitory alterations in consciousness. She would begin to yawn, and occasionally there was some movement, even levitation, of the table during this time.

The moment she slipped into what Feilding calls a "half-trance" was preceded by a great deal of yawning and then an attack of "amazing hiccoughs." This was generally the signal for someone to turn down the lights in the room. During this half-trance, she would continue talking, but now answering questions "in an oppressed and plaintive voice." Her consciousness seemed divided during this period—partly conscious enough to know what she was doing, and partly given over to her alter ego, "John King," whom she called her "control," an alleged spirit presence that spoke of things Eusapia herself did not consciously know. When questioned afterwards about this period of the séance, she would seem to have no recollection.

Upon falling into deep trance, the third stage, she seemed to be under the complete control of John King. She seemed on the verge of being overwhelmed by sleep and often spoke in a deep voice and laughed diabolically. Also she was given to throwing herself into the arms and laps of the other sitters somewhat provocatively, her frankly sexual nature being more on display than usual. She would come out of the trance state charged with sexual energy, sometimes shuddering with pleasure. Occasionally she claimed that while she had been in the deep trance state the spirits had brought her an invisible lover (Feilding 1963: 34; see also Blum 2006: 238, 290).

Since the upper-class Victorians who recorded these events tended toward discretion—far more than a Eusapia or a reporter today would do—it is certainly worth noting how many references to sexual arousal have come through in the historical record. This seems a clear indication that the parasympathetic nervous system was functioning in an elevated state, while reports of throwing herself about suggest sympathetic arousal as well. Evidently psychokinesis, as much as remote viewing, requires some sort of unitive brain state.

Eusapia's psychokinetic phenomena

Feilding (1963) lists the physical effects of Eusapia's séances in eleven categories. To understand some of them, it is necessary to know that it was the practice of Victorian mediums to sit at a table with their backs to a cabinet standing in a corner of the room a few feet behind them. The cabinet was generally large enough to allow two men to stand side-by-side inside of it, and its contents were concealed by means of a full-length curtain. This is "the curtain" in the eye-witness accounts. Inside the cabinet it was customary to place musical instruments and other objects that may subsequently be made to sound or to float about the room while the medium was in trance.

Feilding's categories of PK observed when Eusapia was in trance are: movements and levitations of the table, movements of the curtain, bulgings of the medium's dress, raps and bangs on the table, the plucking of a guitar, the transport of objects in the room, touches and grasps by a materialized hand emerging through the curtain, appearance of hands outside the curtain, appearance of other indefinable objects, cool breezes, and the untying of knots. It may be easy for the twenty-first century reader to scoff at some of these phenomena by attributing them to errors of perception, trickery by the medium, or in the case of cool breezes by assuming that there simply was a draft in the room. It should be borne in mind, therefore, that Feilding and the SPR had a horror of being tricked. They believed that the organized religions had been up to that game far too long, and they were determined to learn whether there was any irrefutable evidence that spiritual entities like the soul really exist or that some sort of material effect resulting from the action of spirits could be ascertained. Consequently they went out of their way to imagine every sort of natural explanation and track down the possibility that it may have been the true cause of what they had experienced. Only phenomena judged to be genuinely inexplicable by ordinary means were accepted.

I shall describe only one or two instances that have been vividly described in some detail. At the Cambridge series of SPR séances in August 1895, F. W. H. Myers was very cognizant of Eusapia's unsavory reputation for fraud and therefore was indisposed to accept any evidence that her powers were genuine. Consequently, the observations of his wife, Mrs. Myers, are very interesting. On August 4, 1895, she was sitting on the floor at Eusapia's feet, holding them to make sure they were not being used to falsify phenomena. Looking up, she could see against the ceiling of the room ectoplasmic projections emanating from Eusapia's body. Mrs. Myers saw a third arm with hands and fingers holding a chair. She also saw two long pseudopodia looking like "the neck of a swan," one of them prodding Mr. Myers on the back. Meanwhile a stumpy pseudopodium emerged from Eusapia's hips and was prodding Mr. Myers in the lower ribs (Gauld 1968: 236f).

One has to assume that Eusapia knew which of the experts she needed to convert and was doing her very best to force Mr. Myers to notice. Immediately after the sitting, Mrs. Myers helped undress Eusapia and reports finding "no sign of any machinery" under her clothes with which she might have produced some of the effects Mrs. Myers had witnessed. At the same series of sittings with Eusapia, Charles Richet, whose intelligence, cunning, and integrity are eminently convincing, attested that he had seen extra hands emerging from Eusapia, even while he could clearly see that both of her bodily hands were being held by SPR members. Once he had held one of those extra hands for about twenty-five seconds (Gauld 1968: 241).

That Eusapia had some control over some of these events, at least some of the time, is suggested by incidents reported by Richet and Myers at the sitting the SPR held on July 21, 1894. The two men were holding the hands and knees of the medium, as was customary, when Richet felt a hand laid on his head and mouth, and a small round table—not the large one they were sitting at—approached them, moving across the floor in jerks that were coordinated with the jerks of Eusapia's body. Following that, an accordion fell to the floor and began playing single notes coordinated to the movements of Eusapia's fingers, which the investigators were easily able to feel, since Richet and Myers had her hands in theirs (Gauld 1968: 226f).

Eusapia's trickery

Feilding says that "the opinion of practically all scientific men" was that, allowing for some fraud, the evidence was clear that Eusapia possessed some sort of supernormal faculty which could not be explained (Feilding 1963: 27). When she was in good humor, she made no objection to any controls the witnesses wish to impose, the lights were stronger, and the inexplicable phenomena most numerous. But when she was out of sorts, she would object to everything and the phenomena would be fewer and less interesting (Feilding 1963: 33).

Since mood or state of mind is essential to every sort of psychic performance, it seems likely that when she knew she was not "on," she would still hope to impress by trickery, and that would require fewer and weaker controls. Thus, on August 7, 1895, three days after the remarkable session Mrs. Myers described just a few paragraphs above, Mr. Myers and Henry Sidgwick brought SPR member Richard Hodgson in to observe. He had not been present earlier, and "passed himself off as an amiable imbecile" to lower Eusapia's suspicions. He observed that she managed during the séance to get both Sidgwick and Myers holding the same hand, which left the other free "for mischief" (Gauld 1968: 238).

Some psychics, like Alexis Didier, Rudi Schneider, and D. D. Home, were always cooperative and graciously allowed any sort of condition an expert could think up. They were not always able to produce impressive phenomena, but they understood that being above suspicion was essential. Others, like Eusapia, apparently were unable to grasp the fact that being caught cheating even once threatened to invalidate all their good work. Such was surely the impression of Ronald

Rose concerning the Aboriginal clever men he observed. He and his wife found "skillful use of hypnotism [as well as] imposture and fraud, superstition and delusion, distortion, exaggeration, and sheer fancy" (Rose 1956: 9). The typical clever man, who may indeed produce wonders, aimed above all to "maintain an atmosphere of credulity about himself. And he will descend to sly opportunism and even outright deceit to keep this atmosphere or enhance it" (Rose 1956: 178).

Feilding (1963) concluded that Eusapia's genuine phenomena could not be explained by physical dexterity, and it was impossible that she had an accomplice. Consequently the only alternative to her having some sort of supernormal power was that the SPR members and others who had observed her "had been hallucinated." Perhaps they imagined phenomenon that had not occurred: but in the case of objects transported, they remained in their new locations even after the lights were back up to full strength and the observers were clearly in ordinary consciousness. If not that, then perhaps they only imagined they had control over her hands and feet: but in this case, they would all have to be hallucinating the whole time and their hallucinations would all have to agree at every moment. Furthermore, since they were also orally reporting their observations as they occurred so that a shorthand writer could place everything into the record, their state of mind would have had to be both altered and normal at the same time. Therefore "with great reluctance, though without much personal doubt as to its justice, we adopt the latter alternative [that] some hitherto unascertainable force was liberated in her presence" (Feilding 1963: 51–4).

D. D. Home

Daniel Dunglas Home (pronounced "Hume"), who lived between 1833 and 1886, is probably the greatest of the Victorian physical mediums, for not only was the range of his marvels remarkably broad, but also he was never found to engage in any trickery. Indeed, he went out of his way to satisfy his observers. He performed his wonders in relatively bright light and could boast of an extraordinary "number of seemingly disinterested persons who were prepared to testify" to the genuineness of the phenomena they had seen (Gauld 1968: 216).

Home began having visions at the age of four, in Edinburgh, where he was born; he reports that at the age of thirteen he had a vision of a cloud that accurately announced the death of one of his childhood friends. Another vision announced his mother's death when he was seventeen, and from then on the visions and other phenomena became quite frequent. He moved to England in 1855 at the age of twenty-two and performed as a medium for the next twenty-five years.

Physical phenomena

Philosopher Stephen Braude (1986) lists fifteen types of psychokinetic phenomena that Home regularly performed, and the list excludes apparent healings of sick people and other such feats that are impossible to verify.

The phenomena are: raps and knocking sounds, not only on the séance table itself, but also everywhere in the room, including the ceiling; the levitation and moving of objects, including pianos and tables, while several people sat on them; moving tables sharply, while the objects on top of the table remained undisturbed, and extending to other sitters the ability to command tables and other objects to move; changing the weight of objects; making lights and luminous objects appear; making partially or fully materialized forms appear; causing touches, pinches and other tactile phenomena to be experienced by sitters while everyone's hands were visible on the table top; producing auditory phenomena, voices and music, odors, earthquake effects and the appearance of hands, "supple, solid, mobile and warm, of different sizes, shapes and colors," animated and solid for a time and then dissolving; playing untouched musical instruments; handling of hot coals with bare hands and enabling the observers to do so; elongating Home's own body by twelve inches or more; and levitating (Braude 1986: 73f).

Conduct of the séances

Evidence of distinct trance states is spotty in the case of Home. Sometimes he spoke from the standpoint of what other mediums might call their "control spirit," for he addressed himself as Dan or Daniel. But usually he spoke in a conversational manner of ordinary everyday affairs with the sitters. Sometimes he remained silent, perhaps until a change in consciousness occurred, and some sitters reported that he spoke very little. But he made a point of urging his sitters to talk freely among themselves because he wished no one to suspect that he was hypnotizing anyone and thereby fooling them with suggested illusions. When disembodied voices were heard, Home himself talked constantly so that no sitter could accuse him of ventriloquism. He also made a practice of asking one of the sitters to sit underneath the table so as to report that there was no trickery going on down there out of sight.

When heavy tables or bookcases began to move across the room, Home would invite those present to try to prevent them. Such volunteers often found themselves dragged along with the furniture. In other reports, Home would walk to the fireplace, run his hands through the blazing coals, and remove a large one with his bare hands. On one occasion, he handed the coal to a sitter, who held it in his own hand without feeling any pain. Then Home pushed the coal off the sitter's hand with his finger and onto a sheet of paper which immediately burst into flame. A Mr. Hall had coals put on his head and reported that it felt warm but not hot, although his wife reported that the heat was so intense on her face that she had to retreat. When Mr. Hall brushed his hair before retiring that night, he found it contained a quantity of cinder dust (Braude 1986: 74–85).

Testimony of William Crookes

William Crookes (1832–1919), a prominent English chemist and physicist who discovered the element thallium and invented devices to observe and measure radiation, decided in 1870 to lend his prestige to the D. D. Home phenomenon. He observed Home at the latter's regularly scheduled séances and also devised some sessions with special test conditions. He took notes at those sessions and published them as an attestation to the genuineness of Home's marvels.

A storm of outrage followed. Crookes' veracity and competence were questioned, and he became enraged. In fact, Crookes had expected his reputation would convince the critics, and he had not gone into minute detail about every aspect of the séances, as Feilding (1963) had done, with the location of each piece of furniture and every sitter clearly defined, including who was holding which hand or foot. The criticism did force Crookes to be more specific about test conditions. But the damage had been done.

Eventually he published letters he had received from prominent scientists who "clearly refuse to investigate or think seriously about his claims—and, in fact, decline invitations to attend formal experiments with Home" (Braude 1986: 87). In view of this reaction, one hardly has to wonder at the dishonesty and evasion with which members of the French Academy of Sciences treated the psychics who asked to be observed under scientific conditions (Méheust 1999). Because these things "can't happen," scientists have to be wary of being seen associating with them.

Rudi Schneider

Born July 27, 1908, in Brunau-am-Inn, Austria, just across the river from Bavaria, Rudi Schneider began his career as medium at the age of ten. There are several conflicting stories purporting to explain how his family learned about mediumship and séances, but all agree that they succeeded on their first try. Rudi's older brother Willy, age sixteen, fell immediately into a trance when a spirit guide announced herself to be Olga, mistress of the former King of Bavaria. Various forms of ectoplasm were projected from and hung upon Willy's body (Gregory 1985: 1–10).

After a month of sittings as Willy's control, in March, 1919, Olga announced, "I need Willy's brother, Rudi." Rudi, who had been asleep in an adjoining room, thereupon entered the séance chamber, sleep-walking. Willy received a new guide, Mina, and the form of his trances underwent a transformation, while Rudi simply took over with Olga and her style of trance where Willy had left off. Willy and Rudi were by no means the only sibling mediums. Among the famous pairs were the Fox sisters and the Didier brothers. It is apparently not unusual for such talents to run in families. Careful records of all of Rudi's séances were begun on December 8, 1923, when Rudi's father, always known simply as "Vater Schneider," began keeping a systematic and comprehensive account of each meeting. There was space at the end of each account for the witnesses to sign their names, attesting to the genuineness of what they had seen. The notebook constitutes primary evidence for Rudi's early career, and it is where the signatures of C. G. Jung and Eugen Bleuler appeared on June 21, 1925, during a visit Rudi and his entourage made to Zurich (Gregory 1985: 14–20; 74f).

Some early successes

Rudi's séances were held in faint *red* light, on the advice of an Italian count named Logothati. Not all accounts of the famous mediums are clear on the color of light used, but as we shall shortly see, red light may well enhance the visibility of ectoplasm. Rudi moved objects, perhaps with ectoplasm, and hands materialized and dematerialized; but his primary talent seems to have been levitation. The faint red light presented problems for the witnesses to ascertain that they were seeing a body floating, unsupported. Consequently, Rudi was provided with "séance pajamas" that were beset along the arms, legs and trunk with numerous pins, each with a head the size of a hazel nut and painted with luminous paint (Gregory 1985: 23). Rudi, as Rudi, always complied with whatever demands were made on him regarding the arrangement of the sessions and the controls required by scientific investigators. Occasionally Olga would ask for and get some rearrangements after Rudi entered his trance, but all agree there was never any effort to conceal or deceive (Gregory 1985: 151).

Regarding the levitations, notes from Vater Schneider's notebook on December 8, 1932, record the following incidents. At 9:01pm, Rudi levitates out of his chair, straight up about five feet. He floats horizontally while the controllers continue to hold his hands. Their role is to verify that he is not using his hands to push or pull himself up. The audience can see by the luminous pins that Rudi's trunk and limbs are lying on thin air. Three minutes later, he falls back into his chair. At 9:10, he rises again, but this time falls horizontally with some force directly onto the floor. Nine minutes later, he levitates directly from the floor, rises and drops several times, and finally pulls his hands free of the controllers and claps them together to show that the controllers are not holding him up (Gregory 1985: 23f).

Having studied Willy Schneider's séances in Munich, the parapsychologist and sexologist Baron Albert von Schrenck-Notzing visited Brunau to see Rudi in 1924. He was a colorful and controversial figure, independently wealthy through marriage, and able to devote full-time attention to whatever interested him. He believed that mediumistic phenomena were the products of the unconscious psyche and not disembodied spirits, and he took good care of Rudi, shepherding his career until his death in 1929. During those first ten years, 1919–1929, Rudi was well protected, felt most comfortable, and produced his best work.

With the death of Schrenck-Notzing, Rudi "was almost immediately plunged into the whirlpool of international psychical research" (Gregory 1985: 129). Harry Price, an ambitious and fairly unscrupulous self-promoter, brought Rudi to London and made him into a newspaper celebrity. Rudi could neither understand nor speak English, and being in no position to take care of himself, he trusted Price implicitly. Price adopted and took credit for Schrenck-Notzing's idea to produce a scientific-seeming device that he believed would insure no fraud was being perpetrated during a séance. It involved a battery and lights in a circuit that would be closed when all sitters and Rudi were holding hands while wearing metalized cotton gloves and also kept their pot-scrubber-sock-clad feet on metal plates placed on the floor. The lights would go out if anyone "broke the chain." The SPR believed it a mere gimmick that distracted attention from the psychic phenomena they were there to witness. Nevertheless, as long as Harry Price was happy, so was Rudi. The difficulties arose the very next year, when Rudi traveled to Paris to be investigated by Dr. Eugène Osty at the Institut Métapsychique International, where more sophisticated apparatus led to an interesting discovery.

Scientific evidence

Osty set up a séance room rigged with cameras and an experimental table bearing objects for Rudi/Olga to move with their "psychic force." The table was criss-crossed with infrared light beams so that if a target object were moved or if some material instrument should try to move it, a beam would be broken and the cameras triggered. Osty hoped to catch the psychokinetic agent in the act, or at least unmask a fraud.

When Rudi entered his trance and Olga announced that an object was about to be moved, Osty and the other sitters could see a thick, grayish mist, about a foot across, moving slowly toward the table. Cameras flashed, but the film showed no gray mist and no movement of the object. After fifteen failures, the cameras were replaced with bells. Now bells rang and objects were moved. Osty hypothesized that (a) ectoplasm is some form of matter or energy broke the beam by absorbing at least 30 percent of the infrared light; (b) ectoplasm is transparent to white light, since it cannot be photographed; and (c) ectoplasm and its movement were under the psychological control of Rudi/Olga, since they were able unfailingly to announce its approach (Gregory 1985: 171–87). Further tests showed that intense red light inhibited the effect of ectoplasm, but that dim red light provided a much reduced inhibition. Ultraviolet light did not inhibit it at all (Gregory 1985: 194f).

Thus it seems there is good reason for the folkloric notion that physical séances work well in dim red light. More than that, however, it seems there is some sort of "psychoid" effect. Something material enough to break a beam of infrared light responds to an intention made by an individual in an altered state of consciousness. Something "transgresses" the psyche/matter divide. It is impossible to say whether psychic states can "condense" enough of the gas or quantum particles in the atmosphere to produce pseudopodia or clouds of mist. But Osty's experiment at least shows that some such "transgressive" phenomenon is possible.

Unfortunately for Rudi, however, Osty's success threw Harry Price into a state of envy, which increased with every new piece of good publicity Osty received. After three years, Price was so beside himself that he sought to destroy the French scientist's reputation by renouncing Rudi for a fraud—no matter that it also rendered his own successes worthless. Anita Gregory (1985), the scholar who has assembled all of the Rudi Schneider material, has devoted 122 pages of her book to examining Harry Price's accusation and found the whole story to be self-contradictory. She saves Rudi's reputation for us, long after his death. But the damage was done at the time. A single newspaper story accusing fraud was enough to ruin a psychic. Rudi was nowhere near as tough as Eusapia Palladino, who survived numerous truthful accusations of trickery. Rudi needed constant emotional support, and Price's betrayal damaged the frame of mind he needed in order to be able to produce good psychic phenomena.

Rudi's altered states

What Rudi needed most for a good performance was "an atmosphere of jollity and good fellowship," what the Germans call *Gemütlichkeit* (Gregory 1985: 145). It helped him to feel accepted, valued and upbeat, which in fact describes the frame of mind that is most conducive for anyone's success at psychic tasks. Perhaps this was the reason Olga usually insisted on the sitters incessantly singing and reciting. By all accounts the séances were noisy, chaotic affairs, which certainly does not seem to be the atmosphere to encourage concentration, but perhaps it assisted in fostering a certain isolation from the crowd of witnesses and distraction from the ordered thinking of ordinary consciousness.

Another regular practice of Rudi's, although irregularly reported, appears to be a marked increase in breath rate. In the séance summarized above where he levitated several times, it was recorded that six minutes before the first levitation his breathing became audibly faster (Gregory 1985: 23). Osty made systematic notes. He found Rudi's breathing speed to increase to fifteen times the normal rate, although inhalations were shallow. Osty noted that Rudi could keep up such a pace for two to three hours while the pH level (acidity) of his blood remained unchanged. Osty theorized that the human body may be regarded as a reservoir and transformer of energy that it collects from the environment (Gregory 1985: 199–201).

Osty reported as well that not only Rudi but also all the major physical mediums he had studied displayed neuromuscular rigidity and hyperarousal while producing their effects, and Gregory adds that the Italian parapsychologist Lombroso reported the same of Eusapia Palladino (Gregory 1985: 202). Contrasting with these findings are reports of visible sexual arousal during and semen stains on his clothing following Rudi's successful séances: one from the SPR, one from Schrenck-Notzing, and one from a Dr. Probst (Gregory 1985: 123–5). Thus, it is again evident that a major physical medium manages simultaneously to elevate both halves of his autonomic nervous system, thereby producing, presumably, unitive brain states.

Ted Serios

Ted Serios' psychic phenomena were produced in the mid twentieth century and present us with an entirely different genre. He gets distant scenes to appear on photographic film while pointing the camera at himself, and occasionally at other improbable objects. His case was studied in the 1960s by psychoanalyst and Clinical Professor of Psychiatry at the University of Colorado, Jule Eisenbud, in *The World of Ted Serios: "Thoughtographic" Studies of an Extraordinary Mind* (1967).

Ted was a sort of rascal psychic, his career marked by truancy, delinquency, and lies. He was often drunk and arrested for speeding or driving recklessly, sometimes assaulted the officers who pulled him over, and initiated bar fights that he regularly lost. His insecurity often resulted in his going missing just before an important demonstration of his skills had been scheduled. He might be considered a sort of male version of Eusapia Palladino, except that it was impossible for him to fake his results. Eisenbud kept his film in sealed packages until the moment they were loaded into the camera. Thus there was nothing for Ted to do but trigger the shutter, and the psychic photographs either came out or they did not.

His story begins in 1955, when he was hired as an elevator operator at a Chicago hotel and made friends with a colleague, Johannes, who dabbled in hypnosis. Ted turned out to be an excellent subject and the two of them came up with a Tom Sawyer scheme to have Ted visualize the location of buried treasure while in hypnotic trance. Ted came up with many images of desert islands, but none distinctive enough to find on a map, so Johannes suggested he make the pictures appear on film. Strangely it worked. After more than 300 photos, Ted began to fear he was a "fake," and went to a professional hypnotist to get an opinion. The hypnotist, as a post-hypnotic suggestion, told him it was all a dream, and Ted destroyed the pictures. After a time, he wondered about it again and consulted a second hypnotist, this time demonstrating his power by taking six photos of India while aiming the camera at the wall of the hypnotist's office. This professional encouraged him and also made the suggestion that Ted aim the camera at himself. By the end of this process, Ted could perform his "thoughtography," as he called it, only when *not* hypnotized.

Thoughtography

Getting psychic images to appear on photographic plates has been reported since the beginning of photography. Eisenbud (1967) says such experimentation was quite a fad between 1860 and 1880. Between 1919 and 1923, there was a Society for the Study of Supernormal Pictures in Europe. And in Japan in 1931, Tomokichi Fukurai published a book of his own "thoughtographs," which he had taken between 1910 and 1913 (Eisenbud 1967: 245).

Ted used a Polaroid camera, model 95, the old-fashioned type of self-developing camera with a lens at the end of a corrugated structure that telescoped out and in from the camera box. He also used what he called a "gismo," a small object clutched near the lens which caused a great deal of interest and suspicion among witnesses of his demonstrations. The gismo, however, was nothing more than a short length of empty plastic tubing, part of the developing mechanism that came with every package of film. It had no conceivable function other than to serve Ted as a sort of good luck talisman (Eisenbud 1967: 24).

"Thoughtography" is an ambiguous description of what Serios was doing, especially if one is led to think that he was photographing his own thoughts. In fact, he rarely got the image he was trying for, and most frequently no image at all. Yet what he produced was almost always "impossible" according to all causal theories. Even the biggest disappointments, the ones he called "blackies" because they looked as though not a single photon had entered the lens of the camera, were "impossible" in view of the fact that the lens cap had been off and the shutter had opened in a lighted room. The "whities" were also interesting—those that were uniformly white, without a single feature—for the camera had been pointed at Ted's face, and should have shown at least some fuzzy or overexposed image of the thoughtographer himself. It seems every snap of the camera produced something that "couldn't happen," even if it was rarely what he was hoping for.

Turning to the shots that did produce images, Eisenbud (1967: 283) says, "On most occasions, what Ted gets on film appears to be as independent of what he is able to visualize as dream-images would be." All of these so-called "misses" are extraordinarily interesting. For instance, when he was trying for an image of the Chicago Art Institute, specifically the carved lions in front of it, he got, first, what was later identified as a Jain temple in India with two lions facing one another, and on a second try, the Lion Gates of Mycenae (Eisenbud 1967: 45). It is possible he had seen pictures of either of these monuments in books, but regardless of whether he had ever seen them, it seemed that lions of every sort were emerging in dream-like fashion. So the process is recognizably that of the human imagination and thoroughly acausal: a wonderful, if inexplicable, demonstration of the psychoid principle.

On another occasion, Eisenbud's daughter, Joanna, was handed the camera and gismo and asked to take a picture of Ted. What emerged from the Polaroid was a picture of Joanna herself from Ted's perspective, and superimposed over her figure was an unidentifiable triangle (Eisenbud 1967: 143). Double or triple exposures were common and never explicable.

Whether Ted got a picture of the scene he wanted or not, it seemed he had no control over the perspective. Often structures were photographed as from a helicopter or from the roof of a nearby building. It was as though Ted had taken the camera with him on an out-of-body journey. Eisenbud comments:

> We have got used to thinking of the mind in terms of space—it is "in" the body, "in" the brain and moves from place to place only with the body and the brain—and seem to have lost sight of the fact that what we may actually do is quite the reverse, that is, experience space in terms of the properties of the mind.
>
> (Eisenbud 1967: 237)

This is an amazingly "Jungian" statement. It is "Kantian" in the sense that space is a necessary structural principle of the knowing apparatus; it also suggests Jung's comment that psyche and brain may be connected by synchronicity just as psyche connects with the image of a distant object or event synchronistically.

One final acausal issue: Eisenbud (1967: 277) asks, "How is it that Ted always manages to affect only one print-sized film rectangle at a time, and nothing from the adjoining film or (except rarely) the rest of the roll?" Everything about the process is synchronistic. It is surely as much a demonstration of psychokinesis as lifting a piano with ectoplasmic pseudopodia, and it is far and away more interesting than affecting a random number generator.

Ted's altered states

The picture of Ted Serios we get from Eisenbud's book is quite harmonious with what we have seen regarding the altered states of every psychic. Like most novice parapsychologists, Eisenbud (1967) began with the idea that he was going to prove beyond all doubt that Ted's thoughtography was real. He devised laboratory conditions to serve that goal, but found that Ted was uncomfortable and unable to produce images. Eventually he had to allow Ted a more spontaneous set-up. On the other hand, Ted was not demanding or temperamental. He never protested any one of his witnesses doing "anything he pleased by way of scrutiny and examination, physical or otherwise" (Eisenbud 1967: 26).

Ted's relationship to the work was often rather childlike, from the early days with Johannes and the search for buried treasure to "the uninhibited shrieks of astonishment and delight ... or groans of disappointment" with which he greeted the development of each snapshot. He was always just himself, with "no scientific self-image" to defend or maintain. When children were present, he was in his best frame of mind and most given to "flights of improvisation" (Eisenbud 1967: 126).

The deliberate fostering of altered states of consciousness, however, did not disappear when he gave up on hypnosis. Alcohol seemed to be essential, for I do not think Eisenbud describes a single séance for which he did not provide Ted all the beer and scotch he wanted. Despite the story of the six images of India produced in the office of the second hypnotherapist, which seemed to imply that he was sober and unhypnotized, most of the work he did for Eisenbud was done in a very intoxicated state of mind. He surely felt under pressure to succeed, especially with an audience of skeptical witnesses. He probably took on the alcohol as an aid to the parasympathetic system and to silence the chatter of his ordinary mind.

There seemed to be plenty of evidence for sympathetic system arousal. Ted volunteered before his first demonstration with Eisenbud that the concentration for a shoot was very difficult and often left him bleeding from the mouth and anus (Eisenbud 1967: 24). Eisenbud observed other evidence of this:

> When about to shoot, he seemed rapidly to go into a state of intense concentration, with eyes open, lips compressed, and quite a noticeable tension of his muscular system. His limbs would tend to shake somewhat ... veins standing out on his forehead.
>
> (Eisenbud 1967: 25)

* * *

These four "physical mediums" make it clear that spontaneous PK events do happen and that they have something to do with the mental state of the psychic. But it is impossible to say what that relation is. Results are about as predictable as dreams, even though the psychics in question usually seem to know when a significant effect is about to be produced. No one ever seems to have composed a relevant question about these effects, apart from whether they involve fraud. Even Jung's proposed psychoid field only seems to make the occurrence of such incidents less unlikely, while failing to provide any suggestion for why they should take the form they do.

Perhaps, since we cannot predict the themes or images of our future dreams, we should not be disturbed on this last point. For that we *have* dreams, no one doubts; and that they have something to do with psychic processes that are outside of our conscious control seems self-evident and not at all difficult to accept. That dreams may be *useful* is widely accepted. What psychokinesis, telepathy and clairvoyance challenge us with is the problem of knowing and acting at a distance, the problem of understanding causality and synchronicity.

Chapter 11

A crisis of metaphysics

Accounts of ESP are always fascinating, especially if we merely hear about them. Those suddenly forced to deal with unexpected psychic phenomena, however, are often frightened at first. Robert A. Monroe lived in terror for at least a decade, every time he took one of his out-of-body journeys. When caught unaware by a powerful instance of parapsychology, the safety and dependability we have been taking for granted is called into question; *for if these things can happen, the world is not at all what we have believed it to be*. This, it would seem, is the challenge of parapsychology. If we can be surprised by suddenly realizing things we have no business knowing, if premonitory dreams and visions—to say nothing of PK effects—can make us think we may be responsible for plane crashes and other disasters, if the world can disintegrate into "whizzing molecules," if our psyche will not stay put in our brain, and if other people can read our minds: then the world is far more dangerous than what appears in our worst nightmares.

We have a collective Western account of what is real that comfortably has no place for parapsychology. It also has no way to understand life or consciousness or what produces the leaps forward that the evolutionary record shows. Our picture of reality, our metaphysics, is full of holes, and we are insulted—if not frightened—when something happens to challenge our "rational" assumptions. There are understandable reasons for our denial of everything that lies outside of our comfort zone in the borderlands of exact science. On the one hand we do not want to be thought loony for accepting what everyone else rejects, and on the other we do not dare question the fragile illusion of solidity on which we stand.

The challenge of parapsychology

The philosopher Stephen Braude (1986) rightly points out that if we are willing to admit that some PK effects are real, then logic requires us to "be open to the possibility of PK on a grand scale." If Ingo Swann can alter the oscillations of a super-shielded magnetometer by focusing his mind, how can we tell whether a heart attack or an auto accident is as "normal" as it seems and not "produced" by psychokinesis—perhaps brought about by some innocent but nevertheless effective agent who is filled with envy but does not know he is "shamanizing" (Braude 1986: 222)?

Our situation at present resembles what anthropologist Jeanne Favret-Saada found in 1980 among the peasants of the Bocage region in Western France. Those people believe in witchcraft, the usual symptom for which is the sickening of their domestic animals. Evidence of witchcraft is presented by crafting a narrative that summarizes the empirical events and gives them magical meaning. "Like any narrative," Favret-Saada (1980) says,

> [I]t must be told and repeated, but only to someone . . . who would be ready to share the protagonists' "blind spots." The narrative must not give rise to any questions; the listener is simply meant to be fascinated. If he then speaks, it must only be to evoke other narratives of the same kind, aimed at producing exactly the same type of fascination.
>
> (Favret-Saada 1980: 77)

This description surely fits New Age types, who eagerly share with one another stories about paranormal events and theories and avoid telling the same stories to those who will not respond with more fascinating tales of the same sort. If we do not want to belong to that gullible group, we neither tell nor listen to such stories.

But do not scientists do the same thing? Only other scientists in the same field really understand what they have to say, and can respond with similar stories of their own. All the rest of us—including scientists in other fields—have to take their pronouncements on faith. One is not really allowed to say much about fields in which one is not an expert. Thus when James Lovelock, a physician and president of the Marine Biology Association, wrote his first book on "Gaia," the theory that the Earth with its oceans, atmosphere, and biota functions holistically like a sort of organism (Lovelock 1979), he outraged many scientists. Many refused even to look at the book, others read it and mischaracterized what he had said in it. Lovelock responded with a science-fiction novel about making Mars habitable by applying the same principles to that planet that the Gaia hypothesis applied to this one (Lovelock and Allaby 1984). Because the narrative form of a novel removed the Gaia hypothesis from the realm of "real" scientific discourse, it stirred up serious attention among scientists. Indeed, three scientific conferences were organized to discuss the subject (Lovelock 1988: 185f).

Favret-Saada (1980) says that witchcraft stories "must be told . . . only to someone . . . ready to share the protagonists' 'blind spots.'" Chapters 8, 9 and 10 on parapsychology have explored some of the blind spots in Western metaphysics. Referring to one of the largest of them, Bertrand Méheust says, it seems scandalous to know "that time and space do not exist for the somnambulist in a state of lucidity" (Méheust 2003: 106). One of Targ and Puthoff's (2005) gifted psychics, Duane Elgin, put it a bit more colorfully:

> Once you discover that space doesn't matter, or that time can be traveled through at will so that time doesn't matter, and that matter can be moved

by consciousness, so that matter doesn't matter—well, you can't go home again.

(Schnabel 1997: 162)

The facts of parapsychology, if we taken them seriously, cause us to question all of our usual assumptions. If telepathy and clairvoyance are universal human talents, psyche must not be located in our brain. Descartes' problematic soul moves his body and makes it live; it, too, has a location and cannot go flying about the empirical world while his body sits in his study. But Descartes raises a disturbing issue. If my soul *can* fly about, or—what is even more disturbing—if it is non-local (exists everywhere and nowhere at the same time), does my body live and think on its own? What "animates," "gives soul to," the insensate and lifeless molecules that comprise my body if some sort of soul-substance does not live within it? Duane Elgin and Alexis Didier participated in a cosmic reality that is hidden behind our Western blind spots. We need a metaphysics that excludes none of the reality we experience.

No hypothesis to test

The greatest fallacy concerning parapsychology is that "science disproves it." We have seen over and over again that science has never disproved parapsychology. Indeed, scientific experimentation clearly shows that parapsychological events really do happen. The conflict is not with science but with our metaphysics. Our metaphysics declares parapsychology impossible, and behind this stand lurks our latent terror that the world may be completely irrational and undependable. Like fundamentalists, we cling to a simple doctrine of what is real and true for the illusory comfort it gives us.

We will not have hypotheses to test until we accept the whole reality that we live every day. There are four monumental realities our metaphysics has no place for. Something makes *life* possible when molecular arrangements become sufficiently complex. We assume that molecules are thoroughly lifeless. If so, how does adding up a lot of them into a complex structure make them live? Second, life always exhibits *intentionality*, at least in the minimal sense that every living organism strives to maximize itself and to choose in every instance whatever is most conducive to its survival and comfort. Intentionality always implies some minimal degree of *consciousness*—certainly not ego-consciousness, probably not the ability to represent the world to itself in imagery, but the ability to distinguish and choose what feels better from what feels worse. *Parapsychology* presents us with the fourth elephant we refuse to see, the non-locality of the psyche, the fact that consciousness is not limited to what the sense organs present.

The need for a new metaphysics

Parapsychology cannot get past the initial stage of proving that "non-ordinary" events happen at rates that surpass chance. Normally a science would move on to widespread acceptance of the proven reality and then begin investigating how and why such things happen. Century after century, however, nothing carries parapsychology past stage one because we lack a view of reality that not only has room for ESP but also will enable us to formulate hypotheses.

We need a new metaphysics, an account of reality that includes life, consciousness, organism, and parapsychology—four things that are manifestly real. It has to be a *modest* metaphysics, one that does not claim too much. The history of philosophy has known too many grandiose metaphysical systems; and since the late nineteenth century—since Nietzsche at least—professional philosophers have treated the metaphysical enterprise with extreme prejudice.

Today, we do not need a grandiose scheme, we need a tentative proposal, one that leaves itself open to revision, but that has at least two qualities to recommend it. It must include everything we know to be real; and it must align itself as much as possible with what science has discovered, for these testable matters have become for us the very paradigm of the real.

When we recall that a century ago we were shocked to discover that matter and energy were not separate realities but alternate aspects of the same single reality, perhaps it will not be too shocking today to suppose that matter and *mind* might be alternate aspects of one underlying thing. Instead of trying to imagine how consciousness can "emerge" from the inertia and insensibility of Newtonian matter, does it not make more sense to consider consciousness, not as something added on, but rather as something that has been there all along—as a "primitive," rudimentary "psychoid" quality inhering in everything that exists? We now know matter and energy are interchangeable in a quantum realm that is characterized by non-locality. In the chaotic sea of sub-atomic phenomena, where minute particles are popping in and out of existence, distance is irrelevant. Would it be too much of a stretch for us also to see psyche as non-local in its behavior and capacities?

The explanatory value of fields

If our modest metaphysics is to be harmonious with modern science, there can be no more powerful concept than that of the *field*. Two centuries ago, Michael Faraday brought the "dubious" (for his day) quality of magnetism into the mainstream of Western science when he showed that an electric current running through a wire generates a force that will deflect the needle of a compass. Electricity and magnetism are related phenomena, and what ties them together is the magnetic field that not only revolves around a current-carrying wire, but also flows through and around a bar magnet in a doughnut-shaped pattern. A phenomenon that had formerly been puzzling, in that it suggested action-at-a-distance, made sense as soon as scientists stopped considering magnetically attracted bodies as isolated entities projecting something invisible through space. Instead, it was clear that space itself unified those two objects as a single phenomenon, organized by a field.

A century ago, Albert Einstein found that the apparent problem of gravity (action-at-a-distance, again) could be solved if space-time itself were seen as a single field that is depressed by the mass of each heavenly body, thereby forming a basin of attraction that holds smaller bodies in orbit around itself. With the gravity field and the electromagnetic field, the objective realities of everyday life are pretty well described: day and night, the seasons of the year, water running downhill, and light from distant stars bending around massive bodies on its way through space in our direction. This is the realm of local causes and transmissions, the horizontal axis of Figure 11.1.

The vertical axis describes the much more mysterious and invisible realm of acausality. From the chaotic quantum sea has precipitated the material world of the gravity field as well as the photons and electrons of the electromagnetic field. In 1924 Louis de Broglie unified the quantum field by proposing that its particles could also act as matter waves—just as light takes the form of both particles and waves. Particles and waves are aspects of fields, and fields are descriptions of space. In this way, fields have become more fundamental in all of physics than matter; they have replaced the medieval idea of "soul" as the invisible organizing principles of the universe (Sheldrake 1992: 83). Faraday and Einstein essentially said, Let's stop looking for mechanical, billiard-ball-like explanations; let's just accept that the universe is built this way. Eventually we are bound to say something very similar about life, consciousness, intentionality and parapsychology. These things happen, they are part of our reality, and they have to be taken into account.

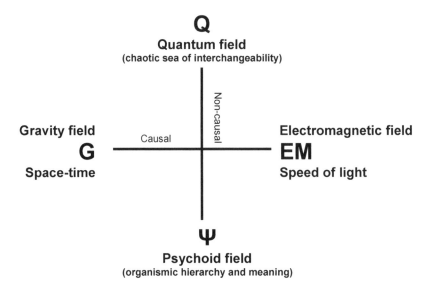

Figure 11.1 The four fields that describe the universe.

Source: original digital diagram by John Ryan Haule.

Modest proposal

My modest proposal is to regard Jung's psychoid principle, the essence of the theory of synchronicity, as the fourth universal field. In contrast with the chaotic sea of the quantum realm, the psychoid field provides an influence which gathers matter into organisms, giving them inherent meaning as living forms active in a world that is always meaningful as safe/dangerous, comfortable/uncomfortable, etc. and which organizes non-living forms as well into wholes greater than the sum of their parts. All of nature is organized as wholes nested within larger wholes, and therefore has an "organismic" character even when we would not want to call a particular whole "alive."

We need to consider what it would mean for Westerners to see the world and ourselves—all of reality—as governed by an organismic, psychoid principle. The argument will proceed in three steps. This chapter outlines the history of field theory in physics in order to establish that the movement toward holism—the tendency to understand discrete phenomena as modifications of a whole—has been the overall trend in physics for the past two centuries. Problems that have seemed insoluble from the standard Western point of view, in every case involving the problem of action at a distance, have been solved by understanding them in terms of a field. To date three have been agreed upon: gravity, electromagnetism, and quanta. Consequently, the addition of a fourth field that adds the realities that our present picture lacks would seem to be consilient with the overall trend of scientific thinking. In Chapter 12, we sketch a picture of how an organismic principle may be imagined by describing what living beings do, and follow this up with some examples from contemporary evolutionary biology that reveal a picture of organismic functioning to be slowly emerging. After these preparations, we describe how the organismic principle may be conceived as a *universal* factor, i.e. as a description of how the universe itself is organized.

The holistic trend in physics

In *The Holistic Inspirations of Physics: The Underground History of Electromagnetic Theory* (1999), Val Dusek, Professor of Philosophy at the University of New Hampshire, shows that despite Western science's self-image as reductive, mechanical and atomistic, its most important breakthroughs and enduring achievements have been made when a holistic (field) theory suddenly made new sense of the parts and how they interact. Consider, for instance, "elementary particle physics," a specialty of "quantum mechanics." Both titles imply the pre-eminence of particles as the "building blocks" of a mechanical universe. Yet precisely *this* branch of physics "has the most developed field theory," even as its self-designation reveals a "deep cultural bias toward atomistic as opposed to field theory" (Dusek 1999: 3). Atomism in Western science, Dusek (1999: 5) points out, is no accident, as it parallels historically the rise of individualistic, competitive societies.

Dusek's point is similar to Jung's, although each man is attending to a different aspect of the contemporary Western world. Dusek sees that "individualism" biases science in favor of a mechanical universe in which the independence of each "building block" is overemphasized, leaving us with the problem of explaining what might cause mutual influence. Jung sees "individualism" as a distortion of individuation, whereby the independence of the ego is overemphasized, leaving the modern Western individual with the problem of recovering a connection with the archetypal "rhizome" that we all share. In every crisis Western science has faced over the appearance of "action at a distance," the solution has taken the form of the holistic image of a field. And the inspiration for the field model can ultimately be traced to Chinese metaphysics. Jung describes the metaphysics of synchronicity with the help of the philosophy behind the *I Ching*, and he urges us to balance our extraverted Western bias by acquainting ourselves with an introversion that is characteristic of the East.

In physics, the idea of a *field* implies that space itself has a structure. A field is a non-material region of influence. Regarding the apparent celestial "eros" of gravity, the adoption of field theory means that the Earth and its moon do not radiate an invisible attractive force toward one another across empty space. Rather the space between them is bent. That bent space describes the field of gravity. Space is bent by the masses of the bodies it contains, and the way it is bent determines the motion of those bodies. Field theory says that a body is where it is because it has found its place within a field of force (Dusek 1999: 52), while our unexamined Western bias assumes that if a body occupies a particular place, it must have been pushed there by another body. Fields provide us with wholes that are greater than the parts and make sense of the matter and energy they contain.

The problem of the magnet

On account of our Western atomistic prejudice, the Chinese solved the problem of magnetism long before we did. They discovered the lodestone near the north pole fifteen centuries earlier; learned how to make a magnet of iron by heating it to the Curie point and then cooling it six centuries earlier; discovered the discrepancy between magnetic north and true north four centuries earlier; and invented the mariner's compass a century earlier.

Western mechanical thinking made magnetic attraction a problem. We wondered how a body can influence another across the empty space lying between them, while the Chinese grasped immediately that the Earth itself is a magnet with north and south poles, just like a bar of magnetized iron. They did not need a separate model to explain what turned the compass needle. They started with the idea that the universe is a whole that organizes its parts, while we started with separate parts and tried to imagine an influence operating between them (Dusek 1999: 50). The world presupposed by Chinese language and culture is not an aggregate of separate things but a continuum that can be divided up in a variety of ways. Seeing reality as a continuum, an organic system in which each element has its place and orientation, "allowed the Chinese to accept and investigate magnetism" (Dusek 1999: 91, 204).

The larger question of this chapter is analogous: "How do life, consciousness, intentionality, and parapsychology arise when the separate parts of nature come together?" These things mystify us because we are missing the larger (psychoid) picture.

China and Leibniz

The first Westerner to realize that China might be right was Gottfried Wilhelm Leibniz (1646–1716), a mathematician, philosopher-scientist and diplomat. As a diplomat, he was fascinated with China, considered it a sort of Oriental anti-Europe, which he wished to convert to Christianity by operating diplomatically through Russia. He derived most of his ideas about China from the Jesuit missionaries who had hoped to convert China by becoming experts in the philosophies and religions of the Chinese, Matteo Ricci (1552–1610), Athanasius Kircher (1602–1680), and especially Joachim Bouvet (1656–1730), who introduced Leibniz to the *I Ching*. Leibniz came to believe that the Chinese holistic universe was a superior conception to the Western atomistic view (Dusek 1999: 194–205). The philosophy of Leibniz and the metaphysics of the *I Ching* were major contributors to Jung's theory of synchronicity.

Leibniz eventually integrated three holistic traditions that contributed to field theory: first, neo-Confucian cosmology, second, Renaissance notions that the whole universe is reflected in each of its parts, and third, the Romantic idea that force is the essence of matter (Dusek 1999: 194). In this regard, it is interesting to note that Leibniz was a contemporary of Isaac Newton (1642–1727). While Leibniz was formulating a holistic philosophy—a universe comprised of nested organisms moving in pre-established harmony—Newton remained thoroughly in the atomistic tradition of Descartes and Gassendi, who were born a half-century earlier. In Newton's thinking, matter was barren and passive; spirit, alone, was able to move matter. Gravity was ultimately as inexplicable as Descartes' mind/body problem (Dusek 1999: 185). Ironically, however, Newton and Leibniz were on the same page in knowing exactly what a dependable science required; for simultaneously and without communication between them, each of them separately invented the calculus, which has been modern science's most important tool.

The way forward

In 1600, William Gilbert (1544–1603) was the first European to describe the Earth as a planetary magnet, with north and south poles (Dusek 1999: 141). Being right was not enough, however. Because his contemporaries believed that magnetism was a quality inherent in "certain isolated features of the surface of the

Earth," his discovery was ignored for more than two centuries (Dusek 1999: 146). Gilbert gained his insights through a number of experiments that were "extraordinarily clear-headed and precise for his day." Although there was much he missed, he was led to a view that was essentially correct—that "each little bit of magnetic Earth is a mirror of the great Earth mother herself"—just as when magnets are cut into pieces, each piece becomes a magnet with a north and south pole of its own. He even speculated, correctly according to modern views, that the Earth's core is responsible for the planet being a magnet (Dusek 1999: 144–6).

The first scientist to connect electricity with magnetism was Hans Christian Ørsted (1777–1851), who discovered in 1820 that a compass needle would swing around on its pivot until it stood perpendicular to the direction of current running through a wire. Some of the leading scientists of the day declared this finding "impossible" and "just another German dream" (Dusek 1999: 251). Ørsted was a Dane and a *Naturphilosoph*: he belonged to an intellectual movement centered in Germany whose members described themselves as "philosophers of nature." Outside of Germany, the Philosophy of Nature stood for backward science and bad metaphysics (Dusek 1999: 253). Other "nature philosophers," however, made significant contributions, the most important of which for our argument is Faraday's notion of the magnetic field. Other *Naturphilosophen* who advanced our understanding of the world include Friedrich Schilling (1775–1854), who "organized the universe in terms of polarities in the manner of primitive thinking," leading him to correctly predict the ultraviolet spectrum on the basis of the discovery of the infrared. The infrared spectrum was discovered by another *Naturphilosoph*, Johann Wilhelm Ritter (1776–1810), who was ridiculed for his interest in dowsing (a parapsychological talent) but nevertheless "can be considered the founder of research in general bioelectricity" (Dusek 1999: 253–6).

These developments prepared the way for Michael Faraday (1791–1867), who as we have seen was the first to propose the idea of a magnetic field with a definite shape and vector of force. Faraday was the son of a blacksmith and uneducated in mathematics, the language of science. Therefore, it is particularly noteworthy that he was able to conquer the field through a combination of "careful, ingenious experiments and qualitative metaphysical speculation." Faraday showed that metaphysical theorizing, when rigorous enough, could be used to make predictions that could then be tested experimentally (Dusek 1999: 259, 265).

The mathematical formulation of Faraday's ideas was not accomplished until 1861, when James Clerk Maxwell (1831–79) unified the phenomena of electricity, magnetism and light with a set of equations he understood to be describing fields of stress imposed upon "ether," the very subtle fluid that had for millennia been assumed to fill empty space and to be the medium through which the heavenly bodies moved. Maxwell's ether was a form of matter, but Faraday's field was not. Faraday's speculations involved empty space, itself, as a field. It was not until Einstein that space-time, alone, became the field and the ether-hypothesis was abandoned (Dusek 1999: 268).

Thought experiments

Einstein's gravity field is the first pure field theory, where points in space-time are quantified. If Jung's psychoid field is ever established, it will also be non-material. But unlike the fields of Einstein and Faraday, the psychoid field will not emphasize position in space. The psychoid field better resembles the quantum field in being completely non-local and non-causal. Nevertheless, it is encouraging to note that Faraday's magnetic field and Einstein's space-time were both achieved through what Einstein called "thought experiments," i.e. controlled and rigorous metaphysical speculations that were consequential enough to make predictions that can be tested.

Clearly parapsychology is unlikely to be the domain within which to test the psychoid hypothesis. The very nature of ESP renders it inappropriate for strict laboratory conditions. Spontaneity and the right mood are essential, and the transition from limbic reception to cortical report always leaves plenty of room for error. The first efforts to describe a psychoid field, therefore, ought to look to one of the other three aspects of psychoid process—intentionality, consciousness and organismic function. Of these, the organism is the most observable, dependable and fundamental. There is no intentionality, consciousness or parapsychology outside of organisms. Consequently thought experiments applied to the psychoid field will have to begin with the observation of living organisms.

Therefore, in our effort to understand what the proposal of synchronicity means for understanding the world we live in, we begin in Chapter 12 with a description of the process that is evident in every living organism. Organismic process will stand as a sort of prototype against which we can understand the effects of a universal psychoid field. With this image in mind, we will be able to appreciate how it is that an inchoate notion of organismic process is already at work in some recent, highly respected discussions of evolutionary biology.

Chapter 12

Darwin's dilemma

Evolution needs a psychoid principle

Just as Newton was embarrassed by his accurate mathematical description of gravity because it seemed to require an explanation of action-at-a-distance that he could not supply, so Darwin was embarrassed by the fact that his *Origin of Species* accounted only for "natural selection," the filtering process whereby unfit organisms are excluded, and that he had no way to explain how new species come into being. The source of novelty in evolution has been called "Darwin's Dilemma."

The so-called "Modern Synthesis" that allies natural selection with genetics has described the mechanism whereby inheritance is highly dependable and also how mutations can occur from time to time that may occasionally give rise to new species. But what the Modern Synthesis knows is a haphazard mechanism that seems inadequate to describe the rapidity with which new species develop after certain "bottlenecks" have caused massive species die-offs, such as at the end of the Permian period, 251 million years ago, or the end of the dinosaurs 65 million years ago.

It really looks as though evolutionary theory needs the notion of psychoid process to support the facts in the fossil record, whereby meaningful change can occur much more accurately and quickly than the slow accumulation of random mutations would seem to allow. Even with the discoveries of the Modern Synthesis, Darwin's Dilemma has not been solved, for it leaves us with an image of evolutionary novelty that resembles the efforts of a thousand monkeys banging away at keyboards while an observer waits for *Othello* to emerge from one of them.

A psychoid principle suggests that things happen meaningfully because what we see as isolated facts belong to the process of an organism. There is a whole organizing its parts, analogous to the fabric of space-time giving rise to galaxies and solar systems. To understand this way of seeing things, we shall examine how organisms behave.

Jung was already on the path that led to his "psychoid" proposal in 1933, when he expressed regret that, "We Westerners can only see psyche as an appendage of the brain" (*CW8*: ¶743). In his view, even protozoa have a primitive psyche, which is "the quintessence of life in the body," where "mind and body [may] ultimately prove to be the same thing" (1926: *CW8*: ¶621). In 1927, he made it most explicit:

> This whole psychic organism corresponds exactly to the body ... still pre-
> serves elements that connect it with the invertebrates and ultimately with the
> protozoa. Theoretically, it should be possible to "peel" the collective uncon-
> scious, layer by layer, until we come to the psychology of the worm, and even
> of the amoeba.
>
> (*CW8*: ¶322)

Psychic process in simple organisms

Recent discoveries support these statements of Jung's. Amoebas, for instance, act
as though they remember their past. As they move about in a "non-random"
manner foraging for food, they "tend to remember [their] previous steps."
Obviously such a memory capacity, small though it may be, is an asset in the
struggle for survival, since it "increases the microbe's chance of finding food in
new areas" (*Science News*, March 31, 2007: 205).

Other species of amoeba manifest more remarkable abilities that we normally
associate with brains, or at least with nervous systems. *Physarum polycephalum*,
an amoeba with multiple nuclei, acts as a kind of "protoplasmic slime." In laboratory studies, it has been shown to have the capacity to remember a rhythmic
pattern of shocks it has received in the form of puffs of dry air. The rhythm of the
puffs may be as slow as once every hour or hour-and-a-half:

> When the amoeba *Physarum polycephalum* is subjected to a series of shocks
> at regular intervals, it learns the pattern and changes its behavior in anticipa-
> tion of the next one to come, according to a team of researchers in Japan.
> Remarkably, this memory stays in the slime mould for hours, even when the
> shocks themselves stop. A single renewed shock after a "silent" period [of six
> hours] will leave the mould expecting another to follow in the rhythm it had
> learned previously.
>
> (Ball 2008: 385)

The anthropologist Jeremy Narby (2007) reports on a visit he made to the Peruvian
Amazon in 1989, where he observed the same slime mold, which he describes as
"a single cell [that] behaves as though it has a brain," in that it consistently solves
maze problems. The largest of such organisms can be the size of a human hand
and able to reassemble itself if cut up into small pieces. When Narby sprinkled
pieces of the slime throughout a maze, the fragments spread out until they occupied its every corridor. When food was placed at the two ends of the maze, the
multinucleated cell would reduce "itself down to a tube that covers the shortest
distance between food sources" (Narby 2007: 44).

Narby also found a vegetable that acts as though it has a brain. Dodder, a leaf-
less plant, is unable to photosynthesize its own food and therefore is totally dependent on other plants for nourishment and water. It parasitizes its host plant by
wrapping itself around its stem. The number of coils it makes amounts to an

estimate of how fruitful dodder expects the host to be. "Botanists have found that dodder makes the right decisions about when to stay and when to move on with the same mathematical accuracy as animal foragers" (Narby 2007: 44).

The ubiquity of process

In all these extraordinary instances, psyche reveals itself in an organism's process. It is always on account of what appear to be "choices"—which direction to forage, when to flinch in expectation of a shock of dry air, how many coils to wind—that we recognize psychic, or at least psychoid, behavior. Psyche, then, inevitably refers to a meaning-giving or meaning-recognizing process within a living being.

If psyche is essentially a form of process, it will not be surprising to discover that science as we know it today has no place for process of any sort. In *Creative Evolution* Henri Bergson (1911), who was admired by Jung for his emphasis upon flux as a fundamental aspect of reality,[1] points out that everything in nature is constantly changing. Science, however, tries to understand things by studying "snapshots" of process—dead, static moments extracted from the flow. "It is the flow of time, the very flux of the real that we should be trying to follow" (Bergson 1911: 342).

To grasp Bergson's idea of snapshots instead of process, consider how the primary mathematical tool of science, calculus, works. The typical question that calculus addresses is what sort of change does x undergo over the course of a short snippet of time (Δt). In effect, the question asks how does the snapshot of x taken after the interval differ from that taken before. Calculus tries to approximate process by imagining the time interval (Δt) as it gets smaller and smaller, approaching zero. But in every case, it is comparing snapshots.

In place of this series of snapshots, Bergson would have us attend to process itself, rather in the style of Aristotle, who described *psyche* as the "entelechy" of a living body—the principle by which a body strives in every moment to meet its needs optimally (Bergson 1911: 350). *Entelechy* means to have the goal (*telos*) within (*en*). Jung wanted to claim precisely this quality for psyche and brought it up in his writings from time to time, but always nervously; for he feared his readers would mistake his intentions and jump to the conclusion that the *telos* inside might be a sort of pre-established blueprint—as though each acorn has a tiny oak tree inside.[2]

For Jung, entelechy, the principle by which an organism strives in every moment to achieve the best overall conditions for itself, describes the process of "self," psyche's wholeness. An amoeba, indeed every living cell, marshals its thousands of components toward the best holistic solution for its organism, not only internally but also in the context of the world it senses surrounding it. In every instant a situation is unconsciously felt, a solution unconsciously chosen, and a new situation produced. This new situation then becomes the past for the next instant of choosing. Process is an endless flow of split-second moments, in each of which an incremental change is unconsciously envisaged and chosen. Life, Bergson (1911: 71) said, proceeds by *insinuation*.

If an amoeba has a "psychology," psyche must be the "entelechy" located in the animal's wholeness, the process whereby all the parts work together (even in the absence of a brain) on behalf of a common, ever changing goal. Psyche, therefore, is the wholeness of an organism's process and the process of the whole organism. In Jung's words:

> *The* self, [the hero's] wholeness, which is both God and animal [is] not merely the empirical man, but the totality of his being, which is rooted in his animal nature and reaches out beyond the merely human towards the divine.
>
> (*CW5*: ¶460)

Some three decades later he compared psyche to a tree, "the self depicted as a process of growth" (*CW13*: ¶304). Bergson had a similar view, comparing an organism to a tree (Bergson 1911: 16).

Process in amoeba

In each moment, the living amoeba is a different configuration of the molecules that comprise it: sub-societies of molecules in its cell wall, its cytoplasm, its energy-producing mitochondria, the variously deployed genes curled up in its nucleus, and the protein skeleton that changes the animal's shape by in-and-out telescopic movements. In each moment, the configuration of the amoeba's whole is responding to a different past and intending a different future. In the moment before last, for instance, the sensory proteins embedded in the north side of its cell wall had not detected the presence of food. But now, in the moment just ending, they have interacted with nutrient molecules dissolved in the soil's moisture, and a cascade of chemical reactions begins unfolding in the cytoplasm. In the next moment, the telescopic protein microtubules of the cell's skeletal structure will begin stretching out pseudopodia to engulf the morsel.

None of these rough "moments" detailed from a split-second in the life of an amoeba involves only a few or even a hundred of the elements comprising the animal. Each element in the organism participates, feels its place in the organismic order of the whole. The process philosopher, and one of the very few metaphysicians of the twentieth century, Alfred North Whitehead (1861–1947) argues that the amoeba, like every biological cell, is a tiny universe of "concrescence" within itself, and also together with its environmental surround (Whitehead 1929: 243). The notion of "concrescence" is essential, the perspective whereby in every moment there is a growing-together (*cresco*, to grow up, to spring forth; *con*, with, together). Psyche manifests itself as an endless process in which the many components of organism grow together through a series of momentary choices, each in pursuit of a new momentary goal.

Whitehead's "concrescence," in the case of amoeba, means that while every component molecule has its own function and its own meaningful surround, it participates in the larger growing-together flow that is the life of the whole organism. Thus the behavior of each molecule is governed by a larger purpose, one that it could never envisage on its own, so to speak. It participates in and finds its higher purpose in the wholeness, entelechy, or psyche of the larger organism. Entelechy is interior goal-directedness that does not look minutes, much less years, into the future. The flow of process "chooses" new instantaneous configurations ceaselessly: this is what it means to be an organism.

Process in a neuron

The uninterrupted flow that is an amoeba's life is essentially the same as that of a neuron in the brain. Although a neuron does not move about in search of food, its every moment consists in attaining organismic balance—the concrescence of its molecular constituents in making holistic responses to its ever changing immediate surround. For a neuron, the surround has much to do with the established neural networks to which it belongs as well as novel events occurring at its dendrites when other neurons seek to "wire" new pathways. Furthermore, as we have seen in *Volume One*, electromagnetic fields set up in the neuropil cause tiny AM waves in regions only millimeters across, and these tiny regions coordinate with others to form larger patterns of waves that entrain ever larger numbers of neurons.

The entrainment of neuronal societies by AM waves describes the hierarchical nature of an organism. Smaller societies are nested within larger ones. Thus, each neuron is an organism with respect to its constituent molecules but participates in networks and wave fields which incorporate it into larger organisms. Meanwhile, the full complement of neuronal societies is governed by the concrescent wholeness of the brain. In each case, an organism does not merely assemble its own components into an individual whole, it does so under the guidance of the larger living organism to which it belongs. Psyche as we usually understand it is the "regnant" (reigning) organism at the top of the hierarchy, the concrescent wholeness of brain, heart, lungs, liver and all the rest.

Process in a zygote

If life in an amoeba illustrates the holistic nature of psychic process and if life in a neuron illustrates its nested, hierarchical structure, then life in a zygote reveals psyche's potential for growth and expansion. A zygote comes into existence within moments after a sperm penetrates an ovum. At that point the new individual is about as simple as an amoeba: a cell wall containing cytoplasm, mitochondria and a nucleus with a full complement of chromosomes. According to the organismic perspective articulated here, the psyche of a zygote is no more complicated than that of an amoeba—a view that stands in stark contrast to the idea that God injects a fully formed human soul into every zygote of *Homo sapiens*.

That theological idea assumes a metaphysics of soul-as-separate-substance rather than soul-as-process.

Zygotes, however, become more complex than amoebas at their first cell division. Before that point, the same mitotic process of cell division can be observed in both zygote and amoeba: chromosome pairs separate along spindle-like fibers and the single cell splits into a pair of clones. For amoeba, the clones are free and independent individuals. Two simple psyches are engaged in two separate life processes where moments before there was only one. In the zygote, however, a single psyche remains. One regnant process governs both clones. Two identical cells, each with its own subordinate psychic process, cooperate in a way that two amoebas cannot, as parts of a larger, more complex organism. The psyche of the former zygote has already become substantially more complex than that of an amoeba. In a many-celled organism, mitosis is more than a duplication of matter; it is also a process that elaborates an emerging self.

As cell division continues in the new being that once was a zygote—through four-, eight- and sixteen-cell entities—a single psychic process marshals all the cells in the interests of a single organism. The complexity and scope of that regnant psyche doubles at each cell division, but a huge jump in complexity occurs when the ball of cells folds in on itself to differentiate into three different cell types. At this point the outer layer or "ectoderm" develops a specific entelechy that will lead to nervous tissue and skin; the middle "mesoderm" will move toward producing skeletal bones and muscle, while the inner "endoderm" will over time elaborate internal organs. This in-folding "gastrulation" that begins these developments, therefore, implies a complexity of psychic process that is incomparably more elaborate than that of an amoeba or a neuron. Psyche grows from zygote through fetus, infant, language-learning tot and on into adulthood and death. Psyche is a process that is always changing, always growing, never the same from one moment or one decade to the next. Whitehead (1929: 128) expressed the issue vividly: "All life in the body is the life of individual cells. . . . So what needs to be explained is not dissociation of personality but unifying control."

Where is psyche?

The unexamined assumptions of our Western culture lead us to expect that if a thing is real it must be located somewhere specific. Therefore, as long as we took primates like ourselves as our primary objects of study, it was convenient to follow the Western assumption and locate psyche inside the brain. We did so cautiously. To avoid naive materialism, we distinguished the psychological lived-brain from the meat-like laboratory brain. However, now that we have granted psychic process to protozoa, individual neurons and the gastrula in a primate's womb, we seem to have reopened the question of psyche's locality and found it to be mysterious.

We can say no more than that every living body is pervaded by psyche. Psyche belongs to our material being, but has no specific location within it. It is not in the brain or the heart or the liver but is the organismic process that brings the functioning of all those parts into concrescent harmony. Jung liked to say that the self is a circle whose circumference is everywhere and center nowhere.[3] Whitehead (1929: 207) had a similar conception, "Our bodies are largely contrivances whereby some central actual occasion [read "*psyche*"] may inherit these basic experiences of its antecedent parts."

Evolution and the psychoid field

Our examination of psychic process in amoebas, neurons and zygotes was designed to reveal how a psychoid principle is at work within a living organism. To make a case for a universal psychoid field, however, requires us to examine larger processes, and in particular whether anything like psychic process is evident in the course of evolution itself. I think there can be no doubt that evolution betrays psychoid traits such as organizing individual cells into societies, societies into organisms, and organisms into species of growing complexity. To make this case, we shall consider the major transitions through which the evolution of life has passed, according to the classic brief account by John Maynard Smith and Eörs Szathmáry, *The Origins of Life: From the Birth of Life to the Origins of Language* (1999).

Non-living psychoid processes

Smith and Szathmáry (1999) describe the evolution of life in eight steps. But most important for us are the two preliminary steps that precede the emergence of living organisms. This brings the full number of evolutionary stages to ten (as numbered below). Evidence for the preliminary steps is not merely imagined or deduced by logic; it is all around us, in the sea and in our own bodies.

I Simple autocatalysis

There can be no evolution without reproduction and no reproduction without growth: "The essence of growth is autocatalysis" (Smith and Szathmáry 1999: 6). Autocatalysis is a process by which a single molecule multiplies itself by undergoing a series of interactions with other molecules in its vicinity. Thus in Figure 12.1, molecule **A** reacts with raw material x_1 to produce molecule **B**. B splits off waste product **y** to become molecule **C**. C takes on raw material x_2 to produce molecule **D**, which in turns splits into two separate molecules, **A**. In this manner, the entire cycle of reactions results in a multiplication of the original molecule; and this is the foundation of growth. Molecules of **A** are being "grown."

Cycles of molecular interaction like this have been found to occur in nature under a variety of conditions, and are universally held to be an essential aspect of the "primordial soup" out of which life is believed to have first appeared. Similar cycles occur extensively in our bodies, in metabolism, energy production and the

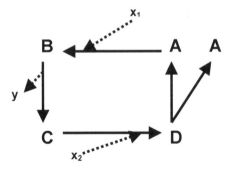

Figure 12.1 Autocatalysis.

Source: digital diagram by John Ryan Haule summarizing Smith and Szathmáry (1999: 6).

like. We may call such an elementary process "psychoid" in the sense that there is primitive organization, cooperation among parts, and the fact that such autocatalytic cycles occur ubiquitously in living organisms. Responsiveness, the minimal form of psychoid behavior, makes all "growth" possible.

2 Molecular autocatalysis

In the second stage before identifiably living organisms could have evolved, autocatalysis had to have reproduced long, chain-like molecules, each "bead" of which is a "module," a relatively complex sub-molecule, one of perhaps four types, that can be assembled in any order. RNA is the prototype of this sort of molecule, where an existing molecule serves as the template on which the next molecule is assembled. RNA, like DNA, is comprised of strings of "bases," only four in number, and the order of their arrangement carries "information" related to the building of proteins.

When autocatalysis has become complex enough to produce the prototypes of cellular reproduction like these, we are only a step away from the simplest of living forms. A psychoid principle must be operating to favor not only growth, and not only growth in complexity, but also the emergence of meaningful complexity—what is everywhere called "information"—in the form of the modular "language" that reaches its highest form in the DNA of living cells.

From molecules to cells

In the two stages of autocatalysis just described, chemical reactions occur in the open. Perhaps sometimes in the open ocean, but more likely in tidal pools, where molecules of various sorts can become concentrated and their temperature raised by the sun.

3 The emergence of compartments

RNA-like strings reproducing themselves are far too simple to be considered alive. Living things build secondary structures—proteins, for instance, to carry out additional functions. Such proteins and their constituents all have to be concentrated in the same small area if they are to function cooperatively. Therefore, it was necessary as a first step toward life that the interacting components all be contained within some kind of membrane. Perhaps the first such enclosure was as simple as a globule of oil, something to separate the water-borne molecules cooperating in their simple proto-living project from the larger tidal pool.

4 The development of chromosomes

If the cell-like enclosures just described are to reproduce themselves, they need to have all their genetic material connected so that it can be reproduced entirely and exactly for each individual that emerges from the original entity. Smith and Szathmáry (1999) conclude that an organism with a single chromosome, all of its genes linked together end-to-end, would be the most likely proto-cell capable of exact reproduction. "When one gene is replicated, all are. This coordinated replication prevents competition between genes within a compartment, and forces co-operation on them. They are all in the same boat" (Smith and Szathmáry 1999: 17).

The first single-cell organisms

The previous two steps in the evolution of life are merely logically necessary. We have no evidence in the world today that such entities exist. Perhaps the virus comes closest, in that it contains a short string of DNA inside a capsule of protein and is very good at both self-propagation and rapid mutation to enhance its survival. But the virus is both more advanced and less viable than the supposed "compartmented" entities that single cells presuppose: more advanced because of the very well-developed capsule and less viable because viruses cannot function on their own but require living cells whose metabolism and reproductive mechanisms they can subvert to their own ends.

Thus, though there is evidence for evolution's two autocatalytic steps abundant in the world about us, the two proto-cell stages are only required by the evolution hypothesis. The psychoid feature of the universe must proceed through stages. Without "intending" biological cells in any anthropomorphic manner, the psychoid tendency to self-organization and the meaning-laden response every entity has to its surround, encouraged ever more successful organizations of matter that could perpetuate themselves in the style of organisms—even when all the conditions for a living being were not present.

From here forward in the Smith and Szathmáry account of evolution, every stage described has living descendants abundant in the world around us.

5 Prokaryotes

Prokaryotes are living cells that lack a nuclear membrane to separate the genetic material from the rest of the protoplasm. Examples of prokaryotes in the world about us include the common bacteria that help digest the food in our intestines and the blue-green algae (cyanobacteria) that transformed the atmosphere of the Earth from a condition that was hostile to life as we know it today, being very high in carbon dioxide, to today's oxygen-rich environment. The cyanobacteria transformed the Earth through millions of years of photosynthesis: using the sun's energy to split the carbon out of carbon dioxide and combine it and hydrogen from water molecules into sugars for their own nourishment and propagation. In the process, the oxygen freed from carbon dioxide and water was released into the atmosphere. Another type of prokaryote has recently been discovered in the vicinity of hot vents deep in the seabed, living on the sulfur released there.

The advance prokaryotes made over the proto-cells that preceded them is primarily the division of labor made possible by the evolution of DNA. General agreement among evolutionary biologists holds that an "RNA-world" preceded the emergence of prokaryotes, where all of the reproductive work was done by RNA. RNA's cousin, DNA, however, is ideal for the job of preserving the genetic code. Its double-helix structure lets it duplicate itself simply by unwinding into single strands and then assembling by chemical attraction mirror-image strands to restore its double-helical structure. Every unwinding of DNA, therefore, results in two complete DNA molecules, each a perfect duplicate of the other.

6 Eukaryotes

All the animals and plants we are familiar with, including ourselves, are eukaryotes: organisms whose cellular organization includes encapsulated structures in the protoplasm. The most important and definitive of these is the nucleus, which keeps the genetic material separate from the rest of the cell's components. But other "organelles" are also quite characteristic and universal in eukaryotes. Mitochondria are the power-plants of a cell, and in plants chloroplasts perform the work of photosynthesis. Current belief among evolutionary biologists holds that these organelles arose as certain prokaryotes engulfed others, and instead of dissolving the "morsels" and metabolizing their components, the engulfed entities were allowed to survive and cooperate in the life of a single, more complex organism.

Because mitochondria have their own DNA, they appear to be a perfect case for the "engulfment" hypothesis. They really appear to be prokaryotes that have "consented" to perform a single function on behalf of a larger entity. Cooperation like this stands as a striking example of psychoid process: radically new possibilities were in some way "recognized" and incorporated. The psyche of an engulfed bacterium, say, remained as the organizing process of a new organelle while cooperating in turn with the psyche of the engulfing entity. The containing cell's psyche became the regnant, organizing process for the whole, more complex eukaryote. That psyche grew, proportionately, much as the psyche of a zygote becomes progressively more complex and responsive to more and more levels of meaning as zygote becomes gastrula, embryo, infant, and so forth.

7 Sexual propagation

The most mysterious "jump" that evolution has made involves the introduction of sex. All of the organisms described to this point reproduce by simple splitting (mitosis), when a cell divides into two identical clones. How and why sex arose is not clear. But the process by which it occurs is well known. The double endowment of every chromosome, based in the double helix of DNA, is cut in half. The gametes (ova and sperm) result from unwinding the DNA and encapsulating each strand in a separate gamete so that the zygote that results from the union of ovum and sperm will receive a double helix—one strand from the father and one from the mother.

The advantages of sexual reproduction are easier to state than the mechanism by which it first came to be. The rate of evolutionary change is enhanced insofar as each new individual inherits from two parents, so that the possibility of the new individual receiving a useful mutation is doubled, and such mutations can spread much more rapidly through the population. At the same time, evolutionary change gains a certain stabilization in that the effects of harmful mutations will be reduced by the fact that each mutated gene will likely be paired with an unmutated gene. Finally, the behavior Darwin identified as "sexual selection" gives a role in evolution to each individual's choice of mate. Those potential mates better adapted for survival will likely be seen as more sexually attractive by the opposite gender (Smith and Szathmáry 1999: 82–4).

While it may be hard to discern a "psychoid" pressure toward the process of chromosome splitting in the production of gametes, it is nevertheless clear that a new use (splitting) has been found for an old enzyme (the one that repairs DNA damage). This represents at least the ("psychoid") discovery of a new meaning in an old entity.

Multicellular organisms

In one step, Smith and Szathmáry (1999) move from single-cell creatures to every sort of animal and plant comprised of many cells. Thus sponges, starfish, clams, lobsters, insects, fish, amphibians, reptiles, birds and mammals are all accounted for in one step. Later in this chapter, we discuss the issue of how evolution has gone about engineering new body plans in the Animal Kingdom. Here, we consider only what multicellularity means.

8 "Endless forms most beautiful"

With this phrase, Darwin ends his *Origin of Species*. Such variety comes about when cells learn to cooperate with one another to constitute a single, complex organism. Since all the cells of a given animal or plant carry identical information in their genes, evolution has had to provide a way for different groups of cells in a single organism to "turn on" specific genetic instructions, while "turning off" others. This is where the psychoid process within a single individual becomes truly complex, with cells organized into tissues, tissues into organs, and organs into a single body, operating as a unit within the process of a single regnant psyche. Biochemistry describes the situation in terms of local concentrations of certain chemicals. Genes are turned on, perhaps, when the concentration is high and off when it is low. Chemical concentrations are meaningful realities within a developing embryo and reveal the psychoid processes by which multicellular organisms construct themselves.

9 Colonies

Smith and Szathmáry (1999) see the development of colonies of social insects—ants, termites and bees—as a major step forward in evolution, in that a whole colony of individuals is organized by an order of meaning higher than any one of them. One dimension of importance of this sort of organization can be measured in biomass: one-third of the weight of all the living beings in the Amazon forest is comprised of colonizing insects (Smith and Szathmáry 1999: 18). Each individual ant or bee is a complete organism in its own right—more self-evidently than each of the neurons in its own body. Each is more independent of the others than a body's cell, and yet each finds its place within the higher psychoid process of the colony. They cannot live alone but rely upon a psychoid principle that reaches beyond the individual organism to a higher reality which is more elaborately organismic than the individual insect.

10 Primate societies

The best and most consciously organized of all world societies are those of the primates, whose survival strategy is based in their sociality. Here the psychoid nature of connection between individuals is unmistakable; and among humans it is assisted and differentiated by the psychically intensive activities of myth and language. Through language, indeed, evolution itself can be served: "A trait that is adaptive, and that *must be learnt* in the first place, can evolve to be hard-wired into the brain, because learning can guide natural selection" (Smith and Szathmáry 1999: 166).

With this brief summary of evolution, we can see that a psychoid principle is evident at each transition: among the relatively simple autocatalytic processes of the primeval soup, forming cells, building simple organisms into more complex societies, always favoring complexity and the processing of more and more meaning. Intentionality cannot be said to have appeared before the first cell, but the psychoid principle was already at work in the process of autocatalysis, illustrating that what Jung meant by "psychoid" was truly elemental, a basic trait of all reality, that which makes sensitivity, response to meaning, and intentionality possible.

The psychoid process encompassing an organism and its surround

According to Neo-Darwinism and its modern synthesis, evolution is a purely Newtonian, mechanical enterprise. Gene mutation provides random, mostly hopeless changes, and natural selection filters out the poorly adapted gambles so they cannot propagate. Novelty is slow, hesitant, and mostly a failure, while natural selection is immediate, decisive, deeply rooted in the past, with no view to the future, and without purpose or guidance (J. S. Turner 2007: 5).

Quite apart from their thirst for theological justification, therefore, the proponents of Intelligent Design have a point, of which even Darwin was painfully aware. Within a dozen years of the publication of *Origin of Species*, the American paleontologist E. D. Cope and the British zoologist St. George Mivart both published books that searched for a theory to explain how novelty might be favored by the process of evolution. The origin of the new had to be explained, and not just the filtering out of the unfit. In the twentieth century, however, addressing the issue of novelty was as unfashionable as metaphysics. It is therefore good to find that this rigid situation may be changing. J. Scott Turner, Professor at the SUNY College of Environmental Science and Forestry, at Syracuse, says:

> The biggest of [the unexplainable] gaps confronting Darwinism today is the problem of biological design. Bridging that gap will mean coming to grips with the problem of intentionality, which Darwinism will be unable to do as long as it remains wedded to the atomist doctrines of Neo-Darwinism.
>
> (J. S. Turner 2007: 138)

Turner's title, *The Tinkerer's Accomplice: How Design Emerges from Life Itself*, suggests the psychoid process for which we are searching. The book, he says, is the product of an insight that changed his approach to evolutionary biology:

> I had been subscribing to the conventional notion that a living structure is an object in which function takes place. That's all wrong, I came to see. A living structure is not an object, but is itself a process, just as much so as the function that takes place in it. Even the conventional dodge that structure and function are inextricably linked is wrong, I decided. That implies that structure and function are somehow distinct, just as peanut butter and bread each retain a distinct identity when they are inextricably linked into a peanut butter sandwich. But living structures are not distinct from the function they support; they are themselves the function.
>
> (J. S. Turner 2007: 21)

Termite chimneys

Turner was taught his lesson in South Africa and Namibia by termites. He was attracted by the magnificent chimneys they built and wanted to demonstrate to his students how the chimneys were designed to maintain a steady flow of air through the termite nest underground (Figure 12.2). Tunnels open out of the sides of the chimney-topped mound through which the insects travel to gather wood, which they chew to provide a medium for their fungi gardens. (Fungi do the intermediate work of digesting the wood for the termite colony.) Turner thought, and textbooks declared, that if he were to inject a traceable gas into one of those side tunnels, the gas would be detectable leaving the colony by way of the chimney. He failed repeatedly to prove the standard theory correct, with two different species of termite.

Eventually, he found he had completely misconstrued the termites' relationship with their mounds. He had imagined the termites as one sort of entity

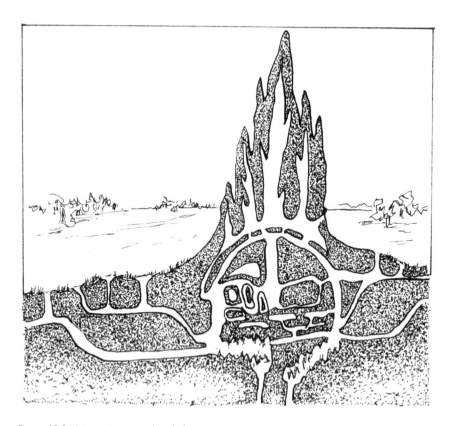

Figure 12.2 A termite mound and chimney.

Source: original pen and ink drawing by Ann Yoost Brecke.

(a community of living insects) inhabiting another sort of entity (the inanimate tower-topped mound). This is, in fact, the standard Neo-Darwinian point of view: animals "adapt" themselves to ecological "niches." In fact, he discovered, there are no pre-established niches that "are simply imposed on living creatures," rather "environments are not imposed, but are created by living systems" (J. S. Turner 2007: 218).

He came to see that the termite mound is the "colony's lung," where ten pounds of termites and twenty pounds of fungi are expelling carbon dioxide, water vapor and heat constantly, and in quantity about equal to three times the output of an adult rabbit. He envisioned the core of the nest as highly concentrated with these waste products of living processes. The concentration would be greatest at the base of the nest and diminish as it approached the inner wall of the mound. Because hot gasses would rise, the concentration of carbon dioxide at the very top of the mound would be greatest. Consequently, it seemed that termites were carrying grains of sand from points of high carbon dioxide concentration to points relatively lower in the gas (J. S. Turner 2007: 26, 24).

As a result, the very top of the mound was selectively hollowed out and a chimney gradually rose. Furthermore, all chimneys rose in a northerly direction—not on account of the prevailing winds, as was the general opinion—but at an angle midway between the average zenith of the sun at noon and a point directly overhead. This resulted from the termites' moving grains of sand in such a way that the chimney was heated equally on all sides, for south of the equator the sun's zenith is in the north.

The "tinkerer's accomplice"

Turner came to see that termites are not organisms occupying a pre-established niche, but rather that termites and mound were interrelated processes. "Organisms . . . are not things but . . . processes that *do* . . . [they are] transient assemblages of ordered matter that are sustained by an ongoing flow of matter and energy through them" (J. S. Turner 2007: 145). Genes do, indeed, begin the process of making termites and ourselves what we are. This is the role of Darwin's "tinkerer," the agent that replicates and produces mutations that prepare an organism to produce "slapdash solutions to adaptive problems as they arise" (J. S. Turner 2007: 6). But the tinkerer is not alone in this enterprise, rather the physiology of the organism, the tinkerer's "accomplice," goes to work on the environment to shape it, and leaves behind an environment shaped for the next generation of termites to inhabit and continue to reshape. A mound and chimney is there in advance when they emerge from their eggs, a persisting structure that shapes their behavior, even as they continue to reshape it.

The tinkerer's accomplice is "frankly teleological," for it is always looking one step ahead in a process of finding immediate solutions (J. S. Turner 2007: 28). Note that this is no grandiose teleology, no plan that looks minutes or years into the future. In the case of the termites, this modest teleology moves one grain of

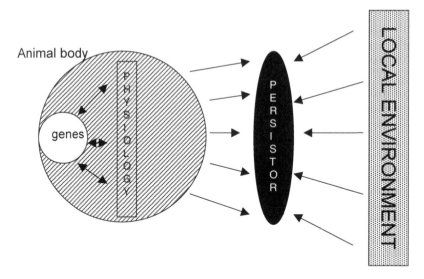

Figure 12.3 Psychoid process: animal/environment.

Source: digital diagram by John Ryan Haule summarizing the argument of J. S. Turner (2007).

sand from a high carbon dioxide location to a lower one. Here are the instanta-neous but meaningful "choices" facilitated by the universal psychoid field. A nest of a million termites, over the course of years, creates a persisting niche designed to shape subsequent generations of termites.

In the end, Turner comes to understand the relationship between DNA and an animal's environment as a process involving several "players," as depicted in Figure 12.3. At one end is the genome of the animal, and at the other is the envi-ronment as it would be in the absence of the animal. The genes produce bodies as they interact with the physiology of the animal's developing body. A termite hatching in a termite mound is shaped by the "extended physiology" of termite activity in the mound, just as a human child is shaped by its interactions with its mother and the wider cultural world of which she is a part. The termite mound, itself, is a "persistor," a persisting structure that has resulted from termites inter-acting for hundreds of years with their environment. The persisting mound, there-fore, resembles the cultural world into which a human child is born. It is a veritable monument of psychoid process.

Tinkerer and accomplice inside an animal's body

Turner gives a number of examples for how this same process, where an organism (a cell, in this case) interacts with its surround and thereby creates an animal's body. The tinkerer throws out a slapdash attempt at a solution, and the accomplice shapes it into a viable "design." Turner applies these principles to the construction of muscles, blood vessels, bones, intestines, and more. We shall consider only muscles, as the same principles are involved in every case.

Fibroblasts are specialized cells that begin the work of building muscle. They "weave a meshwork of fibrous protein threads . . . [by secreting] trails of fibrous protein as they wander about . . . Like a termite mound, the connective tissue is embodied physiology" (J. S. Turner 2007: 32f). The process carried out by fibroblasts building muscle tissue corresponds to the termites building their chimney.

After the first fibroblasts lay down a network of collagen fibers, a second population lines up along the fibers, "holding onto footholds called fibronectins." These fibroblasts are as responsive to tension in their fiber as termites are to carbon dioxide. When the tension rises, they relax their grip, when it drops they take up the slack until the tension is restored. "Collagen networks, like termite mounds, are dynamic structures. New fibers are being continually laid down (fibrogenesis), while old fibers are continually dismantled (fibrolysis)" (J. S. Turner 2007: 34). Fibrogenesis lays down parallel fibers where the tension is high, while fibrolysis dissolves fibers where tension is lacking. In this way, as muscles are used by the growing embryo or exercising adult, new fibers are built as needed to reinforce the fibers that are carrying the load, while those that carry no load fail to survive.

The first move in the process is random—collagen fibers laid down chaotically. The second move, responding to tension, the work of the accomplice, is more evidently psychoid. We have already seen a similar process in the building of an infant's brain. A great superfluity of neurons is created initially by the tinkerer, but only those that fire regularly and become wired by psychoid process into neural networks are retained by the accomplice. The others die and are metabolized.

Psychoid process and the evolution of novelty in anatomy

Another recent approach to "Darwin's Dilemma," the problem of identifying a principle by which novelty enters the evolutionary process, takes note of the fact that the development of new anatomical forms has consistently been "facilitated" at every step along the way. Marc W. Kirschner, Professor of Systems Biology at Harvard Medical School, and John C. Gerhart, Professor at the University of California, Berkeley, argue in *The Plausibility of Life: Resolving Darwin's Dilemma* (2005) that evolution consistently biases itself in the direction of developing new forms. In place of the pure randomness of mutations envisaged by Neo-Darwinism, Kirschner and Gerhart (2005: 13) find that genetic variation is "biased to be viable . . .; biased to produce functional outcomes; and biased to be relevant to the environmental conditions." The psychoid principle is evident in each of these biases.

A theory of evolutionary novelty, the authors say, can be considered for the first time, now that we have begun to understand how molecular biology, cell biology, and developmental biology have contributed to evolutionary history by building flexibility and variation into organisms at every level of function (Kirschner and Gerhart 2005: xii). To simplify the heart of the argument, we might say that molecular "decisions" are made on the basis of changes in the immediate surround of the molecule—decisions that can easily be reversed when conditions change. Processes are engaged with processes, influencing one another very much like Turner's termites and their mounds.

Thus, "allosteric proteins" are capable of folding into two different configurations, and as they respond to changes in their environment, they fold and refold themselves repeatedly. The hemoglobin molecule, for instance, folds one way in the lungs to facilitate the uptake of oxygen and another way in the muscles to shed oxygen. In the intestines, the bacterium *E. coli* eats only glucose. But when we eat a meal high in milk products, our intestinal levels of lactose rise. Some of the lactose binds to the DNA in the bacterium, resetting a genetic switch which enables the *E. coli* to eat lactose. At low lactose levels, it switches back (Kirschner and Gerhart 2005: 100, 112–18). Switches like these, built into organisms at all levels, facilitate evolution, revealing it to be a psychoid process.

Core processes

To understand how evolution promotes change, Kirschner and Gerhart (2005) would direct our attention away from the giraffe's remarkable neck and toward the processes occurring in its cells. All present-day organisms retain the properties of their ancestors, including the properties that allowed them to change in the past. These conserved processes that enabled change in the past, they call "core processes." They can facilitate change again in the future, particularly when combined with one another in new ways. Body structure (the giraffe's neck) "is never inherited as such, but merely types of adaptive cell behavior . . . adaptive responses to differing conditions" (Kirschner and Gerhart 2005: 36). Evolution is marked by epochs of inventiveness interspersed with long periods of stability.[4] Environmental change triggers the reshuffling of core processes, resulting in new forms.

When the authors ask themselves what kind of novelty can be "stored" in an organism until a mutation establishes it as a potential solution for an environmental stress, they point to the same characteristic that Turner (2007) describes with the metaphor of tinkerer and accomplice. When core processes can "tinker" with a variety of possibilities—precisely the way muscle cells, bone cells, and vascular system cells lay their fibers down randomly and then allow the "accomplice" to reinforce the ones that carry the load and dismantle those that do not—new solutions are facilitated (Kirschner and Gerhart 2005: 143–6). A particularly rapid and flexible example of this is the way that the microtubule skeleton of a cell—that process that enables an amoeba to extend and retract pseudopodia, for example—is continually growing, disintegrating and regrowing. Kirschner and Gerhart describe processes of this type as "dynamic instability." The cell, an organism in its own right, builds, dissolves and rebuilds in response to "stabilizing agents acting peripherally" in its dynamic surround (2005: 150–2).

In consequence of dynamic instability, an organism makes itself receptive to its environment, shaping itself optimally. When a new solution is arrived at in this way, a mutation or genetic reassortment can stabilize the new structure, in a process called "dynamic restoration." In this way is "generate[d] a class of significant phenotypes [body plans] with reduced lethality. Evolution can achieve new forms of somatic adaptation so readily because the system, at all levels, is built to vary" (Kirschner and Gerhart 2005: 108).

The emergence of adaptive cell behaviors (evolution in four steps)

Kirschner and Gerhart (2005) tell the story of evolution in four episodes, each of which attends to the establishment of different sorts of core processes.

Stage 1

About three billion years ago, when prokaryotes first appeared, novel chemical reactions were made possible, including most of the biosynthetic pathways that are still used by all the creatures on Earth. Molecules from the environment could be incorporated, metabolized, and used for cell building or, along other chemical pathways, for energy production. Information could be retrieved from the genome when necessary, as we have just seen exemplified in the case of the prokaryote *E. coli* as it switches its digestion back and forth between glucose and lactose (Kirschner and Gerhart 2005: 46–50).

Stage 2

Between two billion and one billion years ago, eukaryotes appeared. These cells were capable of growing much larger than prokaryotes; and the enclosure of their genes inside a nuclear membrane made it possible to regulate much larger combinations of genes, vastly increasing the range of cellular functions. Very little has changed in this respect between the emergence of the first protozoan and that of *Homo sapiens*. The genes of eukaryotes are organized into small chemical circuits that can be linked up in a variety of ways for high flexibility of function. "Transcription factors" came into play for the first time, internal proteins that turn genes on and off in response to pressures from the cell's surround. The complexity of genetic activity in eukaryotes made it possible to control protein levels in the cytoplasm, so as to facilitate some functions and hinder others in response to processes in the cell's vicinity (Kirschner and Gerhart 2005: 50–4, 119).

Stage 3

About 1.2 billion years ago, multicellular organisms emerged. New adaptive cell behaviors include the ability of cells to stick themselves together with proteins and eventually to assemble an epithelium, a sheet of cells "so tightly welded together that virtually nothing can pass between them." This, in turn, enabled multicell creatures to control the fluid environment inside the organism by pumping water and salts through the epithelial membrane in one direction or the other. Finally, cell differentiation is a crucial core process that survives in all multicellular living forms today: the development of cells for specialized functions in different parts of the organism (Kirschner and Gerhart 2005: 55–7).

Stage 4

Around 600 million years ago, the first "body plans" arose, which bore the familiar homology that links our anatomy with that of all mammals, birds, fish, insects, and so on. All are characterized by a gut that runs through the body from mouth to anus, thereby differentiating head from tail, right from left, and front from back. This is the stage at which the third, middle, layer of embryological tissue first developed, mesoderm, the tissue out of which bones and muscle develop (Kirschner and Gerhart 2005: 57–61).

It is out of mesodermal tissue, primarily, that the segmentation of the body plan is located, where the so-called "Hox" genes are differentially turned on and off in different segments to generate arms, wings and other anatomical structures. This set of core processes was established so early in Stage 4 that, by 543 million years ago:

> the locus of the battle had shifted from who could make the best body plan to who could make the best jaw and appendage on an adequate body plan. The days of the body-plan wars had ended; a different technology was at stake.
> (Kirschner and Gerhart 2005: 69)

The segmented body plan has brought the compartmentalization that makes eukaryotes more flexible than prokaryotes into the design of the multicellular body. Each segment is a compartment within which a separate "gene expression space" exists. Certain genes can be turned on in one compartment, while they remain off in others nearby. In this way, evolutionary change can be localized and interference with gene expression in other compartments is avoided (Kirschner and Gerhart 2005: 213f).

In consequence of these and other core processes, each creature retains a focused sensitivity to a variety of environmental processes in each of its parts, so that each can respond quickly with its own version of "dynamic instability" and not interfere with the focus of other parts of the animal. This, evidently, is how Darwin's finches were able to evolve such a variety of beak types.

The psychoid field in biology

All such changes are evidence for the influence of a psychoid field, expressing itself as a force that encourages the organization of processes and guides them to interact meaningfully with one another. The psychoid field makes psyche an evolutionary possibility—the organizing and holistic process of every living organism, which becomes more complex and differentiated as its organism grows and differentiates. Psyche is not something separate from a material organism itself but is that organism's life and process.

To say that all these processes from the molecular through the cellular and on up are *psychoid* is not to attribute consciousness to them in the sense that humans or chimpanzees or robins have consciousness. The essential psychoid quality might rather be described as "responsiveness." Molecules and cells "respond" to one another in a meaningful way; they have "information" for one another. Furthermore, no structure is permanent; each is a momentary configuration of a material process that is always changing. Everything that happens to and within a cell is a meaningful event. Psychoid process, therefore, is evident in all the tiniest component process as well as in the larger process within which they find their higher significance. Psychoid process manifests itself, therefore, most characteristically in nested hierarchy, which is everywhere characteristic of living beings: molecular processes organized into a cell's process, every cell's process organized into its tissue's process, and so on up to the organization of the whole animal. We call all these processes "psychoid" because there is something minimally psychic—at least responsive—in every part of every living being. Life is always psychoid.

Although we would not wish to call an amoeba's life conscious, we cannot deny that it is thoroughly psychoid, even "intentional"; for everywhere we observe psychic process, intentional traits are unavoidable. The psyche of an amoeba is a holistic process that intends the best vigor, best nutrition, optimal temperature, moisture, salinity, and so forth, within the constraints offered by its surround. It does not intend in the trivial sense whereby my neighbor intends to file his income tax well before the deadline every year and always fails to do so. The amoeba intends unswervingly, yet without knowing that it does so. Facts such as this demonstrate that it is not just that there can be no psychology without intentionality, there can also be no biology without it.

Walter Freeman (1995), the neuroscientist we have often cited for his description of brain-states described by AM waves falling into their basins of attraction, gives us a highly differentiated definition of intentionality. He notes that the term has been made trivial by analytic philosophers who "have reduced intentionality to mere 'aboutness'; leaving biologists free to inject it with life." Freeman calls intentionality "the process of a brain in action," manifesting unity, wholeness and intent (Freeman 1995: 18ff). Now that we have seen psychic function in the absence of a brain, we shall have to take intentionality as the process of a *psyche* that manifests Freeman's three qualities.

Intentionality implies *unity*, in the sense that it is the process of an integral organism. We could call it a "self," if it were limited to humans; but we have also recognized that bacteria and protozoa are more unified than we, for our conscious ego is very often at odds with our greater self, while such conflict never appears in an amoeba. Intentionality implies *wholeness*, namely that "the entirety of life's experience is brought to each moment of action . . . a blind, organic striving toward realizing [one's] full potential within the constraints of heredity and environment" (Freeman 2000: 18). Finally, intentionality implies *intent*, in the sense of the capacity, flexibility and unswerving determination to modify oneself in adaptation to the non-self.

Intentionality is what emerges between the tinkerer and the accomplice, between the termite and the mound, between the core processes and the environment. It is a distinctive symptom of psychoid process and characterizes every aspect of the living world. Turner says, "The living world is . . . in its peculiar way, an intentionally designed place" (J. S. Turner 2007: 227). He does not mean the grand intentions of a designing deity. He means the momentary choices that are made by termites, fibroblasts and molecules that fold themselves one way in the presence of oxygen and another way in its absence. Design is the upshot of an infinite number of instantaneous decisions that are simultaneously occurring everywhere and followed up instantaneously by another infinity of decisions. That is what psychoid process is.

In the end, then, the psychoid field, whose recognition the biological sciences seem to be inching toward, provides a foundation for everything we have missed in our Western account of reality: life, intentionality and "responsiveness," that rudimentary form of consciousness that can accumulate and achieve greater awareness as living matter is combined in ever more complex and redundant ways. The entire sum of all biological processes, evolution itself, is also psychoid. At every step, each organism is engaged with its environment in a process in which both of them are transformed. All of the living world is described as processes within processes, patterns within patterns, patterns changing in response to others, proceeding by *insinuation*.

To say that the universe is governed by a psychoid field is to say that it is characteristic of all processes in the universe to be responsive. It is as fundamental as every particle having mass and every current exerting magnetic influence.

Chapter 13

Sketches of a universal psychoid field

Chapter 12 provided a sort of phenomenology of living processes, simply a description, supported by the work of leading scientists, of what life and its patterns of interaction are about. It leads us to a metaphysical question, however; for we have had to say that every organism and its every component manifest the psychoid quality of responsiveness. While we may not blanch from claiming that every cell, every tissue and every organ is psychoid in that sense, it is probably the case that few of our contemporaries are willing to grant a psychoid nature to molecules, atoms and subatomic particles. But if these "building blocks" of life are lifeless and devoid of psychoid responsiveness, life and consciousness must come from somewhere else, some Cartesian "soul." Our description of the psychoid nature of reality, therefore, must go further and truly become a universal psychoid field, like electromagnetism and gravity. Psychoid responsiveness must go "all the way down" to the most inorganic-seeming of entities. Anything less, and we make living processes an exception to universal physical principles.

In our view, Jung's psychoid argument implies that everything that is, every particle of reality, is responsive in the psychoid sense. Otherwise no matter how many molecules we heap together—even if we find a way to strike them with lightning—they will never spring to life and never become psychoid, much less aware. To demonstrate the inevitability of the psychoid principle, we have to show that the West's metaphysical assumption that matter is dead, inert, and incapable of responsiveness does not accurately describe the reality we experience. Ultimately, we need a new description of reality, a new metaphysics. But first let us consider some of the evidence that matter may not be as insentient as we have assumed.

Toward a metaphysics of the psychoid field

First, it seems that the insentience of matter is less a matter of common sense than a consequence of a theological decision taken only about 400 years ago. The philosopher of parapsychology David Ray Griffin (1997) says the doctrine of matter's insentience derives from an effort in the sixteenth and seventeenth centuries to save the Christian belief in an eternal soul. Educated people of the time thought that if matter were animate, i.e. possessed soul inherently, soul would be a property of matter. Four centuries ago, it seems, the psychoid nature of matter appeared to be self-evident and had to be declared invalid by the theological authorities. The defenders of the faith feared that on the basis of matter being deemed psychoid, the death of a biological being would result in its soul ceasing to exist. There might be no afterlife of reward and punishment. Such concerns forced Descartes, Mersenne, Boyle, and others to argue "that matter does not have the power of self-movement" (Griffin 1997: 131). Soul had to be conceived as a separate, non-material substance that could never be affected by insentient matter. Theological victory, therefore, was achieved at no little cost. We were left with the monstrosity we call the mind/body problem.

A second reason to doubt that matter is as insentient as we have been led to believe is the self-evident fact that our consciousness has a great deal to do with our brain. The prevailing doctrine among neuroscientists and philosophers is that matter, when it gets complex enough, as in the human brain, somehow permits consciousness to "emerge." This is the doctrine of psyche/brain identity, which we have already found to be absurd given that brainless creatures like amoeba manifest psychic process. It is much more reasonable to assume that matter is subtly sentient—psychoid—and on that account growing complexity results quite logically in higher orders of conscious functioning.

Unless matter itself were psychoid, psyche would not be able to emerge at any level of material complexity. Yet it does. The world is populated with psychoid creatures of almost infinite variety. Every one of them is made up of the same material stuff as the inanimate world. Living organisms come into existence at specific instants, grow, reproduce, and die. During the time that they are alive, ordinary matter and energy pass constantly through them, changing their molecular make-up and even their form, as in the case of larvae becoming adult insects. But before they are alive and after they are dead the matter that makes up living beings is indistinguishable from that of the inanimate world. If psyche is not some separate substance imposed from without, the psychoid qualities that make life, intentionality and sentience possible must somehow belong to matter itself.

A fourth reason to suspect matter capable of sentience is the clear evidence that all living beings are to some extent conscious. Human consciousness is simply the most complex and far-reaching form of the same power that organizes the life force in all organisms. In each case it is the concrescent process that we call "psyche," a sort of entelechy that typically proceeds from the state of affairs established in the moment just passed and intends a subtly different new reality in the moment just now arising. Higher, more complex capacities of consciousness can intend specific events further into the future. A cat, for instance, may spend several minutes and solve several problems while holding the single far-reaching intention of seizing a mouse. But even the author of the Great American Novel, during years of work, lives a process that springs anew with promise and then becomes petrified in accomplishment, instant after instant.

Fifth, several philosophers of the early twentieth century have shown us the way forward. Henri Bergson (1911: 272) said: "Matter or mind, reality has appeared to us as a perpetual becoming. It makes itself or it unmakes itself, but it is never something made." The american philosopher Charles Sanders Peirce (1838–1914) was even more explicit: "Matter is merely mind deadened by the development of habit to the point where the breaking up of these habits is very difficult" (quoted in Sheldrake 1995: 14). In a letter to C. S. Peirce, William James expanded the argument: "If . . . one takes the theory of evolution radically, one ought to apply it not only to the rock-strata, the animals and plants, but to the stars, to the chemical elements, and to the laws of nature" (Sheldrake 1995: 14). More recently, Christian de Quincey, Professor of Consciousness Studies at John F. Kennedy University, makes the same argument, that the central insight of Darwin extends to all of reality: "Evolution . . . is a story of matter feeling its way forward toward ever increasing complexity and higher levels of order and organization. Matter is adventurous" (de Quincey 2002: 41).

The paleontologist Pierre Teilhard de Chardin (1881–1955) developed probably the most comprehensive idea of a psychoid field in his book, *The Phenomenon of Man* (1959), an argument deeply rooted in evolutionary biology and inspired by his own mystical Catholicism—although it is an argument the Catholic Church still regards as "dangerous to the faith." Teilhard's argument resembles Jung's proposal that amoeba has something fundamental to tell us about the psychoid realm. Teilhard said, "By means of the cell, the molecular world 'appears in person,' touching, passing into, and disappearing in the higher constructions of life" (Teilhard de Chardin 1959: 81). Teilhard saw no clear dividing line between life and non-life. Rather, all of reality coheres in a single reality. What we have long called "life" and treated as an exceptional development unique to this blue planet has inevitable precursors: "a 'pre-life' [that extends] as far back before [life] as the eye can see" (Teilhard de Chardin 1959: 57). Teilhard draws our attention to a planetary stratum beginning with mud and extending up through water and the atmosphere, a several-mile-thick shell about the earth, filled with "ultra-micro grains of protein." He says, "If pre-life has already emerged in the atom, are not these myriads of large molecules just what we would expect?" (1959: 73).

Process and Reality

These five arguments reveal our need for a metaphysics of process and of organism. Fortunately there is one. The philosopher and mathematician Alfred North Whitehead (1861–1947) caught the significance of extending Darwinian evolution beyond life forms in both directions: "down" into molecules, atoms, and the quantum sea, and "up" to the planet, solar system, and galaxies. In the 1920s he observed: "The whole point of the modern doctrine [in biology] is the evolution of complex organisms from antecedent states of less complex organisms. The doctrine thus cries aloud for a conception of organism as fundamental for nature." For Whitehead, "Biology is the study of the larger organisms; whereas physics is the study of the smaller organisms" (Whitehead 1925: 107). By "smaller organisms," he means to include molecules, atoms and quantum phenomena. Organisms, therefore, do not begin at the complexity of bacteria or protozoa. They go "all the way down" to the "building blocks" of material reality, that evanescent cloud of vibrating force fields or "strings" that physicists call "quantum space-time." Furthermore, if every organism owes its organismic nature to something resembling a psyche, then psyche, too, goes all the way down. In some sense, matter itself must be sentient. Christian de Quincey, heavily influenced by Whitehead, says, "The assumption of consciousness and matter as coextensive and co-eternal is the most adequate 'postmodern' solution to the question of consciousness in the physical world" (de Quincey 2002: 48).

Whitehead's systematic development of "a conception of organism as fundamental for nature" is the most original of modern descriptions of the world: *Process and Reality: An Essay on Cosmology* (1929). It is a radical approach to metaphysics, for it discards the view we in the West naively take for granted, the idea that matter, static substance, is fundamental, and posits instead the *event*, a slice of process, an "actual occasion" as the root of all that is real.

> "Actual entities"—also termed "actual occasions"—are the final real things of which the world is made up. There is no going behind actual entities to find anything more real. They differ among themselves. . . . But, though there are gradations of importance and diversities of function . . . the final facts are all alike, actual entities; and these actual entities are drops of experience, complex and interdependent.
>
> (Whitehead 1929: 23)

An actual entity is a moment of process, in which what has come into being in the moment just passed becomes the occasion for a new choice, a new concrescence, as factual details of the moment are "felt," selected among, and chosen with a view to an instantaneous future. Whitehead's actual entities answer to the same description we have been giving to moments in the psychic process of an amoeba. What Whitehead (1929) adds to the description is his distinction between what he calls the "physical pole" and the "mental pole" in a moment of process. The physical pole is the result of what has been chosen an instant before and now stands as an established fact for the present living instant. The mental pole, on the other hand, is the activity of feeling the past and choosing an instantaneous future. The physical pole is the established past, and the mental pole the living, feeling, choosing present. It is the psychoid element in process.

Whitehead, therefore, calls process "the becoming of experience." "There is nothing in the real world which is nothing but an inert fact. Every reality is there for feeling: it promotes feeling; and it is felt" (Whitehead 1929: 193, 364). "Feeling" or sentience is "the mental pole of process," the most rudimentary form of consciousness. It is matter's psychoid dimension. The physical pole of process is the pure givenness of what has come to be, while the mental pole "feels" the physical and intends what is growing together in the concrescence of the present moment. In virtue of the mental pole, each moment is subtly different from the last. Mentality is the dynamic principle in process.

The mental pole does not much resemble "thinking," but "feels" the world and itself somewhat as an amoeba does. In every moment of concrescence a variety of feelings occur as the multiplicity of the immediate past is sensed. Oppositions will be felt, choices will be made (Whitehead 1929: 290). This is the mentality that goes "all the way down" through molecules and atoms. As we follow mentality upward through levels of greater and greater complexity, we pass through the psychology of amoebas and of worms and eventually arrive at levels of consciousness that are recognizably human. "Mind is the action or process by which matter moves itself" (de Quincey 2002: 249).

Atom and molecule

The idea that matter is inert becomes absurd as soon as we look closely. The simplest bit of matter, the hydrogen atom, has a single electron whose presence surrounding the atomic nucleus can take any of the twelve shapes depicted in Figure 13.1, each resulting from a different energy pattern. Each looks "smeary" and out of focus because it is a somewhat inexact "probability region," the zone where that single electron is most likely to stop being pure energy and "pop into

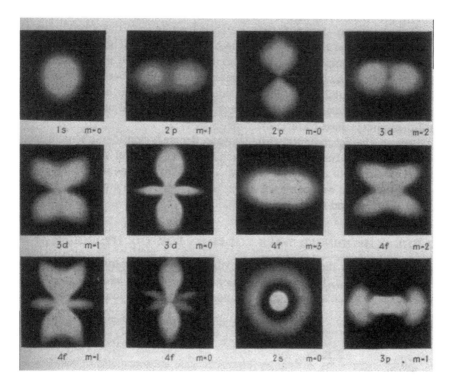

Figure 13.1 Electron cloud configurations in a hydrogen atom.

existence" as a particle. Atoms and molecules are incessantly in motion as their quantum-level components alternate instantaneously between "energy smear" configurations and discrete particles. Although not much mental "originality" is possible at the atomic level (de Quincey 2002: 205), novelty explodes when we reach the level of the living cell. Atoms and molecules, by contrast, have a fixed set of allowable vibratory states; experience teaches us not to anticipate any radically new "behavior" from a hydrogen atom.

Even an atom, however, is not a single thing but rather a "society" of sub-atomic components, each following its own rhythms, but falling in with the higher-level governance of the atom's holistic process. A molecule is a larger society still, which draws each of its constituent atoms into a single "life history," the "historic route" of processual instants, each characterized by the specific quanta which it feels and marshals into concrescence (Whitehead 1929: 96, 98).

Such, then, is the nature of Teilhard's "pre-life." The molecules that comprise a biological cell like that of an amoeba are themselves "societies of simultaneous occasions," as each electron, proton, and neutron falls into a series of organic assemblages, each guided by a concrescent process. The process of the society of atoms comprising a molecule, therefore, closely resembles the society of molecules comprising an amoeba. A living cell is immensely more complex than a molecule, but insofar as each is an organism in process there is no essential difference between them. In this picture of reality, this metaphysics, there is a coherent principle holding it all together. Mentality goes all the way down, even as it becomes pared down to its essential psychoid nature, feeling or responsiveness.

The cosmos

Organic process seems to be the universal principle that organizes and moves all the smaller entities we have discussed, from protons to protozoa and primates. It does not stop with humanity, however, for the cosmos itself appears to reflect the same overall structure: organisms nested within one another and hierarchically organized.

In *The Conscious Universe: Part and Whole in Modern Physical Theory* (1990) Menas Kafatos of the Department of Physics at George Mason University, Fairfax, VA, specializing in astrophysics, general relativity, and the foundations of quantum mechanics, has teamed up with Robert Nadeau of the Department of English at the same university, a student of cultural history and the history of the philosophy of science. Convinced that even most physicists do not grasp the unthinkably revolutionary implications of today's science, Kafatos and Nadeau are partisans of a coherent scientific description of reality. They describe the cosmos at large in imagery that is closely harmonious with Whitehead's, that is as a hierarchical organization of organisms within organisms. "Galaxies now appear to cluster themselves in increasing hierarchies of clusters, called superclusters, and may even form larger structures . . . which approach a sizable fraction of the radius of the known universe" (Kafatos and Nadeau 1990: 155).

We will consider this description of the universe in the next section. Only one implication needs to be mentioned here. In an organic hierarchy, each organism is sensitive to, feels, and guides the process of all its constituent organisms, even as its own process is guided by the organisms that contain it. There is constant communication, however tenuous, in every growing-together instant between the lowest and simplest of organisms and the highest and most complex. No organism is ever isolated, each participates in cosmic process.

The process of the universe

Whitehead (1929) follows the logic of nested hierarchies all the way up to the universe itself, as the greatest nest, the organism whose process governs every single thing and every society, regardless of size. "The universe is always one . . . always new" (Whitehead 1929: 270). Its always being *one* means that its process governs everything that is, in the same sense that an amoeba is one and governs all its molecules. Its always being *new* means that the universe itself is a process, arising anew in every instant and then becoming the concrete past for the next instant of arising. In each concrescence, the many entities that comprise the universe are assembled into a unique momentary cosmos. Each item within the universe, an organism in its own right, becomes "subordinated to the novel one" (Whitehead 1929: 243). Universal process subordinates each of its components, every hydrogen atom and every supercluster of galaxies, in exactly the same way that the amoeba's psychic process marshals each of its organelles and each of its molecules into an organismic whole. The implications of universal process, however, go both ways. Each entity is subordinated, but each one also participates in and becomes "the whole universe in the process of attaining a particular satisfaction," i.e. the momentary goal that is intended (Whitehead 1929: 231).

Organism implies interdependence. Just as an amoeba cannot become what it is unless each of its molecules becomes what it is, so it is with the universe. Every nested hierarchy is a "complex, interlocking network" of organisms. Every part contributes to the whole, even as the whole's process governs all the subprocesses nested within it (de Quincey 2002: 31). Whitehead expressed this interlocking principle vividly: "All origination is private. But what has been originated, publicly pervades the world" (Whitehead 1929: 364). He means that every molecule, every neuron, every human, every galaxy proceeds in the present moment to realize its "private" organic goal. But having achieved that goal in the moment just passed, every organism has become "public" data, information that will be felt in the new moment just arising.

Anima mundi

In the very first pages of *Process and Reality*, Whitehead (1929) begins talking about "God" in a manner that must be confusing for the unprepared reader. He does not mean Yahweh, Allah or Vishnu. He means the mental pole of the universe, the psychoid capacity by which the immediate past of the cosmos is felt and a proximate goal (or "satisfaction") intended. He might have made it clearer if he had called this principle the "cosmic psyche" or "world soul," referring to the *anima mundi* of medieval philosophy. Whitehead's "God" is an immanent "urge toward the future based in an appetite in the present" (Whitehead 1929: 37). There is very little similarity between such immanence, inseparable from the matter of the cosmos, and the transcendent personal God prone to irrational outbursts of rage and miraculous suspensions of causal relations that the Bible portrays. Whitehead's God more closely resembles the Tao of ancient Chinese religion or the impersonal pervading force of brahman described in the Upanishads.

Still, Whitehead (1929: 288) betrays his Western background when he speaks of God "intervening": "Apart from the intervention of God there could be nothing new in the world and no order in the world." Intervention is a strong word, since it usually suggests something reaching in from outside to make changes. But Whitehead's God is not outside the universe. His God is rather the mental pole of universal process, each moment of which is "an intermediate step toward fulfillment of [God's] own being." Far from being "immutable," as traditional theology holds, Whitehead's God is always *in* process, changing along with the universe. Whitehead often uses the word "value" to describe the intentions of God, the cosmic psyche. God's primary value is the cosmic order "from which each temporal concrescence receives that initial aim which its self-causation starts" (Whitehead 1929: 125, 286). Whitehead's vision places the "self-identity" of the whole in the parts and the parts in the whole (de Quincey 2002: 170).

Analogous metaphysical systems

As startlingly original as Whitehead's metaphysics has been for twentieth-century Western thought, there are quite a few analogies in the larger world. We have already mentioned Taoism, in which the whole is always changing, and each moment has a unique character that qualifies everything that occurs in its duration. The unique character of each Taoistic moment corresponds directly to the "value" intended in that same moment by Whitehead's "God." The Buddhist doctrine of co-dependent origination represents another ancient parallel, the idea that what seems "substantial" and unchanging to the naive mind is actually part of a universal process by which things are constantly arising out of the disintegration products of previous entities and then disintegrating in their turn. There are also several interpretations of quantum mechanics which strongly imply a process metaphysics. David Bohm's undisputed but largely ignored mathematical calculations describe a universal totality that is "implicate" (folded in on itself and invisible to the senses) but which governs all the sub-wholes that have unfolded for our experience (the "explicate" order) (Factor 1985: 86). Bohm describes the universe as a nested hierarchy that is in constant process. He likens the universe to a hologram, in which each part contains an image of the whole—but as it is incessantly dynamic, he finds "holomovement" a more accurate description.

Kafatos and Nadeau (1990) stress the principle of quantum non-locality, the fact that any two "entangled" particles go through parallel transformations simultaneously regardless of how far apart they stray in the course of time. Kafatos and Nadeau reason that all the particles that comprise the universe have been "entangled" with one another since the Big Bang (when they were all in the same place). All the particles that comprise the cosmos, therefore, comprise a unified system in which each part is in relation with every other (Kafatos and Nadeau 1990: 73). A genuine whole results "when the universal principle of order is 'inside' the parts, and thereby adjusts each to all so that they interlink and become mutually complementary." This, in turn, means that the universe is "self-reflectively aware of itself" (Kafatos and Nadeau 1990: 176, 178). In the end, Kafatos and Nadeau appear to agree with Whitehead that the proper name for such a mental pole of the universe is "God." They use Aristotle's term, however, which is perhaps a more appropriate description: "the unmoved mover" (Kafatos and Nadeau 1990: 168). For just as an amoeba's unmoved mover is its psychic process, so is that of the universe.

The descriptive power of fields

The gravity field is described as the propensity of space-time to bend in the presence of mass. The electromagnetic field is described as toroidal vectors of magnetic force surrounding an electric current, or as the same configuration around a body of iron, nickel, cobalt or their alloys in which the molecules have been aligned while in the molten state and then allowed to cool. Quantum fields describe the probability that energy waves will "collapse" into particles and vice versa. Each of these well-known fields has its own dynamics, as the plus or minus charge and spin of a particle determines both its magnetic behavior and the state of its quantum field. Particles and waves are susceptible to the bends in space-time, and the huge masses of stars and planets that bend space-time represent different configurations of quantum fields—from the chaos of plasma in a star to the orderly molecular structure of the metals, rocks, liquids and gasses comprising a planet.

When the psychoid field is added to the description of the cosmos, the holistic factor that makes sense of the parts is the process of organism. Everywhere from quanta to superclusters of galaxies, process manifests as the mental or psychoid pole of an instantaneous occasion. Every part, however small or large, responds to the factuality of its past to grow its parts together into an instantaneous future. Every occasion "reigns" ("is regnant") over all of the subordinate organisms that comprise it, while being responsive to and informed by the process of the larger organisms within which it is nested. The nested nature of organism means that the entire universe evolves as a single organism along with every smaller organism nested within it. Because everything is in process with everything else, the non-locality of psychic functioning—or indeed that of the quantum realm—is no more mysterious for the universe as a whole than it is for an amoeba and its immediate surround.

Gaia: a case in point

We have taken amoeba as the prime example of an organism. A large collection of diverse molecules, clearly not alive on their own, function holistically as parts of a living animal. The process that makes it an organism is teleological, intentional and psychoid. Just one or two steps up from non-living chemistry, psychoid process is unmistakable. We conclude that there must be something pre-psychoid in the molecules themselves, some propensity for being governed by a psychoid principle that resembles the other three universal fields of physics. We do not propose that something non-material is added on to the universe, rather that all of reality just *is* psychoid. The same energy/matter that manifests as gravity, electromagnetism and quantum uncertainty also manifests as organismic process.

Just as Jung's term *psychoid* means "psyche-like" or "proto-psychic," so *organismic* means "organism-like" or "proto-organic." Even things that, strictly speaking, have no psyche and are not themselves alive nevertheless manifest psychoid and organismic features. James Lovelock's idea that the Earth itself manifests organismic process eloquently makes the case for expanding the notion of organism to such border zones of life. Here amoeba represents the midpoint between entities too simple to manifest life and those complex enough to be called "alive."

Lovelock (1988) made this expanded notion of organismic process explicit when he said we should not think of the Earth as a big rock but more as a giant redwood tree. The core of a tree and its bark are dead wood. What is alive is a ring of cells between the two dead areas, just as the living part of the Earth is that same ring of organisms from the mud through the water and the atmosphere that Teilhard de Chardin (1959) pointed to. A tree would not be a tree without the structure and protection of core and bark. Even including the massively predominating dead areas, the tree is a living organism. By analogy, the Earth functions very much as an organism, although its living elements are comprised of separate species that do not all carry the same DNA.

Lovelock (1988) cites a list of earlier scientists who discovered the organismic nature of the Earth, including: Y. M. Korolenko, an independent Russian philosopher and scientist, more than a century ago; James Hutton, the integrator of modern geology, whose views were initially rejected by his peers (Gould 2007: 130), called the Earth a "superorganism" whose proper study should be physiology, in 1785; and Eduard Suess, who first proposed the term "biosphere" in 1875. More recent contributors have been "Alfred Lotka, the founder of population biology, Arthur Redfield, an ocean chemist, and J. Z. Young, a biologist." In 1911, Vladimir Vernadsky wrote, "The biosphere is the envelope of life, i.e. the area of living matter ... the area of the Earth's crust occupied by transformers which convert cosmic radiations into effective terrestrial energy: electrical, chemical, mechanical, thermal, etc." (Lovelock 1988: 9–12).

Living planets

A "dead" planet will have an atmosphere that is in a state of chemical equilibrium. By contrast, the gaseous mixture of the Earth's atmosphere has been driven well away from a simple state of balance, or entropy. Entropy is the physical process whereby everything naturally "runs down," from a high state of tension to a low one. Energy differences between warm and cold air masses, for instance, generate storms. Air molecules move rapidly and produce high pressure when warm and move slowly, producing low pressure, when cool. Entropy is the process whereby the warm and the cool mix with one another until all the molecules are moving at the same speed. Energy differences are lost, and a uniform air mass produces no storms.

Ludwig Boltzmann (1844–1902), who was largely responsible for the kinetic-molecular theory of gases just described, "defined entropy as a measure of the probability of a molecular distribution." Thus, Lovelock (1979) says, whenever we find a highly improbable mixture of atmospheric gases, living process must be responsible. Entropy, the "running down" of physical processes toward equilibrium, is always opposed by living processes, which by their very nature produce imbalance, a condition of higher tension that is called "negative entropy." Life always moves a planet's atmosphere away from equilibrium and toward negative entropy (Lovelock 1979: 34).

Earth's atmosphere has levels of methane, nitrous oxide and nitrogen that are "tens of orders of magnitude away from equilibrium." In the absence of life, methane, for example, would readily be broken down in the presence of oxygen to produce carbon dioxide and water vapor. Earth would return to the atmosphere it had before life began: high in carbon dioxide and low in oxygen and methane. A billion tons of methane have to be released into the atmosphere every year to maintain our present levels of imbalance. These enormous quantities are produced primarily by the digestion of organic matter by bacteria in the soil and in the guts of higher organisms. We have discussed how the high levels of oxygen are produced: cyanobacteria transformed the atmosphere billions of years ago, using the light of the sun to remove the carbon from carbon dioxide, leaving oxygen behind as a waste product, "poisoning" the atmosphere for themselves but preparing it for us.

The massive amounts of oxygen and methane in our current atmosphere are highly improbable from a purely chemical perspective and are the result of constant manipulation from the Earth's surface by living organisms (Lovelock 1979: 6–10). For this reason, Lovelock (1988) concludes that a living planet is either rich in life and boasts an improbable atmosphere, or its atmospheric gasses are at equilibrium and no life at all is present.

> Long before Viking set course from Earth, I felt intuitively that life could not exist on a planet sparsely; it could not hang on in a few oases, except at the beginning or at the end of its tenure. As Gaia theory developed, this intuition grew; now I view it as a fact.
>
> (Lovelock 1988: 6)

Atmospheric temperature, too, is an indicator that Earth is not in a state of physical equilibrium. Because the Earth rotates around the Sun, which is "an uncontrolled radiant heater whose output is by no means constant," the laws of physics would expect its surface temperatures to vary widely. But they do not. "Right from the beginning of life, about three-and-a-half [billion years] ago, the Earth's mean surface temperature has not varied by more than a few degrees away from its current levels" (Lovelock 1979: 52f).

"The greenhouse effect" that we have recently become very much aware of constitutes the essence of that manipulation. Changing levels of radiation affect the vigor and numbers of Earthly organisms, which by their metabolism change the levels of greenhouse gases: "Only by pollution do we survive" (Lovelock 1988: 26). The overproduction of that same pollution by burning fossil fuels has recently begun to endanger the Earth's long-range temperature control. If we do not adjust, the Earth will have to re-establish itself without us. We humans are but a part of the greater organismic process that is the Earth.

Interactive ecology

The Earth's atmosphere exemplifies, therefore, not a state of chemical or physical equilibrium, but a very dynamic and interactive "biological steady state." "Gaia did not awake until bacteria had already colonized most of the planet. Once awake, planetary life would assiduously and in essence resist changes that might be adverse and act so as to keep the planet fit for life" (Lovelock 1988: 72, 76). Furthermore, as evolution proceeded and the diversity of species increased, the flexibility and subtlety of its atmospheric manipulations grew. "Anything that makes the world uncomfortable to live in tends to induce the evolution of those species that can achieve a new and more comfortable environment" (Lovelock 1988: 178).

Gaia theory, therefore, agrees with J. Scott Turner's discovery that termites and their mounds cannot be understood separately. Organism and environment constitute a single, complex interactive process. Consequently, the Neo-Darwinian view that species evolve to adapt themselves to pre-existing niches in the environment is again revealed to be too simple. Every organism and each of its neighbors act constantly upon the material environment, changing it for themselves and for one another.

> It is no longer sufficient to say that "organisms better adapted than others are more likely to leave offspring." It is necessary to add that the growth of the organism affects its physical and chemical environment; the evolution of the species and the evolution of the rocks, therefore, are tightly coupled as a single indivisible process.
>
> (Lovelock 1988: 63)

Even Earth's rocks are involved in evolutionary process. The nature of this claim is made sense of by two historical facts. First, Darwin's treatise, *The Formation of Vegetable Mould Through the Action of Worms, with Observations on their Habits* (1881), demonstrated how rapidly and effectively worms reduce stone to garden soil (Gould 2007: 155–65). Second, it is a well-known fact that millennia of microscopic shell-bearing organisms dying in the sea and falling to the bottom produce sandstone when the calcium carbonate they contain is gradually compressed by their own weight and the pressure of deep water.

Gaia, therefore, is simply the sum total of all the individual modifications made by each of the interconnected and mutually interdependent species that have evolved in the seas, on the land, and in the air. The material constituents of the planet—including its Sun and Moon—are also part of the dynamic of life that makes up Gaia's very complex organismic process.

Objections to the Gaia hypothesis

After about a decade of being ignored, the Gaia hypothesis fell under heavy attack from scientists in the late 1970s. Some resisted the evidence that organism and environment constitute a single, mutually interactive system, and claimed that the chemical and physical forces of geology, alone, produced the niches that living species had to occupy. Others understood Lovelock to have claimed that the planet itself is an organism rather than an organismic process in which a vast collection of interacting organisms and material constituents are engaged. A third type of objection misunderstood entirely the role of teleology in Gaia. In this simplistic view, the biota had to have had the foresight to plan optimal living conditions. We have tried to make it clear that simple forms of life are teleological only in the sense that they respond to current conditions so as to maximize their situation for an instantaneous future. This is not planning, and whatever momentary "foresight" might be ascribed to the process belongs necessarily to life itself.

Lovelock took the criticism in good humor and decided that he had not made his points with sufficient clarity. He devoted most of his attention to the issue of teleology. To answer objections, he designed a computer program he called Daisyworld. A planet about the size of Earth circling a star resembling the Sun supports two species, dark-colored daisies and light-colored ones. The conditions of the Earth over the past 3.8 billion years were built into the program, including the fact that the Sun has increased in luminosity by about 30 percent. In the computer program, the absorption of heat from the Sun is regulated by the relative numbers of dark and light daisies: dark ones heating the planet by absorbing light, and light ones cooling the planet by reflecting light. Daisyworld demonstrated the heat regulation on a virtual planet just as the Gaia hypothesis had proposed for Earth, and all without planning, just by responding to changing conditions (Lovelock 1988: 35–9). Later Lovelock (1988: 52) refined the program by adding gray daisies, plus rabbits to eat the daisies and foxes to eat the rabbits. Daisyworld II was as successful as its predecessor.

The point of the Gaia hypothesis is that it is a *way of looking at* the Earth, not a literal claim that the planet is alive. It is a perspective that does not reject the findings of science but sees relationships that "exact science," well back from its "border zones," cannot see. It is a holistic view like the ones that have been necessary in other regions of physics. Indeed, it now appears that seeing Gaia as organismic process is very far from a fatuous exercise in philosophy. We must all learn to appreciate the organismic nature of Earth if we are to avoid ecological disaster. We resist it today for short-sighted financial reasons, our fear that the costs of reducing our polluting way of life will be too painful. However, philosopher John Gray points out that we may be running away from the Gaia hypothesis for a more terrifying reason. If Gaia is organismic process, we ourselves are not the independent and self-sufficient beings we would like to believe ourselves to be. We are part of a much larger process that will go on without us if it has to (Gray 2002: 34).

Images of the psychoid field: lessons from Rupert Sheldrake

The one biologist who has been most outspoken and developed the most refined field theory to describe living processes is Rupert Sheldrake, who has been a Research Fellow of the Royal Society, director of studies in biochemistry and cell biology at Clare College, Cambridge, and Frank Knox Fellow at Harvard. Although he has published more than sixty technical papers and a half-dozen books, his entry into the border zones of biology has resulted in his work being steeped in controversy.

In arguing for a field theory in biology, he has noted, for instance, that flat worms can regenerate whole individuals from their parts in a manner that suggests magnets and holograms, well-known instances of a whole that is contained in each of its parts (Sheldrake 1995: 78). Sheldrake links his own notion of a "field" with Faraday's idea that a field is a region of influence connecting things across empty space (Sheldrake 2003: 208). Sheldrake agrees with the many authors we have already cited in asserting that matter is neither passive nor inert, but a pattern of vibrating energy that finds its organization when it interacts with a field (Sheldrake 1995: 115). Although biology is his primary area of interest, he also agrees that a psychoid field—his term is "morphic field"—organizes everything in the universe, not merely that portion of reality that is alive: "A natural extension of the morphic field approach would be . . . to regard entire planets as organisms with characteristic morphic fields, and likewise planetary systems, stars, galaxies, and clusters of galaxies" (Sheldrake 1995: 300f).

Field theory in biology began at least as early as the 1920s, when Hans Speman wrote of "developmental fields," Alexander Gurwitsch of "embryonic fields," and Paul Weiss of "morphogenetic fields." In all these instances, biologists were struggling to find a way to explain how it is that cells in different regions of an embryo develop in characteristically specialized ways—despite the fact that every cell in the embryo carries the same DNA as every other. In his book, *Principles of Development* (1939), Weiss said, "A *field* is the condition to which a living system owes its typical organization and its *specific* activities" (quoted in

Sheldrake 1995: 99f). In 1972 C. H. Waddington, another biological field theorist, called the idea of a field in biology "a descriptive convenience not a causal explanation," because biological systems will always be too complex to be reduced to mathematical formulas and therefore will never enjoy the certainty of physical laws (Sheldrake 1995: 104).

Limitations of Sheldrake's theory of morphic fields

If Sheldrake is the primary modern spokesman for a holistic field of biological organization, the reader may well wonder why I have waited so long to mention his theory of morphic fields. The answer is that he has not considered many of the issues that have been central to our thesis. As a result there are some drawbacks for us in his formulations. Arguing out our differences with Sheldrake, therefore, will provide a convenient occasion to clarify our own thesis. Three issues predominate: DNA and embryonic specialization, psychic non-locality and the inheritance of fields.

On first reading Sheldrake in the 1980s, I was impressed with the argument from embryology that since every cell in the embryo has the same DNA, a separate explanation was needed to account for the fact that cells in different areas of the embryo specialize as mesoderm, ectoderm and endoderm, or later as a proto-heart or a limb bud. I recalled my undergraduate experience in embryology in the early 1960s and how mysterious these facts had seemed to me then. For we saw in the laboratory that if a patch of cells were transferred from one area of a chick embryo to another, they would not only develop in harmony with other cells at the new location if the transfer were made before a certain date, but also develop into the structure (wing or foot) associated with the old location if transferred after that critical date. To me in the 1980s, it seemed that a theory of morphic fields had to be essential. For unless cells were guided by some outside force, there was no way to understand their differentiation into specialized tissues.

Today, however, the new field of molecular embryology that calls itself "Evo Devo," or "Evolutionary Development," never mentions fields, but explains the step-by-step development of an embryo in terms of relative concentrations of crucial molecules. Beginning with a fertilized ovum whose natural polarity determines where its first cell division will occur, and proceeding to the transcription factors that turn genes on and off in different clusters of cells, Sean B. Carroll of the Howard Hughes Medical Institute and the University of Wisconsin-Madison tells a fascinating story of embryonic development without even once having to refer to morphic fields, by whatever name (Carroll 2005).

This does not mean that there are no psychoid fields at all. I believe there are, but let us not make claims for them where they are not necessary. The psychoid field that accounts for the holistic process of an amoeba and an embryo does not render biochemistry irrelevant. Surely, biochemist Sheldrake does not think so, either. The crucial issue is that principles should not be multiplied unnecessarily. We do not need to postulate a set of biological fields acting upon a zygote as though from the outside. Rather the embryo's psychoid field develops right along with the life process of which it is a part. The psychoid field is the mental pole of that process, rather than an addition that seems to move in from elsewhere. Thus, when Sheldrake says: "How does having the right proteins explain the shape of a flower, or the structure of a mouse," he implies that there is no way to change these things without postulating a pre-existing field (Sheldrake 2003: 275). In our view, his notion of a field is too separate and too independent of living beings. Our more subtle and universal vision of a psychoid field locates it in the process that is the flower's or the mouse's living, organic being.

The second issue is non-locality. Parapsychologists are unanimous in their discovery that telepathic and clairvoyant effects do not diminish with distance and also are not interrupted by Faraday cages or other devices to isolate parapsychological effects from electromagnetic transmissions. The only conclusion to draw from these findings is that parapsychology and consciousness in general are as non-local in their operations as are quantum events and that their effects have nothing to do with electromagnetic transmissions. But Sheldrake imagines "morphic resonance" between a brain and a morphic field or between a region of an embryo and a morphic field. He imagines that this morphic resonance travels through space at the speed of light or faster (Sheldrake 1995: 302), that the sender and receiver of telepathic influence send out mental "pseudopodia" in one another's direction (Sheldrake 2003: 264) and that "the morphic field of a social group is stretched when one or more members are separated from the others" (Sheldrake 2002: 94). He also wonders whether parapsychological effects should be understood on the model of a mobile telephone's function, i.e. as a kind of electromagnetic field (Sheldrake 2003: 208). These assumptions, too, would make the psychoid field decidedly local and causal rather than non-local and synchronistic. They do not answer to the facts.

The most crucial limitation in Sheldrake's thinking has to do with how he imagines fields to be inherited. He says there are only two possibilities: some sort of gene-based Platonic mechanism or else a memory that is immanent in organisms. He rejects the first because he says the Platonic realm of eternal forms implies that the morphic fields that made *Tyrannosaurus rex* possible would have to pre-exist the cosmos, whereas morphic fields as he understands them evolve within the realm of nature. This is precisely what we have been saying about the psychoid field. But it is hard to understand why the gene-based mechanism must be Platonic, for we would see every gene as having a mental or psychoid pole as well as a physical one.

Having rejected the Platonic option, Sheldrake settles on the idea that morphic fields "contain an inherent memory . . . the structure of the fields depends on what has happened before . . . they represent a kind of pooled or collective memory of the species" (Sheldrake 1995: 107f). This position is very similar to ours, namely that the mental pole of the present moment gathers the physical realities of the moment just past into a new "growing together." For us, guidance comes from the larger organisms within which each smaller organism is nested. Sheldrake's "collective memory of the species" and "resonance" with a seemingly distant field seem strangely remote. For us there need be no "pooling" of memory, for memory resides nowhere else than in the structures that exist in the present instant—insofar as each structure has evolved from the structures produced in the instant just passed.

Sheldrake seems to believe that a memory of *Tyrannosaurus rex* might exist in a morphic field that has not disappeared from the Earth. He says: "Even the fields of dinosaurs are potentially present here and now; but there are no appropriate tuning systems, such as living dinosaur eggs, that can pick them up by morphic resonance. . . . archaic structures could suddenly reappear" (Sheldrake 1995: 286). Our position would be that something like a *T. rex* would have to re-evolve. There can be no psychoid field for a *T. rex* unless there are living examples of *T. rex*. Psychoid fields have *nothing* in common with Platonic forms. They do no exist in any etheric reservoir from whence they can return. They are the mental poles of material beings. They evolve and go extinct like everything else in nature.

How to imagine the psychoid field

Despite its limitations, Sheldrake's theory of morphic fields has several things to teach us. Most importantly, it enables us to picture how a field accomplishes its effects. Just as Faraday required the image of toroidal vectors to convince his colleagues of the reality of magnetic fields, so Sheldrake has drawn on the proposals of two earlier scientists to sketch the sort of field that gives shape to anatomy and behavior: the English embryologist C. H. Waddington (1905–75), who proposed the idea of form-guiding "chreodes," and the American neurobiologist we have often cited, Walter J. Freeman, with his theory of spontaneously forming basins of attraction among brain waves.

Waddington coined the term *chreode* in his book *The Strategy of the Genes* (1957). He was searching for a way to picture embryonic development in the days before "Evo Devo," the field of molecular embryology, had emerged. Sheldrake defines a chreode as "a canalized pathway of change within a morphic field" (Sheldrake 1995: 366). The ball rolling down the eroded landscape in Figure 13.2 will most likely find its way to the deepest channel or basin of attraction. In similar fashion, certain pathways of structural development are favored by psychoid fields: favored but not determined. The vagaries of the moment may cause the ball to start down the channel on the right of Figure 13.2, which appears to be relatively less deep at the upper end of the slope. In the end, though, the two final legs of that right channel are actually deeper than the main channel on the left. We may take the depth of a basin of attraction as a measure of structural stability. The chreode landscape, therefore, describes a "probability field."

In an earthen landscape—we might imagine a Mississippi delta unaltered by human-built levees—water will always tend to flow through the deepest channel, hollowing it further as the years pass. But alterations in weather and currents will continually force the river to cut new channels, as Mark Twain so wonderfully

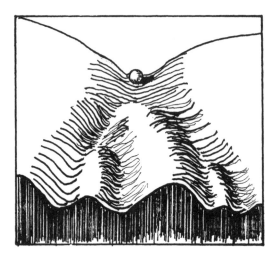

Figure 13.2 The "chreode" shape of a psychoid field: the ball rolls down the steepest slope, as determined by past behavior, and requires a special impetus to roll over a hill into the next valley.

Source: original pen and ink drawing by Ann Yoost Brecke.

describes in his *Life on the Mississippi*. In this way, an amoeba's behavior will be canalized by its experience of its immediate surround, resulting in the evidence for short-term memory that we have cited.

River channels correspond, too, to the basins of attraction that Walter Freeman describes. A familiar scent causes the rabbit's olfactory lobe to generate the same wave pattern, breath after breath, as though the chreode landscape has a single channel. But give the rabbit a new scent, and the entire structure changes. Now there are two basins of attraction, neither in the same location as the old single chreode. In this way, Sheldrake imagines an ever changing morphic (or psychoid) field to be generated around an organism: "Attractors" lying within "basins of attraction in a multi-dimensional phase space, draw the developing organism toward developmental aims or goals" (Sheldrake 2003: 276).

The same nested hierarchy that we have taken from Whitehead's (1929) *Process and Reality* is fundamental to Sheldrake's (1995) concept of morphic fields. Each neuron, for example, is a whole organism in its own right and is organized as a whole, even though it functions as part of a larger whole, the brain. Sheldrake refers to such subsidiary wholes with Arthur Koestler's term, *holon*. Neural networks are higher-level holons, and the brain is a higher holon still, while the holon that describes the entire individual human we call the psyche. At every level, each holon has its own psychoid field that is forever finding its basins of attraction under the guidance of higher-level fields (Sheldrake 1995: 120).

Experimental verification

A new model of reality becomes truly convincing when experiments can be performed to test its accuracy. Faraday's magnetic field was proposed on the basis of a number of clever experiments, and this was enough to add the image of the new field to the tools of science. But the idea was not ultimately confirmed until James Clerk Maxwell worked out its mathematics. It seems unlikely that the theory of psychoid fields will ever enjoy comparable quantification, for everything that has to do with the psyche resists mathematical precision. But this has not held Sheldrake back from proposing and carrying out a number of intriguing tests of the morphic field idea.

One of his favorite examples has to do with what seems to be non-local influence upon processes which are purely physical in nature. Once a laboratory in one part of the world succeeds after much effort in producing a new type of crystal, very often other widely separated laboratories immediately begin to succeed as well. Sheldrake hypothesizes that a new morphic field has been generated and become available everywhere simultaneously (non-locality). The folklore of chemistry imagines, on the contrary, that the information about how to form the new crystal is carried from laboratory to laboratory in the beards of visiting chemists. Perhaps seed crystals are being inadvertently carried about the world this way (Sheldrake 1995: 131). Clearly the folk explanation is a stretch, an attempt to stay within the causal paradigm. To demonstrate the non-causality of this phenomenon, crystallography experiments would have to be designed to include isolation measures, and scientists would have to do their work in the expectation that synchronistic events may be possible. In recent years Sheldrake has been working hard to encourage these kinds of experimentation.

The so-called "evolution of dominance" may be a similar instance in the realm of animal life. House cats readily revert to a feral lifestyle. For some animals, however, anatomical changes accompanying the shift to feral living can be quite dramatic. Pigs, for instance, become more bristly and tend to grow tusks. In the next generation, the young are apt to have regained the stripes of wild boars. Darwin noticed this phenomenon, attributing it to a latent tendency in the species to return to a primitive state. Sheldrake believes that feral living conditions encourage the individual animal to "tune in" to feral morphic fields (Sheldrake 1992: 138). It is difficult to imagine how experimental conditions could be devised to prove the psychoid field hypothesis, but it is appealing in view of the fact that changes in adult living evidently reverse some of the molecular "decisions" made during embryological development. Evidently, re-experiencing feral conditions alters the biology of cells, resulting in bristles and tusks. One thinks of those "allosteric proteins" that refold themselves in response to changing conditions in their surround. Stripes in the young indicate that changes occur in the "Evo Devo" of the next generation, whereby the same genes of a generation ago are now mobilized differently. It would seem that either the environment brings these changes about directly or else lifestyle changes result in the animal "tuning in" to more appropriate psychoid fields.

Experiments run decades ago by I. P. Pavlov (1849–1936) in Russia and William McDougall (1871–1938) at Harvard show that rodents learn mazes progressively more rapidly with each generation. If the first generation required 300 trials to master a maze, the next generation may learn it in 100 trials, the third in 30, and the fourth in 10. Sheldrake argues that the genes could not have changed. What has changed is that morphic fields have been strengthened as each succeeding generation profits from the memories of its ancestors (Sheldrake 1995: 174f).

Sheldrake also suggests that if learning trials were carefully devised for humans, we might produce similar evidence. For example, a new sport like wind-surfing ought to get easier to acquire with each generation. Human wind-surfers would not necessarily have to be the offspring of wind-surfing parents. We would not have to wait an entire generation to begin gathering data. Perhaps we could check in at five- or ten-years intervals, for if Sheldrake is right about morphic fields, they are maintained by living wind-surfers and thereby made available for all novices in the sport. And the more skillful wind-surfers there are, the stronger the psychoid field (Sheldrake 1995: xviii).

An experiment of this type actually performed upon groups of volunteers in England and the United States involved the learning of a Japanese nursery rhyme by English speakers unfamiliar with the Japanese language. The control groups were given a series of syllables of similar sound and identical rhythm that were meaningless in Japanese. About 62 percent found it easier to learn the real nursery rhyme, presumably because that set of rhythmic sounds belonged to a morphic field actively being strengthened with every generation of Japanese youngsters (Sheldrake 1995: 189f).

One of Sheldrake's most ambitious experiments involved homing pigeons. No causal explanation has ever been demonstrated to explain how pigeons find their way back to their loft after being released hundreds of miles away. During the First World War, the Italian navy discovered that the birds would return to lofts that were mounted on ships that moved about continually, and from distances of over a hundred kilometers. Disproved causal hypotheses include the following: that they memorize the twists and turns of their outward journey, that they follow landmarks, that they use the Sun's elevation together with some sort of internal clock, and that they use the Earth's magnetic field.[1]

Sheldrake worked with a pigeon trainer who agreed to mount his pigeon loft on the back of an old farm wagon so that it could be towed to ever new locations. Once accustomed to the mounted loft when it was stationary, the birds had no trouble finding it when it was towed a mile or two away. They did hesitate to enter the loft at its new location, however, choosing instead to perch on nearby branches for a while to get used to it before reentering. A second summer of experiments was to involve much greater distances, but the owner of the pigeons fell ill with pigeon lung disease during the winter and had to give up his birds. It never became clear whether the birds were returning to their loft-mates, to the loft structure itself, or perhaps to their owner and Sheldrake, but there can be little doubt that some sort of psychoid non-locality must have been involved (Sheldrake 2002: 33–68).

Summary

This chapter makes a case for a universal psychoid field to complete the official scientific account of the universe by making room for evident aspects of reality that have up to now been ignored: life, consciousness, intentionality and parapsychology. A view like the one articulated here will probably not gain widespread acceptance until astrophysics or quantum mechanics discovers a need for an organismic principle. At that time mathematical formulation may even become possible and Jung's "border zone" statements about synchronicity will no longer be the subject of misunderstanding. We will probably never see psyche reduced to mathematics; but if the non-living universe can be described by a calculus of organism, psyche's non-locality and partial independence of the brain will no longer seem problematic.

We are not able at this point to make the case conclusively for a universal psychoid field, but we have marshaled at least fifteen converging arguments that make the idea more than plausible:

1   Because the holism of field theory has been solving physicists' most difficult action-at-a-distance problems for the past three centuries, another appeal to field theory would be consilient with and confirm a long-term successful trend in scientific thinking.

2   Jung's idea that the amoeba's life process displays a psychoid nature is consilient with recent discoveries in biology that amoeba and other simple life forms lacking a nervous system manifest memory and accuracy in foraging decisions.

3   Further examination of psychoid process reveals the nested hierarchy of interconnected organisms as well as the natural growth and expansion of psyche as its physical organism differentiates and matures.

4   Overviews of the course of evolution reveal that every stage of development, from simple autocatalysis to the appearance of language-using *Homo sapiens*, manifests psychoid process.

5   Not only the internal life-process of biological organisms, but also the interaction of organisms with their immediate surround, as in the case of the termite colony and its mound, manifests a psychoid process where the organic and the inorganic are no longer separable. Design is a psychoid process resulting from the interaction of tinkerer and accomplice.

6   Darwin's neglected principle, the origin of novelty in evolution, is now being effectively addressed by a number of biologists who are discovering that evolution's core processes facilitate novelty in distinctly psychoid fashion.

7   A nuanced appreciation of psychoid process reveals that intentionality and teleology are integral to all of life and do not imply the long-term planning of a creator-god or any other sort of anthropomorphic principle. For the vast majority of living beings, the future is instantaneous and planning impossible.

8   The alleged inert insensitivity of matter is not self-evident but rather a theological position designed to support an incoherent idea about the nature of the soul.

9   Consciousness could not emerge from matter's complex organization unless matter itself possess some rudimentary psychoid property.

10 Whitehead's metaphysics of process replaces substance with event as the foundation of reality and thereby reveals everything—from sub-atomic quanta to the universe as a whole—to be organismic. Everything physical has a psychoid pole.

11 Several contemporary physicists are coming to see that a holistic starting point is necessary if we are to understand a cosmos full of superclusters of galaxies and a chaotic quantum sea in which every particle has been entangled with every other in a holomovement since the Big Bang.

12 Not only the *I Ching*, which influenced Leibniz, Faraday and Jung, but also Taoism, the Buddhist doctrine of co-dependent origination and the Hindu doctrine of the all-pervading brahman principle reveal the universality of holistic thinking in world cultures.

13 The Gaia hypothesis demonstrates that we do not understand the most basic realities of our home planet until we adopt an organismic perspective. Furthermore, without it we endanger our own survival.

14 The universal psychoid field is effectively pictured as a chreode landscape in which basins of attraction are dynamically being generated and reorganized as living beings encounter ever new challenges.

15 Although the psychoid field is open to experimental verification, and not a few experiments have already been tried, this sort of scientific work will not likely become compelling until a "critical mass" of scientists in a number of different fields begin to take it seriously enough to follow Pierre Janet's advice (1919) and "keep their cultures pure."[2] Crystallographers, for instance, will not refute the folk theory of visiting scientists' beards until they take measures to exclude that possibility of spreading new seed crystals.

Chapter 14

Vision and reality

Jung's ventures into the border zones of exact science have often served his critics as the final piece of evidence that his views are soft-headed, "mystical" in the derogatory sense, and therefore deserving of neglect. We have shown, however, that any fair assessment of the positions he took reveals that in most cases he was out in front of "exact science," formulating sound ideas that have gained more and more support from experts working with experimental methods that were unavailable to Jung a century ago. His vision has become reality a century later. The following positions taken by Jung are well supported and explained by the work of recent scientists working on the assumption that brain and psyche are identical.

Jung's positions supported by science

Archetypes are inherited patterns of behavior that include not only the definable activities themselves but also the emotional, perceptual and imaginal accompaniments that give those activities the subjective meaning and compelling power that they have.

This means that archetypes are top-to-bottom structures, from the visual and auditory areas of the neocortex at the top to fixed action patterns in the spinal cord and hormone deployment from the adrenals at the bottom. Consequently, whenever a pattern is stimulated, at whatever level, the whole structure is activated and we are placed in a characteristic state of body-and-mind. In this sense, "collective representations" are more than images, they are "self-portraits" of an instinct.

The basis for our inheriting such top-to-bottom patterns lies in the structure of the brain and the autonomic nervous system. Neural structures are prepared for by genes but "filled in" and finished as experience builds neural networks.

Human behavioral patterns have analogues in the behaviors and mentality of primates and other animals and some of them can, theoretically, be traced back all the way to the protozoa. Archetypal patterns are shaped by cultural influences, so that identical human themes can take on highly dissimilar cultural expression.

The psyche as a whole manifests an inherent unity of purpose (self) far larger than that of the self-conscious agent (ego). It works unconsciously and incessantly for the well-being of our whole organism. Psychopathology results from an ego that heeds only its own narrow perspective at the expense of wholeness and balance, while individuation is the dialogue between the organismic process of the self and the reflective process of the ego.

Dreams represent an unconsciously generated commentary from neglected elements of our psyche and brain. In this sense, they offer a significant contribution to the self's part in the individuation dialogue. Their vital importance to the psyche is expressed in their utilizing the brain's dopamine-driven "seeking system."

Feeling-toned complexes, based as we now know in the convergence centers of the limbic system, cause us to see and respond to life-situations in stereotypical and poorly adapted ways. They have their origin in innate survival strategies but outlive their usefulness on account of an automatism driven by emotional arousal.

We can gain a certain freedom from our complexes by seeing them for the repetitious patterns they are and engaging our powers of differentiated consciousness (pre-frontal cortex). When the top-to-bottom structure of an archetype is constellated, a nearly irresistible impulse and vision easily overcomes the pull of a complex and can reorient the personality. Conversely the dominance of a single archetypal pattern subverts the wholeness and balance of the self and may take on psychotic features.

Unitive/transformative states of consciousness can occur spontaneously, especially at times when we face an impossible-seeming either/or issue, when two courses of action cannot be reconciled. Such problems can be "transcended" through a unitive brain state that Jung calls "the transcendent function."

Archetypal states of consciousness can also be cultivated. This has been the function of ritual throughout human history, based in archetypal patterns we share with other primates. Religious rituals bind communities emotionally, and focus the attention and motivation of their members on important collective endeavors.

Altered states of consciousness are cultivated by tuning the autonomic nervous system, and individuals who have had a special talent and propensity for doing so have functioned as shamans as far back in human history as we can see. Shamanism, therefore, can be described as the natural religious practice of the human organism.

Human history over the past 40,000 years has been characterized by a process in which free shamanic access to altered states of consciousness has gradually been manipulated and overshadowed by economic, political and religious authorities who have used their control for the accumulation of power and influence. The process has gradually cut us citizens of the West off from easy access to the holistic perspective of our self.

In the past 500 years, our Western emphasis on ego autonomy and a technology based in subject/object dichotomy and mechanistic science has been too rewarding to allow us to doubt the value of our monophasic attitude. Jung describes us as adrift in search of the archetypal roots that shamans have long provided. He employed quasi-shamanic methods of dream-interpretation and active imagination to find his own "personal myth" and to help his patients to do the same.

Crossing into the border zones

Jung's call for a return to a polyphasic attitude in which altered states of consciousness are not only tolerated but also actively and conscientiously explored opens up the border zones where parapsychological events are common and challenges the Western folk-metaphysics which has been accepted uncritically by most scientists.

In the first place, Jung intended his call for a polyphasic attitude as a therapeutic solution for our deep dissatisfactions. It is implicitly a call to incorporate shamanic exercises into our everyday lives: not to abandon the considerable accomplishments precise directed thinking has provided us but to take up the task of integrating the other side of our nature. Some 40,000 years ago, our technology was primitive and our shamanism well advanced. Now our technology is advanced and our shamanism primitive. We have to learn that shamanic practices require significant discipline and that altered states of consciousness can be mastered.

Shamanic practices in themselves are no challenge to science or to the contemporary mainstream view that psyche and brain are not identical. There is no conflict as long as the shaman is exploring his own unconscious, understood to be located in the neural networks of his own brain and the top-to-bottom arousals that they can effect. Shamanic experience, however, claims to do much more than this. Shamans claim that they have learned the medicinal and consciousness-changing secrets of plants in their journeys through the greater cosmos, and have discovered where the animals have gone and where and how they may be hunted. They say they make journeys through the bodies of their patients to learn what is wrong with them and how to cure them, or that they have tracked down their patient's soul as it wanders or has been abducted to distant regions of a greater cosmos. They extract mysterious objects from their patients, which can be seen by other individuals who also happen to be in an altered state of consciousness. Patients are frequently healed by these events. Sometimes the patient herself has glimpses of the shaman's journey on her behalf; and sometimes the shaman's assistant, like the wife of Don Manuel Córdoba, inadvertently witnesses these disturbing events in shamanic dreamscape.

Shamans, in short, claim all the powers that parapsychology explores and therefore serve as our primary evidence that psyche and brain are identical. For shamans it is self-evident that psyche can roam free of the brain and witness distant events (clairvoyance), read minds (telepathy) and effect changes in the empirical world (psychokinesis). When contemporary science asks itself what might cause these things, it has no answer. Such claims seem to be impossible superstitions. Jung agrees that they are not "caused" in any sense that we recognize. He says they are "acausal" and synchronistic. In proposing synchronicity as a universal psychoid field, he invites us to take the inexplicable phenomena of ESP seriously. But in doing so, he has much to say about the nature of science in general.

Science should be in the business of investigating phenomena that clearly occur and not of trying to dismiss them or explain them away; for inexplicable phenomena challenge science to examine its assumptions and reformulate its hypotheses to bring them into line with reality.

Jung identifies the issue to be "metaphysical," in the sense that it has to do with our public agreement on the nature of reality. Our scientific theories have missed a big piece of the world around us. The evidence points to a psychoid factor that makes organisms and their process the primary reality—rather than substances and their localized influences on one another. For giving primacy to so-called building blocks in a mechanical universe makes it impossible to arrive at the self-evident reality that organisms abound and are alive.

Because organisms exist, their component parts evidently possess at least the minimal psychoid quality of responsiveness. Furthermore, it is in the psychoid nature of biological organisms of every type to live and intend.

The organismic perspective that everything in the universe has a psychoid dimension supplies the missing link that helps us understand how novelty is prepared for and enters the process of evolution. Thus Darwin's Dilemma has an answer, namely that the universe itself is characterized as much by a psychoid field as by a gravity field.

The psychoid field explicates not only the cooperative interaction of the parts of living organisms, but also the interactive processual nature of its relationship with its surround—not as fitting into a pre-existing niche, but as partner in a process that shapes both the world and the living creatures that inhabit it.

Psychoid process explicates the tinker/accomplice nature of "epigenetic" processes, the fact that it is not genes alone that determine an organism's structure and function, but that physiology and genetics are equal partners in the process by which a body is built and maintained.

The psychoid field extends beyond biology "downward" into the so-called inorganic realm as far as the chaotic quantum sea. It must do so, for everything that comprises an organism participates in an organismic process and therefore has to be psychoid in the minimal sense of being responsive. The psychoid field, therefore, suggests a model for understanding some of the inexplicable phenomena found in the quantum realm, such as non-locality. Wolfgang Pauli agreed that the psychoid hypothesis might prove useful for quantum physics (*PJL*: 38), and Jung made it clear that he thought the data of quantum mechanics belonged within the realm of synchronicity (*PJL*: 63, 96; *CW8*: ¶965).

In the other direction, the psychoid field helps us to appreciate the organismic nature of our planet as "Gaia" and may well prove useful to astrophysics in understanding the origin and dynamics of the cosmos with its galaxies, black holes and presumed dark matter and energy.

There can be little question that the biological sciences are already creeping toward a psychoid perspective to make sense of evolution and ecology. That the same may be true of the physical sciences it is too soon to tell, but Jung's psychoid field proposal is likely to be found consilient with science insofar as it was made in correspondence with one of the quantum theory's most original thinkers. Furthermore, the argument by which Jung establishes it was thought through according to the model by which physics has solved its earlier action-at-a-distance problems of magnetism and gravity. It would not surprise me if this Jungian proposal, too, is eventually taken up by mainstream science.

Parapsychology and the psychoid field

Having summarized both Jung's agreement with the findings of modern science and his challenge to it, it remains for us to spell out how the postulated psychoid field helps us to make sense of parapsychology and why it is important.

We have said that Jung wished to comprehend the full range of psyche's capabilities. Surely this is true, but his interest in the border zones of exact science had a personal significance for him as well. He was born in the last quarter of a century filled with astonishing scientific discoveries that had thoroughly discredited a naive, literal reading of the Bible, and raised fundamental questions about the meaning of human life, the existence of God and the possibility of an afterlife. Jung was painfully aware of such issues, being the product of a long line of Protestant ministers on both sides of his family. His pastor father had struggled with a series of crises of faith, and his death may have been hastened by the consequent distress he was unable to resolve.

According to his autobiographical *Memories, Dreams, Reflections* (*MDR*), Jung's acceptance of the official Christian story did not survive his twelfth year. The image he could not banish from his young mind, of God defecating on the Basel cathedral, had been a quasi-shamanic experience in its insistence, in its radical challenge to the religious establishment and in the conviction it inspired in the young boy that he had encountered an unavoidable truth. It taught him cautiously to trust his own experience as regards theological claims, while at the same time respecting the *consensus gentium*, as he always put it, the fact that if generations of diverse peoples had agreed on such things there must be something to them. Evidently God—or what counts as God within the psyche—can speak to us. Surely the message is filtered through the human unconscious. But it cannot be ignored.

The theory of synchronicity represents the maturation of such interests, earnestly pursued for seventy-some years. Jung did not clarify how the theory should be applied to the various phenomena of parapsychology; but now, with the integrated understanding of Complex Psychology made possible by recent advances in science, we can attempt a preliminary phenomenology of at least some aspects of parapsychology.

Three modes of psychic functioning

Humans communicate with one another in at least three different modes. The most characteristically human and highest-level mode is deliberate, conscious, goal-directed symbolic communication by way of language and gesture. In this mode we are dependent upon the analytic and creative capabilities of our neocortex and learned skills. It is our most clearly differentiated and explicitly aware mode of operating. The mid-level mode is more innate, less available for conscious manipulation but indispensable for survival, particularly in infancy. This is our automatic and inadvertent capacity for reading one another's facial expressions and body language and responding without thought. In doing so we rely upon a paleomammalian limbic system that is characterized by a more liminal and implicit sort of awareness. These first two modes of communication are explicable in the causal language of neurobiology and, taken alone, support the common opinion that psyche and brain are identical.

The third and most primitive mode of psyche-to-psyche communication is synchronistic and acausal. In principle it resembles the holistic process of an amoeba's moment-to-moment activity and therefore points to a psychic function that is supraordinate to the brain, being the regnant process of the entire human organism, brain included. I have long referred to this sort of communication as characterized by a "self-to-self connection," to emphasize its holistic nature and the fact that it is pre-linguistic and pre-imagistic (cf. Haule 1990). Although the brain may play a vital role in making us aware of such events, they need not ever reach consciousness.

Synchronistic function is a holistic primitive. Imagine, for example, that A communicates synchronistically with B. At the moment such an event occurs, B's whole being is instantaneously brought into resonance with A's being. B undergoes a change of state that aligns her with A. The event can occur without registering in B's awareness, and presumably most times does so. If B is to become conscious of what has happened to her, however, her nervous system will have to interpret her change of state for her.

The nervous system works much more slowly than the immediate, non-causal psyche. While its redundant parallel processing may make analytic, differentiated consciousness of a synchronistic event possible, it is always running to catch up. The locally interactive mechanics of neural networks firing and feeding back on one another slows down the process of awareness. The nature of this slow-down is suggested by Benjamin Libet's work, *Mind Time* (2004), which demonstrates that neuronal activity, as revealed by functional magnetic resonance imaging (fMRI), implies that the brain has already "decided" on a course of action about a half-second before a conscious subject is aware of making the choice (Libet 2004: 34).

Because brain and its consciousness lag behind the synchronistic psyche, however, it is reasonable to conclude that the fMRI evidence of a brain decision is itself preceded by a prior "decision" (i.e. responsive adjustment or change of state) that occurs in the supraordinate psyche. In our example of B picking up telepathic information from A, there would be three moments. The first occurs when B's supraordinate psyche is snapped into alignment with A's being. Nothing "neural" has happened yet. The second event occurs when the limbic system and neural networks in the cortex fire up to interpret the change of state B has undergone. This is when brain processes would register on the screen of an fMRI machine, but it is still a half-second before B is aware of what is going on. The third event occurs when B's ego becomes conscious of the telepathic influence.

Libet says a delay of this sort also confirms Whitehead's suggestion that we ought to cultivate the habit of acting without thinking (Libet 2004: 98f). As regards ESP in particular, the historian of parapsychology Alan Gauld reports that the idea of a subliminal self with superior faculties has been quite common for at least two centuries. He cites a series of literary references collected by F. W. H. Myers revealing that artistic creativity relies on something very much like somnambulism. The French poet and dramatist Alfred de Musset (1810–57) said, "You do not do the work yourself, you listen; it is as though a stranger whispers in your ear."[1] Robert Louis Stevenson said he dreamed the adventures that he later wrote up in his novels, and Mozart claimed that entire musical works "emerged complete and unpremeditated" into his mind (Gauld 1968: 288).

An instance of telepathy

In order to appreciate how the three modes of psychic functioning interact with one another, let us consider a rather commonplace example of spontaneous telepathy. A woman once broke off her conversation with me to say, "Oh! Something good just happened to Matt!" Her son, Matt, who was on a camping trip with his father at the time, telephoned some hours later to tell his mother that "something good" had indeed happened around the time she got the telepathic message: he had caught a big fish.

Synchronistic communications engage the non-local and supraordinate psyche, which has "absolute knowledge" through its participation in the universal psychoid field. The parapsychologist Dean Radin says, "Psi is our experience of the invisible interconnections that bind the universe together" (Radin 1997: 273). Such "interconnections" are the effect of the nested structure of the cosmos. The mother and son of our example are organisms occupying the same familial nest. In principle they are as tuned to one another as two organelles in the same amoeba. "Privately," to use Whitehead's language, organelles perform their functions as though they are separate organisms, but within the life process of the whole amoeba their activities are "public" and deeply attuned.

So it is with mother and son at the invisible level of their familial connection. At the conscious level they are hundreds of miles apart and out of contact, but at the synchronistic level of the supraordinate psyche they react simultaneously, like a pair of distant but "entangled" electrons, as described by Bell's Theorem in quantum mechanics. This is the principle, experimentally demonstrated by physicist Alain Aspect in 1982 (Kafatos and Nadeau 1990: 1), of non-locality—that entangled particles move in simultaneous harmony with one another, even when they are too far apart to be "communicating." Non-locality means that there can be no message. Mother and son undergo a simultaneous change in the state of their being; they experience a whole-body response. Information is not transferred, as by telephone line or radio wave; it is simply known instantly. The son's elation suddenly fills the mother's body as it does his own, a holistic change of state.

In the first instant of telepathic communication, when the response belongs entirely to the realm of the psychoid, there is no feeling, no thought, no image. These things emerge a half-second or more later, after layers of psychoid functioning at the cellular level are subjected to sufficient parallel processing so that higher-order awareness is produced. Emotion is generated when the autonomic nervous system and the limbic system of the brain undergo the holistic change of state. Rapid neural processing in the cerebral cortex brings the holistic change of state to the mother's consciousness as an experience of her son's elation.

A synchronistic response of this sort generates the kind of limbic connection we are already familiar with. It is like the emotional message an infant gets from the look of alarm on his mother's face when she sees him at the top edge of a set of stairs. He knows immediately that he is in danger. The limbic system was designed by evolution for such immediate life-or-death emotional connections, and for this reason it often plays an essential role in spontaneous occurrences of telepathy. It is surely the reason that matters of life and death are so frequently the message delivered in such events. Limbic emotion is the main component of human-human (or, indeed, mammal-mammal)[2] entanglement.

But more than this, the mother knew that it was her *son's* elation—not her own, not anyone else's. No doubt she had felt her son's elation many times before. Memory was involved—another function of the convergence centers of the limbic system, resembling the dynamics described in *Volume 1* in connection with complex reactions.

The vitality of such limbic connections is evidently the reason spontaneous ESP events tend to be so much more interesting and complete than those produced in laboratory exercises. The philosopher of parapsychology Stephen E. Braude is clearly right when he says, "Cases of laboratory psi [should be] regarded [as] degenerate instances of real-life psi" (Braude 1986: 253). Targ and Puthoff (2005) tried to compensate for the laboratory effect when they carefully selected experimental subjects with whom they could enjoy a satisfying and cheerful rapport. No doubt this improved their results, but nothing can compare with the rapport between parent and child, between lovers or between two "entangled" individuals when matters of life and death are involved. Even when parent and child have a contentious relationship, the capacity for telepathy can be very great, as I discovered in the case of a thirty-year-old woman who complained that her intrusive mother, who lived hundreds of miles away, always seemed to know when she returned to her apartment. The telephone would ring with another importunate demand or request within moments of her entering the door.

Our mother/son instance of telepathy includes very little higher-level conscious functioning. The heart of the conscious response seems to end with the contribution of the limbic system; for we have only the verbal report, "Something good has happened to Matt," to attribute to the neocortex. If the mother had had a vision or dream of the big fish being landed, the visual areas of her cortex would have participated in processing the holistic change of state. Such things do happen spontaneously, as might be learned from the story of a gentleman in his ocean liner cabin who was visited in the early morning by the ghostly image of his wife that was also seen by his bunk mate. In our less spectacular case, the mother might have learned about the big fish by practicing Ingo Swann's remote viewing techniques.

The very effort required to produce this sort of detailed sensory information, however, suggests why experiments in clairvoyance produce such mixed results. One can never be sure what the supraordinate psyche is attending to. It may be the experimental target, but it may just as well be its own "mythic" interests—as seems to have been the case with Courtney Brown, whose remote viewing experiments turned up space aliens with a challenge for the human race. In the context of such uncertainty, therefore, it is not surprising that Mrs. Craig Sinclair picked up themes from her husband's musings as he walked along the beach rather than from the drawings he had made earlier. It would be very interesting to know what those musings were and the extent to which they involved the emotion-driven limbic system of his brain.

The role of altered states

An ordinary state of consciousness is oriented to the everyday realities that everyone knows without having to ask probing questions. It is characterized by attention to the sensory conditions before one, by run-of-the-mill opinions, by the incessant fluctuations of beta brain waves and by left-brain linear thinking. All of these conditions conflict with attending to one's supraordinate psyche and to the synchronistic universe within which it lives. Therefore, even when ESP events are spontaneous, common and characterized by matter-of-fact incidents, they always involve a non-ordinary state of consciousness. The instant the mother in our example was overtaken by the experience of her son's elation, she was in an altered state, no longer attending to the sensory field before her, no longer conversing with me. We cannot attend to the nested universe while in the grips of the Western cultural paradigm.

What is intriguing, however, is the degree of clairvoyant accuracy that is possible for people like Ingo Swann, Pat Price, Mel Riley and Joe McMoneagle, the CIA's psychics. These people were not overtaken by spontaneous jolts from a supraordinate psyche collaborating with an overcharged limbic system. Like Jung and Husserl, they simply cultivated a transcendental ego, and it supplied extraordinary information. "Coordinates" produced by a random number generator specified a target that had no emotional significance for them. Any natural bond they might have had with their target was eliminated. That so much could be achieved under these conditions suggests the power of run-of-the-mill entanglements within our nested universe as well as the openness of the transcendental ego. "We might be interacting all the time with the minds of strangers, and acquiring information by ESP of events to which we give little or no conscious attention"

(Braude 1986: 278). If we were consciously in telepathic touch with everyone in our environment, we would be overwhelmed with useless information. Ordinary consciousness, therefore, has a very important role to play. It keeps us oriented to the sensory events going on in our immediate environment; it keeps us alive.

Shamanism and unitive states

Among the access-providing non-ordinary states of consciousness humans have cultivated, those of the unitive/transformative kind are the most interesting. We have seen that they involve a unitive brain state, where the right and left cerebral hemispheres, the limbic system and the brain stem are all pulsing in harmony. They therefore represent not only a whole-*brain* state, but also a whole-*psyche* state. They are the moments when we are in touch with our unitary self, our wholeness; and through that with the synchronistic cosmos.

Shamanic healing journeys unquestionably involve such altered states, which take the form of traveling through a greater cosmos on behalf of the patient. Prior to the journey, shaman and patient have become acquainted over the issue of the patient's illness and the shaman has satisfied herself regarding the patient's life-situation and issues of potential relevance to the reported symptoms. In the course of these preliminaries, shaman and patient will have had a meeting on all three levels of human communication: a conscious exchange of verbal information, a semi-conscious limbic resonance and a synchronistic alignment of their beings.

Evidence that their synchronistic alignment has been effective will appear in the shaman's healing journey, when she finds herself traveling through a dream-scape that belongs to the patient rather than to herself. The shaman may even encounter objects, incidents and people that the patient will later be able to iden-tify as belonging to his past. They are taken to reveal information about the origin of the illness or about what is needed to bring about recovery. More often the shaman encounters scenes the patient has never encountered or imagined, but they nevertheless provide symbolic information about the patient's condition in the manner of a dream. When the healing is successful, all these things are relevant to the patient's recovery.

Psychotherapists may undergo a similar alignment with their patients, called "countertransference." While listening to the patient's story, an attuned therapist will notice bodily changes, memories and fantasies arising, material that comes to mind only now because it is relevant to the patient's story—and to the state of his whole being as he tells it. Limbic resonance may be the foundation of this attune-ment, but in some cases it may also involve the supraordinate psyche.

What is hard for our Western perspective to understand is how the shaman or psychoanalyst can travel through the *patient's* dreamscape or body rather than her own. It is easier to assume that the shamanic state of consciousness resembles active imagination, where one tours a symbolic world that describes the deep holism of one's own being. Thus, we have to assume that the successful shaman aligns her being with the supraordinate psyche of the patient, synchronistically.

Her being snaps into alignment with the patient's disordered state, much as the telepathic mother's being assumed the elation of her son when he caught the big fish. For the mother, it comes naturally and unbidden, as an aspect of the deep connection that exists between mother and son. But the shaman has to cultivate a unitive state and deliberately open her being to that of the patient. The fact that she has done so successfully is demonstrated by the patient's healing.

Jung's cultivation of shamanic states in therapy

A lifetime after Jung's passionate plea for scientific investigation of the border zones of exact science, those border lands had become essential for his daily work as a psychoanalyst. We have described some of the evidence: the fact that he often began to speak without knowing why but turned out to be addressing his analysand's issues in a very helpful way; the fact that he could sometimes know all or part of what his analysand had dreamed the night before; the fact that his analysands sometimes experienced the dissolution of everyday certainties when in Jung's presence so that they spoke of the world becoming whizzing molecules or their losing the distinction between themselves and the furniture in the room; or the fact that he urged trainees at the Jung Institute in Zurich to cultivate a state of mind in which the personification of human wisdom is brought to presence in the session as a two-million-year-old man.

Some of these phenomena had to have been rooted in a non-verbal limbic connection, the kind that infants rely upon to determine their safety and condition of being loved. When we become adults, we do not so much lose this capacity as neglect attending to it. It seems most reasonable, therefore, to conclude that Jung had taught himself to attend to subliminal impressions he gained from his analysand's facial expression, tone of voice, and body language. He allowed his patient's whole body state to affect his own being. He cultivated, in short, a body-centered empathy, tuning his whole being to that of his analysand; and while in this state of deep attunement, he simply spoke what came to mind. Sometimes, apparently, it was only the general theme of his monologue that addressed his patient's concerns. Other times he spoke of Africa and snakes and these specific matters turned out to be of vital interest to his analysand.

Jung claims that he began speaking without knowing why and that his thinking was done unconsciously. ("If someone were to ask me: What are you thinking just now?—I wouldn't know. I think unconsciously.") Such statements imply that he must have been using a modification of active imagination or transcendental ego during his sessions with patients. He waited for the unconscious to give him his thoughts. The images, words and emotions emerged from a state of deep limbic-system attunement. If they were not precisely what the patient was thinking, they were close enough because they were an expression of a nearly identical state of body and mind.

On the other hand, when Jung's monologue came up with some images that the analysand was just then entertaining, narrated pretty much the same stories the analysand was remembering, and even got the analysand's untold dreams right, he was in a state of mind that closely resembles that of the shaman traveling through her patient's dreamscape. At times like that it appears that Jung's supra-ordinate psyche was synchronistically aligned with the being of his patient. Decades of exploring empathy combined, perhaps, with a constitutional openness to the unconscious appears to have given him an advantage in this respect. Certainly he did not always pick up accurately on the analysand's dream of the night before, but he increased his chances of doing so by letting himself be affected by the analysand's limbic state and by holding himself open for whatever "wished" to appear on the screen of his consciousness.

Those of Jung's patients who said that everything became whizzing molecules or that they could no longer distinguish themselves from the furniture while in his presence appear to have experienced a shift in hemispheric dominance. Instead of processing the world of their experience in a linear, serial manner by talking to themselves in words (left hemisphere), being with Jung seems to have induced a condition of right-hemisphere dominance.

The neuroanatomist Jill Bolte Taylor, of the Indiana University School of Medicine, vividly describes her own entry into the experiential world of the right brain as the result of a stroke she suffered at the age of thirty-seven in 1996. She awoke that morning with a headache caused by the rupture of an arterio-venous malformation near the speech area of her left hemisphere. Surgeons later removed a golf-ball sized clot. In the early morning of the incident, however, the pressure on her left hemisphere caused her to lose her capacity to think rationally for minutes at a time. In the intervals when the left hemisphere was silent, her experi-ence closely resembles the testimony of Jung's patients. When her left brain was functioning, she would think, "Hey! We got a problem . . . I'm having a stroke," and she would try to dial the telephone. But the left hemisphere would cut out again before she could finish, and this would deliver her to a state of ecstasy:

> And I lost my balance and I'm propped up against the wall. And I look down at my arm and I realize that I can no longer define the boundaries of my body, I can't define where I begin and where I end. Because the atoms and the mol-ecules of my arm blended with the atoms and molecules of the wall. And all I could detect was this energy. Energy. . . . And at first I was shocked to find myself inside a silent mind. But then I was immediately captivated by the magnificence of the energy around me. And because I could no longer iden-tify the boundaries of my body, I felt enormous and expansive. I felt at one with all the energy that was, and it was beautiful there.[3]

Jane Wheelwright, whose "whizzing molecules" experience we cited in Chapter 7, spoke of being frightened by the dissolution of the ordinary world when she entered Jung's presence. Because she did not completely lose access to the left hemisphere as Jill Bolte Taylor did, she grasped the enormity of the change and found the contrast between the two worlds scary. She pulled herself together with a comforting thought, "Since Jung had descended into this strange world and emerged so could I." She also felt she was not alone, "Two people were caught in a [vise] that was forcing them to undergo an important rearrangement of themselves that had some significance—some meaning far beyond them." Similarly, Rix Weaver had the presence of mind and linguistic capacity to ask, "What is the difference between me and that table?"

Such testimonies support the hypothesis that Jung relied heavily on input from his right brain while he sat in session with his analysands. Probably it was a skill he cultivated by entering frequently into the meditative space of active imagination. Evidently he "tuned" his autonomic nervous system and his hemispheric dominance to induce a mildly unitive/transformative state of consciousness. Analysands who were particularly sensitive and aware of impressions from their limbic systems found themselves drawn into attunement with Jung. Perhaps their "transference" onto Jung, their willingness to place their fate in his hands, stripped them of their natural defensiveness. Jung himself, on the contrary, would have needed his left brain to practice analysis. Thus, we have to conclude that he must have achieved a favorable balance between the two hemispheres. His right brain was aware that the lapping of the waves, the singing of the birds and the tapping of a rose chafer were not separate from the analytic dialogue; and his left brain was able to interpret their contributions.

Finally, Jung's invocation of the two-million-year-old man implies another sort of connection. The experience probably begins as emotional attunement at the limbic level, and it might also include a synchronistic self-self connection at the level of the supraordinate psyche. But in this case it is not just the analyst who is acting as a shaman. *Both* parties enter the receptive psychic space we associate with active imagination. Images emerge out of a psychoid field constellated between them that is anchored in the shared whole-body state of their limbic emotion. In this place of mutuality, either party may begin a dialogue by giving voice to whatever appears on the conscious screen of the transcendental ego. An image, concept or narrative fragment voiced by one will stimulate the other to carry the dialogue forward with whatever thought or image emerges next.

Both parties in such a dialogue will have the sense that there is a third party in the room. For it is inevitable with any practice of active imagination that one finds that images and ideas are *given* to one. Consequently, the practice of active imagination in tandem gives both parties the impression that the common theme they are developing arises from a unitary source that is "neither me nor you," but a third person. Inevitably mythic themes will emerge, for at bottom these are the inherited mental and behavioral structures we share with one another. The invisible third party to the dialogue seems to contribute the wisdom of the human race, as though he had lived through it all. In setting the age of this ancient wise man at two million years, Jung suggests the approximate time that the various *Homo* species, *ergaster, habilis* and *rudolfensis*, are thought to have diverged from *Australopithecus* (Thain and Hickman 2000).

Cosmic unity in mystical states

Shamanic healing supplies the most spectacular evidence of non-local, absolute knowing and the mutual influence that may result. They support a view of reality that includes a psychoid field, where everything that is participates in the holoprocess that is reality. From amoeba to human, every psyche and every photon entails an image of the entire evolving universe. Indeed, we might even suppose that in the quantum realm some sort of proto-emotion at the psychoid level entangles electrons or photons when they undergo simultaneous, non-local changes.[4] For it seems that the psychoid field solves the quantum conundrum of non-locality and saves us from having to suppose that the supraordinate psyche is itself an expression of quantum mechanics, as several physicists have proposed.[5]

Now that we have sketched a universal psychoid field, it appears that we may be under no illusion when our unitive, mystical state tells us that we are one with the universe at large. For if every psyche is moved by the mental pole of the cosmos, each one, while being just itself, also contains the holoprocess of the whole. Thus, upon finding ourselves in touch with the wholeness of our individual being, we must also be in touch with the cosmic Whole. It makes sense of the claims mystics have always made: that they have experienced union with God (the mental pole of the cosmos) or with the cosmos itself, that they have never experienced anything so overwhelmingly true and real. They must really have encountered the underlying coherence of the All, however metaphorically or symbolically it was apprehended.

Psychokinesis

The communication of one psyche with another in telepathy, the capability of a human psyche to "view" distant events, or the ability of a dog or cat's psyche to know when its owner has begun the homeward journey from work all seem rather easy to accept in comparison with PK events. Our mind does not want to believe that D. D. Home could play an accordion that was out of his physical reach, that Eusapia Palladino could nudge F. W. H. Myers in the ribs with a pseudopodium, or that Rudi Schneider could levitate several feet above any possible support and remain there for minutes at a time. These events challenge our Western assumptions more directly than telepathy or clairvoyance. But our assumptions are filled with unexamined leaps of faith so that what we think we know remains just as mysterious as what we believe to be impossible. The helicopter inventor and philosopher of consciousness Arthur M. Young (1976) makes this point vividly, while employing a metaphor that has been essential to our argument:

> What eludes explanation is the nature of the moving force [in psychokinesis]. . . . The pseudopods of the amoeba [are similar] to the ectoplasmic

appendages of mediums, and the psychic libido described by Freud. Now the interesting thing is that this force is no better "explained" in the cases we consider quite normal, like the amoeba, than in the case of the medium.

(A. M. Young 1976: 149)

This is a tempting argument. For although we know some of the molecular mechanisms involved in an amoeba's extending pseudopodia, the psychic process itself is so mysterious that we have had to call it "primitive"—just one of the basic properties of reality that we have to accept without explanation, like mass, length and time. There is a difference between the pseudopodia of an amoeba and those of Eusapia Palladino, however. The amoeba extends its bodily cell walls and the cytoplasm they contain to engulf its food with pseudopodia. But Eusapia's ectoplasm presumably contains no material from her own body—especially when we consider that some of her pseudopodia did not project from her body at all but emerged from the curtain-covered cabinet behind her.

Yet ectoplasmic pseudopodia do seem to have some material substance to them. While Mrs. F. W. H. Myers sat at Eusapia's feet to keep them under observational control, she saw pseudopodia clearly against the ceiling of the room. Evidently the putative ectoplasmic projections interrupted light (probably dim reddish light) reflected off the ceiling of the room. Furthermore, their materiality seemed to be unmistakable when some of them took on the appearance and feel of a human hand and when a cast was made of folded hands with interlaced fingers. The latter case clearly demonstrated that the "ectoplasm" not only became solid enough to support molten wax until it cooled but also melted away and disappeared, leaving a mold to be filled with plaster. From another angle, the work done by Dr. Eugène Osty with Rudi Schneider discovered that whatever was attempting to move the handkerchief psychokinetically was solid enough to break a beam of infrared light.

With these suggestions to guide us, we can speculate that ectoplasm might be studied further in the laboratory to determine whether some sort of dense concentration of air molecules, dust motes or even subatomic particles might be brought about by the physical medium. If so, the pseudopodia under the uncertain control of a medium's psyche would resemble those of an amoeba, even though comprised of matter than is not biological. It would force us to take very seriously Jung's proposal that matter can be influenced through a psychoid principle.

It must be admitted, however, that pseudopodia comprised of ectoplasm constitute only a small part of the psychokinesis mystery. No one saw pseudopodia when musical instruments were played, and pseudopodia are almost unthinkable in the case of Ted Serios' bizarre (but by no means unique) talent for getting images to appear on photographic film. Most importantly, the movement of an amoeba's pseudopodia represents our simplest image of what psychic process can do. At the other end of the spectrum lie human creativity and playfulness; and these, too, belong to the phenomena of PK. Stephen E. Braude would have us "consider the *gracefulness* of a D. D. Home accordion rendition, the *affection* in the touch of a materialized hand, or the *playfulness* or *hostility* of some poltergeist antics" (Braude 1986: 246). He goes on to quote Charles Richet on the "personality" displayed by a table's movement during a séance:

> This lifeless table seems to have a mind; it hesitates, it shows irritation; it affirms energetically; or it sways solemnly. No one who has witnessed such séances can imagine how well diverse sentiments can be expressed by the frequency or the forcefulness, the slow, hesitating, vigorous, or gentle movements. It is an actual language and always interesting.
>
> (Braude 1986: 247)

Just as the mother knows it is her *son's* elation—not her own, not her daughter's, not her husband's—so spontaneous PK events manifest distinct "personality traits." It is clear that a psyche is behind them. Braude (1986) highlights these matters to argue that bottom-up arguments based in the mechanical theories of chemistry and physics will never do justice to psychokinesis. Only an explanation that grants these phenomena the full quirky individuality of a human psyche will satisfy us.

On the other hand, the relationship between the medium's state of mind and the PK effect is by no means obvious. The most common hypothesis is what Braude calls the "copy theory": the idea that the cause of the PK event arises from some intention or desire in the mind of the medium, and that the event itself "copies" that mental content.

The first difficulty with the copy theory is that the medium's mental state is impossible to specify: the number of mental contents and their variety in any moment will be immense. The medium herself will not be able to catalogue fully even those that are conscious, while those that are unconscious are presumably even more varied and numerous (Braude 1986: 229–41). A second problem is the fact that an individual's consciousness fluctuates constantly. Although it can be regulated to some extent by focusing attention and by achieving altered states, a steady focus of consciousness is rare and often fragile. A third issue is the whimsical nature of most PK phenomena. As we noted in the case of Ted Serios' "thoughtography," the images had the unpredictable, absurd and outright playful character of dreams. Ingo Swann captures some of the feel of this "unreliability" in parapsychology when he says of remote viewing, "The cultivation of ESP is an *artistic* performance" (Swann 1987: 72).

A fourth factor in the uncertain relation between the mind of the medium and PK effects is the consciousness of the group. Everyone has had the experience of moving from one group of people to another and finding an immense difference in openness, warmth, suspicion, anxiety, and the like. Every group takes on a unique character, and with cooperation can to some extent become a sort of super-psyche in which each individual participates. A medium will feel these forces, too, and find that the quality of psychic performance changes with the group, resulting in unpredictable psychokinetic effects.

Finally, it has often been argued that the neural activity of the brain constitutes a complex, chaotic system that resembles the uncertainty of the quantum field. According to quantum uncertainty, any particle can pop into existence at any time. Consequently, the wave state is described as an elaborate "superposition," where every one of the diverse possibilities exists simultaneously until something causes one of them to "collapse" into a unique event. Similarly, countless neural networks are simultaneously activated in every moment and eventually (guided by a basin of attraction) "collapse" into a unique brain state with a characteristic content. Probably such a collapse manifests a momentary decision of the supra-ordinate psyche. If so, the brain's collapse into order clearly resembles the collapse of the chaotic quantum sea when an experiment is performed to determine whether a photon is a particle or a wave. The psychoid factor in the quantum experiment emerges when the scientist poses the question. The psychoid factor in the psychokinesis event engages either the supraordinate psyche of the medium or is the result of some psychological situation constellated in the group psyche of the séance participants which induces a "collapse" in the medium's brain-state, or their own.

In any event, the uncertainty is impenetrable. All we can say for sure is that psychokinesis describes changes in material reality that are in some way guided by psychoid influences originating in one or more human psyches.

The rose chafer

It is interesting to speculate about what happened in Jung's primary example of synchronicity: the moment when the rose chafer tapped on his office window while his rigid "Cartesian" analysand recounted her dream of a golden scarab. Recalling that Jung once wondered to Pauli whether psyche might cast a spell on matter or matter bewitch psyche, we note that the rose chafer problem ought to be easier to conjure with. Insects have psyches—far more elaborate than those of amoebas. Thus it falls within the realm of plausibility that an insect may be responsive to non-local events in other psyches. Insects are not responsive to human language, nor do they have a limbic system, eliminating that sort of resonance. Dogs and cats may understand a few words ("walk," "eat," "Fido"), and they certainly manifest limbic responsiveness (reacting to our moods, disappearing in time to miss an appointment with the veterinarian). It would be hard to attribute a responsiveness anything like that to a beetle. But Jung's office, we might speculate, was filled with the idea and image of a glorious golden and deeply meaningful scarab at the time of the tapping. It was probably the transcendent ideal of "beetle-ness." Is it too much to imagine that such an alignment between two supraordinate human psyches might exert a draw upon the psyche of a rose chafer that just happened to be at work near the window? Surely it causes fewer problems for our left brains than the phenomena of ectoplasm.

*   *   *   *   *

In *Volume 1* of *Jung in the 21st Century*, we accepted provisionally and for strategic reasons today's standard doctrine that psyche and brain are identical. This allowed us to review such fields as evolutionary psychology, evolutionary biology, archaeology, anthropology, neurobiology and ethology and demonstrate that Jung's theories of a century ago are remarkably prescient and judiciously articulated. They are consilient with what science has discovered in the highly productive half-century it has enjoyed since his death. Jung appears to be more relevant now than he has ever been. In *Volume 2* we took up psyche's non-local traits and found that psyche cannot be identical with the brain. We found that the non-local and acausal doctrine of synchronicity not only makes room for parapsychology but also brings the long neglected phenomena of life, consciousness and intentionality into our picture of what is real. Some variation on Jung and Pauli's synchronicity hypothesis may eventually prove valuable for quantum mechanics and astrophysics.

We have covered an immense territory. No one on Earth could possibly master all the fields of study we have touched upon. Thus we have imitated Jung who moaned that he was "the most accursed of dilettantes."

My aim in this enormous intellectual journey has not been to give final answers but to suggest a myriad of valuable investigations that remain to be made and to show that they share in a single coherent vision, the pursuit of a reliable and comprehensive picture of the human psyche.

Notes

1 Jung's challenge to science

1 Rossi, E. (1988) "Non-locality in Physics and Psychology: An Interview with John Stewart Bell." *Psychological Perspectives* 19(2): 294–319. See p. 306.

2 Jung on the mastery of altered states

1 I have discussed the technique of using the transcendent function to achieve unitive states of consciousness at great length and in rather different language in my book on St. Francis of Assisi (Haule 2004).

3 The nature of shamanism

1 *Šaman*: "to know rapturously"; "one who is excited" (N. W. Smith 1992: 33).
2 Quoting British anthropologist Graham Townsley in 1993, who lived among the Yaminachua people of the Peruvian Amazon.
3 It was enlarged and translated into English in 1964. That it is still the only worldwide survey is supported by Narby (1999: 16).
4 Daniel C. Noel (1997: Chapter 3) makes this case most convincingly by showing the parallels between Eliade's (1964) book on shamanism and the novel he was writing at the same time, *The Forbidden Forest*.
5 V. P. and R. G. Wasson (1957) *Mushrooms, Russia and History*; R. G. Wasson, A. Hofmann and C. A. P. Ruck (1978) *The Road to Eleusis: Unveiling the Secret of the Mysteries*; R. G. Wasson (1980) *The Wondrous Mushroom: Mycolatry in Mesoamerica*.
6 He often describes it in terms of the "triune brain": (a) the "reptilian brain," with its reflexes and conditioned responses; (b) the limbic system of the "paleo-mammalian brain," with its capacity for emotion, non-verbal processing of social behavior, bonding behaviors, and the like; and (c) the "neo-mammalian brain," located in the advanced neocortex, which is capable of culture, language, logic, and complex problem solving (Winkelman 2000: 30–7).
7 Janet (1903) was apparently the last book of Janet's that Jung read. It opened Janet's study of a hierarchical psyche, which he pursued until his death. Some of the most obviously "evolutionary" pretensions of the project were not specified until the 1920s, in the courses he taught at the Collège de France. Shorthand notes were taken, and the lectures published in the form of a series of books (cf. Haule 1983, 1984).
8 Winkelman does not spell out how such reorganizing of the human brain-and-psyche can be part of evolution. I think we should not take the claim to be Lamarckian, however, i.e. believing that early shamans reorganized their own brains and those of their fellow tribesmen and that these achievements went on to be inherited. Rather, we

may employ Stephen Jay Gould's notion of the "spandrel"—also a part of the medieval cathedral that Mithen favors—which concerns the triangular structures that result from founding a dome upon a rectangular base. It is not intended in itself, but is necessary to the structure and can be used in a variety of ways. Thus, in evolution, a spandrel is an aspect of anatomy or physiology that can be variously mastered and employed by the individuals of a species. Again and again in the course of human history, shamans, yogis, and others have discovered the spandrel of ASC capability and learned how to use it (cf. Gould 2002: 1280f).

4 Mastery of shamanic states of consciousness

1   Citing Husserl's *Cartesian Meditations* (1913: 25f).
2   "Perhaps this saying ['Make the fixed volatile and the volatile fixed'] lies at the root of the word 'spagyric,' from *spáein*, 'to tear,' and *ageírein*, 'to collect'" (*CW14*: ¶685, n. 91).

5 Shamanic mastery: Ayahuasqueros in the Amazon

1   Curandera means a woman who cures. The distinction between shamans and curande-ras is fuzzy, but generally a curandera is thought to be less powerful than a shaman.
2   Strassman (2001) lists one other DMT moment, a favorite hypothesis of his: the moment when the pineal body is formed in the fetus. He calls it "the moment when our individual life force enters our fetal body," and notes it is the forty-ninth day of fetal development, the day that the Tibetan Book of the Dead says that the soul of the deceased enters a new fetus for its next incarnation.
3   By a "natural cognitive domain" he means something that (1) is a cognitive expression of the human mind (2) occurs naturally and spontaneously, (3) is not shared by other domains, (4) every expression of that domain is straightforwardly a member of that domain, (5) the totality of the types belonging to the domain is distinct, and (6) the domain manifests intrinsic regularities and substantial richness and complexity (Shanon 2002: 33).
4   Devereux (1997) *The Long Trip: A Prehistory of Psychedelia*, cited in Wilcox (2003: 48). Other proponents of this view include Dennis and Terrence McKenna, Marlene Dobkin de Rios, Daniel Pinchbeck, and Jeremy Narby.
5   I have heard this attribution but never found documentation for it. Nevertheless, it seems an apt description of intuition.
6   It is always difficult to tell how much interpretation Lamb is applying to Córdoba's testimony. The language in this quotation sounds quite Western.
7   Both the attacks and their healing are described in terms of "darts" (*virotes*) that are cast into an individual by a vengeful shaman to cause sickness. It is said (and seen in visions) that these darts are derived from magic phlegm (*yachay*), "the quintessence of the spirit" which "grows inside the body" and is a "subtle manifestation of the spirits." The shaman who extracts such darts, draws them into his or her own phlegm. Here is yet another realm of manipulation and mastery while in altered states of consciousness (Luna 1986: 110–16).

6 Meditation and mastery

1   Hunt (1995) cites Eliade (1964) and Bourguignon (1973).
2   Nevertheless, Strassman points out that standing waves can be established in the brain during meditation; these waves can cause vibrations in the pineal gland that "weaken its barriers to DMT formation" resulting in a "psychedelic surge" (Strassman 2001: 74f). A very similar argument, together with the evidence to support it, has been made

concerning the experience of kundalini achieved through yogic disciplines and some-times spontaneously (Sannella 1992).

3 "Corby and colleagues (1978) found that the more advanced the meditator, the more actively alert he was during meditation as indicated by measures of skin conductance, frequency of GSR (Galvanic skin response), heart rate, and EEG sleep scoring" (Laughlin *et al.* 1990: 310).

4 The very illusion that Buddhism seeks to free us from.

5 Very likely the crisis experience in near-death and alien-abduction experiences—not to mention this woman's fright—stimulates the pineal gland to product DMT.

6 "He who performs a prescribed action because it ought to be done, abandoning attach-ment and the fruit [of that action], that abandonment, O Arjuna, is thought to be *sattvic* ['spiritual,' 'truthful']."

7 Tri-Shikhi-Brāhmana-Upanishad (II.31).

8 It also corresponds to the view of Sufism's "Greatest Sheikh," Ibn al-'Arabī, who claimed, on the basis of his mystical experience, that God creates the world anew in every instant (Corbin 1969).

9 The Sanskrit term is *ākāsha*, which originally meant "radiance," especially the radi-ance of the Self, which shines like a thousand suns, but has also come to mean the fifth substance (along with earth, air, fire, and water), namely "ether" (Feuerstein 1990).

Part II The border zones of exact science

1 "Between the scornfully skeptical and the eagerly superstitious": this is how Frederic W. H. Myers described his work as an investigating member of the Society for Psychical Research (SPR) in 1894 (quoted in Sheldrake 2003: 71).

7 The lawful irrationality of synchronicity

1 Jung (1958) *Flying Saucers: A Modern Myth* (*CW10*: ¶589–824).

2 For a fuller treatment of this material and what it means, practically, in analytic prac-tice, see Haule (1999c).

3 Historian of the occult Colin Wilson goes to far as to accuse Jung of lying about acau-sality. He says there is causality there, all right, but Jung does not want to admit it. Having thereby eliminated the hard part, Wilson has opened himself a path to demon-strate what a crackpot Jung really was (C. Wilson 1984: 113–16).

4 Zener cards were invented jointly by Rhine and Karl Zener at Duke University in 1930. Charles Richet of the "French School" of dissociation psychology had used similar cards in the same way as early as 1884 (Guiley 1991). The five Zener designs consist of bold line-drawings of a square, a circle, a plus sign, a five-pointed star, and a set of wavy lines.

5 Jung tells Pauli that the idea of absolute knowledge came to him while reading Hans Driesch (1867-1941), the founder of experimental embryology. The study of the drastic and amazing changes an embryo undergoes seemed quite miraculous in the days before molecular biology. No doubt the observations Driesch made in his labora-tory led him to doubt the foundations of Western science, for he eventually rejected the mechanistic view of science (billiard balls) and embraced a *vitalistic* philosophy (the idea that there is some sort of "life principle" that accounts for the difference between living and non-living beings and that drives the living process). Jung asserts to Pauli his resistance to vitalism, but is interested in Driesch's later work in para-psychology (*PJL*: 133).

6 "*Die Erdbedingtheit der Psyche.*" In a later version (1931), he called it "The Structure of the Psyche."

7 Schopenhauer had proposed that an unconscious "will" drives everything.

8   There are, in fact, more than sixty-four types of moment, in that many nuances of each are possible. I have decided not to complicate the description by distinguishing, for instance, between "young yin" and "old yin," etc.
9   The argument is heavily indebted to Dusek (1999).

9 Seeing at a distance and its mastery

1   Gardner Murphy's "Foreword" to Warcollier (1948/2001: xxxvi).
2   By "insects," Warcollier presumably means ants, bees, and termites, the "social insects." We might wonder, though, whether the communication is as "mental" with insects as it is with mammals, since research in the decades since Warcollier's death shows that much, if not all, insect communication occurs through chemicals (pheromones).
3   This paragraph is culled from G. Murphy's "Foreword" and Ingo Swann's "Preface" (Warcollier 1948/2001: xiii–xxxix).
4   One thinks of Jung's advice to therapists to learn all they can and then to forget it when they sit down with their patient.
5   Decades later, he founded a Monroe Institute in Virginia where would-be out-of-body journeyers are supplied with headphones that deliver tones of different frequency to the right and left ears, in an effort to draw the brain into integrated functioning (Monroe 1994). I have discussed Monroe's project and what it means for human consciousness at some length in Haule (1999a).
6   Dictionaries of yoga describe pranayama as any of a number of breathing exercises. Probably Brown's use of the term refers to the practice of manually closing one nostril and then the other.

10 Psychokinesis: mind and matter

1   Jung: "[Maybe] psyche casts a spell on mass . . . or mass bewitches psyche, [but more likely, in] a so-called numinous moment, [the psychoid archetype] causes a joint field of tension" (*PJL*: 62f).
2   For a much fuller discussion of this issue, see Haule 1999b: Chapter 8.

12 Darwin's dilemma: evolution needs a psychoid principle

1   Particularly the notion of "creative duration" (*CW6*: ¶330, 362, 540; *CW8*: ¶278; *CW10*: ¶312; *CW18*: ¶266). As regards Jung's preference for theories that put flux at the center of their description of reality—despite the often static-seeming nature of his own constructs—Heraclitus is perhaps most frequently cited.
2   See *CW8*: ¶937; *CW9i*: ¶278, 282; *CW11*: ¶960; *CW12*: ¶248; *CW13*: ¶248.
3   E.g. *CW6*: ¶790f; *CW9i*: ¶572; *CW9ii*: ¶237; *CW10*: ¶622, 806; *CW13*: ¶457n.
4   The authors clearly subscribe to Stephen Jay Gould and Niles Eldredge's very persuasive theory of "punctuated equilibrium" (Gould 2002: 37). In my view, their new theory of "facilitated novelty" might be described as an exploration of "molecular spandrels"—noting how a molecule that made one change possible in the past can be used again in the future for a variety of others.

13 Sketches of a universal psychoid field

1   Sheldrake says that the magnetism hypothesis was first raised in 1855 and tested vigorously in the 1970s and 1980s, when it was thoroughly disproved. But the idea has not died in "folk science." "Many scientifically informed people will say that [homing behavior] has all been explained in terms of magnetism but won't 'remember the details'" (Sheldrake 2002: 50).

2   Janet (1919) was concerned with the future of hypnosis, which had suffered a severe
     blow to its prestige when it was discovered that Charcot's assistants had inadvertently
     been training his hypnotic subjects with suggestions. Janet believed that hypnosis was
     still a valuable tool, if only the hypnotist were clever enough to avoid giving unwanted
     suggestions.

> We are concerned here with a problem analogous to those which Pasteur had to face
> in connection with his earlier investigations in the matter of pure cultures and spon-
> taneous generation. . . . In the end, a good many investigators abandoned their
> researches rather than take the trouble to keep their cultures pure.

> (Janet 1919: 797)

14 Vision and Reality

1   "*On ne travaille pas, on écoute, c'est comme un inconnu qui vous parle à l'oreille.*"
2   Consider the story in Chapter 9 of the vixen who silently controlled her kits by staring
     intently at them when they began to stray too far from safety.
3   Quoted from the transcript of a talk given by Jill Bolte Taylor. The film of the talk and
     transcript can be seen at www.ted.com/talks/view/id/229. She gives a fuller account in
     My Stroke of Insight: A Brain Scientist's Personal Journey (Taylor 2006: 37–46).
4   Such, in effect, is the proposal of William A. Tiller (1997), Emeritus Professor of
     Materials Science at Stanford University. He argues that "magnons," presently undis-
     covered magnetic particles carrying a primitive form of emotion at speeds many orders
     of magnitude faster than the speed of light, account for part of our ability to send and
     receive telepathic messages. In his view, what Jung calls synchronicity is not immedi-
     ate and non-local, but a genuine transmission that simply travels too fast to be detected
     (Tiller 1997).
5   See, for instance, John Briggs and F. David Peat (1984), Fred Alan Wolf (1994), Amit
     Goswami (1993), and William A. Tiller (1997).

References

Aldhouse-Green, M. and Aldhouse-Green, S. (2005) *The Quest for the Shaman: Shape-Shifters, Sorcerers and Spirit-Helpers of Ancient Europe.* London: Thames & Hudson.

Allman, J. M. (1999) *Evolving Brains.* New York: Scientific American Library.

Ball, P. (2008) "Cellular Memory Hints at the Origins of Intelligence," *Nature 451*: 385.

Barnard, G. W. (1998) "William James and the Origins of Mystical Experience," in R. K. C. Forman (ed.) *The Innate Capacity: Mysticism, Psychology and Philosophy.* New York: Oxford University Press, 161–210.

Baynes, M. (1977) "A Talk with Students at the Institute," in W. McGuire and R. F. C. Hull (eds) *C. G. Jung Speaking: Interviews and Encounters.* Princeton, NJ: Princeton University Press, 360–1.

Bennet, E. A. (1985) *Meetings with Jung.* Zurich: Daimon.

Bergson, H. (1911) *Creative Evolution*, trans. A. Mineola. New York: Dover, 1989.

Blum, D. (2006) *Ghost Hunters: William James and the Search for Scientific Proof of Life After Death.* New York: Penguin.

Bourguignon, E. (1973) "Introduction: A Framework for the Comparative Study of Altered States of Consciousness," in E. Bourguignon (ed.) *Religion, Altered States of Consciousness, and Social Change.* Columbus, OH: Ohio State University Press, 3–35.

Braude, S. E. (1986) *The Limits of Influence: Psychokinesis and the Philosophy of Science.* New York: Routledge.

Briggs, J. P. and Peat, F. D. (1984) *Looking Glass Universe: The Emerging Science of Wholeness.* New York: Simon & Schuster.

Brown, C. (1999) *Cosmic Explorers: Scientific Remote Viewing, Extraterrestrials, and a Message for Mankind.* New York: Dutton.

Calloway, J. E. (1999) "Phytochemistry and Neuropharmacology of Ayahuasca," in R. Metzner (ed.) *Ayahuasca: Hallucinogens, Consciousness, and the Spirit of Nature.* New York: Thunder Mouth, 250–75.

Carroll, S. B. (2005) *Endless Forms Most Beautiful: The New Science of Evo Devo and the Making of the Animal Kingdom.* New York: W. W. Norton.

Charet, F. X. (1993) *Spiritualism and the Foundations of C. G. Jung's Psychology.* Albany, NY: SUNY Press.

Corbin, H. (1969) *Creative Imagination in the Sufism of Ibn 'Arabi*, trans. R. Manheim. Princeton, NJ: Bollingen.

Crabtree, A. (1993) *From Mesmer to Freud: Magnetic Sleep and the Roots of Psychological Healing.* New Haven, CT: Yale University Press.

d'Aquili, E. G. and Laughlin, C. D., Jr. (1979) "The Neurobiology of Myth and Ritual," in E. G. d'Aquili, C. D. Laughlin, Jr., and J. McManus, with T. Burns *et al.*, *The Spectrum of Ritual: A Biogenetic Structural Analysis*. New York: Columbia University Press, 152–82.

d'Aquili, E. G. and Newberg, A. B. (1999) *The Mystical Mind: Probing the Biology of Religious Experience*. Minneapolis, MN: Fortress.

de Quincey, C. (2002) *Radical Nature: Rediscovering the Soul of Matter*. Montpelier, VT: Invisible Cities.

Devereux, P. (1997) *The Long Trip: A Prehistory of Psychedelia*. New York: Penguin Arkana.

Dobkin de Rios, M. (1990) *Hallucinogens: Cross-Cultural Perspectives*. Bridport, UK: Prism.

Dossey, L. (1999) *Reinventing Medicine: Beyond Mind-Body to a New Era of Healing*. San Francisco, CA: HarperSanFrancisco.

Dusek, V. (1999) *The Holistic Inspirations of Physics: The Underground History of Electromagnetic Theory*. New Brunswick, NJ: Rutgers.

Dyczkowski, M. S. G. (1987) *The Doctrine of Vibration: An Analysis of the Doctrines and Practices of Kashmir Shaivism*. Albany, NY: SUNY Press.

Eisenbud, J. (1967) *The World of Ted Serios: "Thoughtographic" Studies of an Extraordinary Mind*. New York: William Morrow.

Eliade, M. (1964) *Shamanism: Archaic Techniques of Ecstasy*, trans. W. R. Trask. New York: Pantheon/Bollingen.

Eliade, M. (1969) *Yoga, Immortality and Freedom*, trans. W. R. Trask. Princeton, NJ: Princeton/Bollingen.

Factor, D. (ed.) (1985) *Unfolding Meaning: A Weekend of Dialogue with David Bohm*. Mickleton, UK: Foundation House.

Fagan, B. (1998) *From Black Land to Fifth Sun: The Science of Sacred Sites*. New York: Basic Books.

Favret-Saada, J. (1980) *Deadly Words: Witchcraft in the Bocage*, trans. C. Cullen. Cambridge: Cambridge University Press.

Feilding, E. (1963) *Sittings with Eusapia Palladino and Other Studies*. Hyde Park, NY: University Books.

Feuerstein, G. (1990) *Encyclopedic Dictionary of Yoga*. New York: Paragon.

Feuerstein, G., Kak, S., and Frawley, D. (1995) *In Search of the Cradle of Civilization: New Light on Ancient India*. Wheaton, IL: Quest.

Fischer-Schreiber, I., Ehrhard, F.-K., Friedrichs, K., and Diener, M. S. (eds) (1989) *The Encyclopedia of Eastern Philosophy and Religion*. Boston, MA: Shambhala.

Flaherty, G. (1992) *Shamanism and the Eighteenth Century*. Princeton, NJ: Princeton University Press.

Freeman, W. J. (1995) *Societies of Brains: A Study in the Neuroscience of Love and Hate*. Hillsdale, NJ: Lawrence Erlbaum Associates.

Freeman, W. J. (2000) *How Brains Make Up their Minds*. New York: Columbia University Press.

Gauld, A. (1968) *The Founders of Psychical Research*. London: Routledge & Kegan Paul.

Goleman, D. (1995) *Emotional Intelligence*. New York: Bantam.

Goswami, A., with Reed, R. E. and Goswami, M. (1993) *The Self-Aware Universe: How Consciousness Creates the Material World*. New York: Tarcher/Putnam.

Gould, S. J. (2002) *The Structure of Evolutionary Theory*. Cambridge, MA: Harvard University Press.

Gould, S. J. (2007) *The Richness of Life: The Essential Stephen Jay Gould*, ed. S. Rose. New York: W. W. Norton.

Goulet, J.-G. (1998) "Dreams and Visions in Other Lifeworlds," in D. E. Young and J.-G. Goulet (eds) *Being Changed by Cross-Cultural Encounters: The Anthropology of Extraordinary Experience*. Peterborough, ONT: Broadview, 16–38.

Grant, C. (1967) *Rock Art of the American Indian*. New York: Promontory Press.

Gray, J. (2002) *Straw Dogs: Thoughts on Humans and Other Animals*. London: Granta.

Gregory, A. (1985) *The Strange Case of Rudi Schneider*. Metuchen, NJ: Scarecrow.

Griffin, D. R. (1997) *Parapsychology, Philosophy, and Spirituality: A Postmodern Exploration*. Albany, NY: SUNY Press.

Grob, C. S. (1999) "The Psychology of Ayahuasca," in R. Metzner (ed.) *Ayahuasca: Hallucinogens, Consciousness, and the Spirit of Nature*. New York: Thunder Mouth, 214–49.

Grof, S., with Bennet, H. Z. (1992) *The Holotropic Mind: The Three Levels of Human Consciousness and How They Shape our Lives*. San Francisco, CA: HarperSanFrancisco.

Guédon, M. F. (1998) "Dene Ways and the Ethnographer's Culture," in D. E. Young and J.-G. Goulet (eds) *Being Changed by Cross-Cultural Encounters: The Anthropology of Extraordinary Experience*. Peterborough, ONT: Broadview, 39–70.

Guiley, R. E. (1991) *Harper's Encyclopedia of Mystical and Paranormal Experience*. San Francisco, CA: HarperSanFrancisco.

Hannah, B. (1976) *Jung: His Life and Work*. New York: G. G. Putnam's Sons.

Hansel, C. E. M. (1980) *ESP and Parapsychology: A Critical Re-Evaluation*. Buffalo, NY: Prometheus.

Harner, M. (1972) *The Jívaro: People of the Sacred Waterfalls*. Berkeley, CA: University of California Press.

Harner, M. (ed.) (1973) *Hallucinogens and Shamanism*. New York: Oxford University Press.

Haule, J. R. (1983) "Archetype and Integration: Exploring the Janetian Roots of Analytical Psychology," *Journal of Analytical Psychology* 28(3): 253–67.

Haule, J. R. (1984) "From Somnambulism to the Archetypes: The French Roots of Jung's Split with Freud," *Psychoanalytic Review* 71(4): 635–59.

Haule, J. R. (1990) *Divine Madness: Archetypes of Romantic Love*. Boston, MA: Shambhala.

Haule, J. R. (1993) *Bushwhacking Through Narcissism: The Making of a Jungian Analyst*, available at www.jrhaule.net/bushwhack.html (accessed May 28, 2010).

Haule, J. R. (1999a) *Perils of the Soul: Ancient Wisdom and the New Age*. York Beach, ME: Weiser.

Haule, J. R. (1999b) *Indecent Practices and Erotic Trance: Making Sense of Tantra*, available at www.jrhaule.net/ipet.html (accessed May 28, 2010).

Haule, J. R. (1999c) "Analyzing from the Self: An Empirical Phenomenology of the Third in Analysis," in R. Brooke (ed.) *Pathways into the Jungian World*. London: Routledge, 255–72.

Haule, J. R. (2004) *The Ecstasies of St. Francis: The Way of Lady Poverty*. Great Barrington, MA: Lindisfarne.

Hayden, B. (2003) *Shamans, Sorcerers, and Saints: A Prehistory of Religion*. Washington, DC: Smithsonian Books.

Hobson, J. A. (2002) *Dreaming: An Introduction to the Science of Sleep*. Oxford: Oxford University Press.

Hobson, J. A. (2005) *Thirteen Dreams Freud Never Had: The New Mind Science*. New York: Pi Science.

Hunt, H. T. (1995) *On the Nature of Consciousness: Cognitive, Phenomenological, and Transpersonal Perspectives*. New Haven, CT: Yale University Press.

Husserl, E. (1913) *Ideas: General Introduction to Pure Phenomenology*, trans. W. R. B. Gibson. London: Collier-Macmillan, 1962.

Janet, P. (1903) *Les Obsessions et la psychasthénie*, two volumes. New York: Arno, 1976.

Janet, P. (1919) *Psychological Healing: A Historical and Clinical Study*, two volumes, trans. unknown, 1925. New York: Arno, 1976.

Jordan, P. (2001) "The Materiality of Shamanism as a 'World-View': Praxis, Artifacts and Landscape," in N. S. Price (ed.) *The Archaeology of Shamanism*. New York: Routledge, 87–104.

Jung, C. G.: see Abbreviations page (p. vii this volume).

Kafatos, M. and Nadeau, R. (1990) *The Conscious Universe: Part and Whole in Modern Physical Theory*. New York: Springer.

Kenrick, D. T. (2006) "A Dynamical Evolutionary View of Love," in R. J. Sternberg and K. Weis (eds) *The New Psychology of Love*. New Haven, CT: Yale University Press, 15–34.

Kirschner, M. W. and Gerhart, J. C. (2005) *The Plausibility of Life: Resolving Darwin's Dilemma*, New Haven, CT: Yale University Press.

LaBarre, W. (1970) *The Ghost Dance: The Origins of Religion*. New York: Dell.

Lamb, F. B. (1985) *Rio Tigre and Beyond: The Amazon Jungle Medicine of Manual Cordova*. Berkeley, CA: North Atlantic.

Laughlin, C. D., Jr., McManus, J. and d'Aquili, E. G. (1990) *Brain, Symbol, and Experience: Toward a Neurophenomenology of Human Consciousness*. Boston, MA: Shambhala.

Le Clair, R. C. (1966) *The Letters of William James and Theodore Flournoy*. Madison, WI: University of Wisconsin Press.

Lévi-Strauss, C. (1966) *The Savage Mind*. Chicago, IL: University of Chicago Press.

Lévy-Bruhl, L. (1922) *Primitive Mentality*, trans. L. A. Clare. Boston, MA: Beacon, 1966.

Lewis, T., Amini, F. and Lannon, R. (2000) *A General Theory of Love*. New York: Vintage.

Lewis-Williams, D. and Dowson, T. (1989) *Images of Power: Understanding Bushman Rock Art*, 2nd edition. Cape Town: Struik.

Lewis-Williams, D. and Pearce, D. (2005) *Inside the Neolithic Mind: Consciousness, Cosmos and the Realm of the Gods*. London: Thames & Hudson.

Lex, B. (1979) "The Neurobiology of Ritual Trance," in E. G. d'Aquili, C. D. Laughlin, Jr., and J. McManus, with T. Burns *et al.*, *The Spectrum of Ritual: A Biogenetic Structural Analysis*. New York: Columbia University Press, 117–51.

Libet, B. (2004) *Mind Time: The Temporal Factor in Consciousness*. Cambridge, MA: Harvard University Press.

Lindorff, D. (2004) *Pauli and Jung: The Meeting of Two Great Minds*. Wheaton, IL: Quest.

Lovelock, J. E. (1979) *Gaia: A New Look at Life on Earth*. Oxford: Oxford University Press.

Lovelock, J. E. (1988) *The Ages of Gaia: A Biography of our Living on Earth*. New York: W. W. Norton.

Lovelock, J. E. and Allaby, M. (1984) *The Greening of Mars*. New York: Warner.

Luna, L. E. (1986) *Vegetalismo: Shamanism Among the Mestizo Population of the Peruvian Amazon*. Stockholm: Stockholm Studies in Comparative Religion.

Luna, L. E. and Amaringo, P. (1993) *Ayahuasca Visions: The Religious Iconography of a Peruvian Shaman*. Berkeley, CA: North Atlantic.

Mack, J. E. (1994) *Abduction: Human Encounters with Aliens*. New York: Scribner's.

McKenna, D. J. (1999) "Ayahuasca: An Ethnopharmacologic History," in R. Metzner (ed.) *Ayahuasca: Hallucinogens, Consciousness, and the Spirit of Nature*. New York: Thunder Mouth, 187–213.

McManus, J. (1979) "Ritual and Human Social Cognition," in E. G. d'Aquili, C. D. Laughlin, Jr., and J. McManus, with T. Burns *et al.*, *The Spectrum of Ritual: A Biogenetic Structural Analysis*. New York: Columbia University Press, 183–215.

Masters, R. E. L. and Houston, J. (1966) *The Varieties of Psychedelic Experience*. New York: Delta.

Méheust, B. (1999) *Somnambulisme et Médiumnité*, in two volumes. Paris: Les Empêcheurs de Penser en Rond.

Méheust, B. (2003) *Un Voyant Prodigieux: Alexis Didier, 1826–1886*. Paris: Les Empêcheurs de Penser en Rond.

Merkur, D. (1992) *Becoming Half-Hidden: Shamanism and Initiation Among the Inuit*. New York: Garland.

Mesmer, F. A. (1980) *Mesmerism: A Translation of the Original Writings of F. A. Mesmer*, trans. and compiled by G. Bloch. Los Altos, CA: William Kaufman.

Metzner, R. (1999a) "Introduction: Amazonian Vine of Visions," in R. Metzner (ed.) *Ayahuasca: Hallucinogens, Consciousness, and the Spirit of Nature*. New York: Thunder Mouth, 1–45.

Metzner, R. (1999b) "Conclusions, Reflections, and Speculations," in R. Metzner (ed.) *Ayahuasca: Hallucinogens, Consciousness, and the Spirit of Nature*. New York: Thunder Mouth, 276–91.

Mithen, S. (2006) *The Singing Neanderthals: The Origins of Music, Language, Mind, and Body*. Cambridge, MA: Harvard University Press.

Monroe, R. A. (1977) *Journeys Out of the Body*. Garden City, NY: Anchor.

Monroe, R. A. (1985) *Far Journeys*. New York: Doubleday.

Monroe, R. A. (1994) *Ultimate Journey*. New York: Doubleday.

Müller-Ebeling, C., Rätsch, C. and Shahi, S. B. (2002) *Shamanism and Tantra in the Himalayas*, trans. A. Lee. Rochester, VT: Inner Traditions.

Murphy, M. and White, R. A. (1978) *The Psychic Side of Sports*. Reading, MA: Addison-Wesley.

Narby, J. (1999) *The Cosmic Serpent: DNA and the Origins of Knowledge*, trans. J. Narby with J. Christensen. New York: Tarcher.

Narby, J. (2007) "An Anthropologist Explores Biomolecular Mysticism in the Peruvian Amazon," *Shaman's Drum 74*: 43–6.

Narby, J. and Huxley, F. (eds) (2001) *Shamans Through Time: 500 Years on the Path to Knowledge*. New York: Tarcher/Putnam.

Neumann, E. (1949) *The Origins and History of Consciousness*, trans. R. F. C. Hull. Princeton, NJ: Princeton University Press, 1954.

Noel, D. C. (1997) *The Soul of Shamanism: Western Fantasies, Imaginal Realities*. New York: Continuum.

Odajnyk, V. W. (1993) *Gathering the Light: A Psychology of Meditation*. Boston, MA: Shambhala.

Ostrander, S. and Schroeder, L. (1970) *Psychic Discoveries Behind the Iron Curtain*. New York: Prentice-Hall.

Panda, N. C. (1995) *The Vibrating Universe*. Delhi: Motilal Banarsidass.

Patterson-Rudolph, C. (1990) *Petroglyphs and Pueblo Myths of the Rio Grande*. Albuquerque, NM: Avanyu.

Pike, N. (1992) *Mystic Union: An Essay in the Phenomenology of Mysticism*. Ithaca, NY: Cornell.

Pinchbeck, D. (2002) *Breaking Open the Head: A Psychedelic Journey into the Heart of Contemporary Shamanism*. New York: Broadway.

Price, N. S. (2001) "An Archaeology of Altered States: Shamanism and Material Culture Studies," in N. S. Price (ed.) *The Archaeology of Shamanism*. New York: Routledge, 3–16.

Radin, D. (1997) *The Conscious Universe: The Scientific Truth of Psychic Phenomena*. San Francisco, CA: Harper Edge.

Reichel-Dolmatoff, G. (1971) *Amazonian Cosmos: The Sexual and Religious Symbolism of the Tukano Indians*. Chicago, IL: University of Chicago Press.

Reichel-Dolmatoff, G. (1975) *The Shaman and the Jaguar: A Study of Narcotic Drugs Among the Indians of Colombia*. Philadelphia, PA: Temple University Press.

Reichel-Dolmatoff, G. (1987) *Shamanism and Art of the Eastern Tukanoan Indians*. Leiden: E. J. Brill.

Reichel-Dolmatoff, G. (1997) *Rainforest Shamans: Essays on the Tukano Indians of the Northwest Amazon*. Totnes, UK: Foxhole.

Ripinsky-Naxon, M. (1993) *The Nature of Shamanism: Substance and Function of a Religious Metaphor*. Albany, NY: SUNY Press.

Rose, R. (1956) *Living Magic: The Realities Underlying the Psychical Practices and Beliefs of Australian Aborigines*. New York: Rand McNally.

Rozwadowski, A. (2001) "Sun Gods or Shamans? Interpreting the 'Solar-Headed' Petroglyphs of Western Siberia," in N. S. Price (ed.) *The Archaeology of Shamanism*. New York: Routledge, 65–86.

Samorini, G. (2000) *Animals and Psychedelics: The Natural World and the Instinct to Alter Consciousness*, trans. T. Calliope. Rochester, VT: Park Street.

Sannella, L. (1992) *The Kundalini Experience: Psychosis or Transcendence?* Lower Lake, CA: Integral.

Sarles, H. B. (1985) *Language and Human Nature*. Minneapolis, MN: University of Minnesota.

Schnabel, J. (1997) *Remote Viewers: The Secret History of America's Psychic Spies*. New York: Dell.

Searles, H. F. (1979) *Countertransference and Related Subjects*. New York: International Universities.

Shamdasani, S. (2003) *Jung and the Making of Modern Psychology: The Dream of a Science*. Cambridge: Cambridge University Press.

Shanon, B. (2002) *The Antipodes of the Mind: Charting the Phenomenology of the Ayahuasca Experience*. Oxford: Oxford University Press.

Sheldrake, R. (1992) *The Rebirth of Nature: The Greening of Science and God*. New York: Bantam.

Sheldrake, R. (1995) *The Presence of the Past: Morphic Resonance and the Habits of Nature*. Rochester, VT: Park Street.

Sheldrake, R. (2002) *Seven Experiments that Could Change the World: A Do-It-Yourself Guide to Revolutionary Science*. Rochester, VT: Park Street.

Sheldrake, R. (2003) *The Sense of Being Stared At and Other Aspects of the Extended Mind*. New York: Crown.

Siegel, D. J. (1999) *The Developing Mind: How Relationships and the Brain Interact to Shape Who We Are.* New York: Guilford.

Siegel, R. K. (1989) *Intoxication: Life in Pursuit of Artificial Paradise.* New York: Pocket Books.

Sinclair, U. (1930) *Mental Radio.* New York: Collier.

Smith, J. M. and Szathmáry, E. (1999) *The Origins of Life: From the Birth of Life to the Origin of Language.* Oxford: Oxford University Press.

Smith, N. W. (1992) *An Analysis of Ice Age Art: Its Psychology and Belief System.* New York: Peter Lang.

Spiegelman, J. M. (1982) "Memory of C. G. Jung," in F. Jensen (ed.) *C. G. Jung, Emma Jung, and Toni Wolff.* San Francisco, CA: Analytical Psychology Club of San Francisco, 87–9.

Strassman, R. (2001) *DMT: The Spirit Molecule.* Rochester, VT: Park Street.

Swann, I. (1987) *Natural ESP: The ESP Core and its Raw Characteristics.* New York: Bantam.

Targ, R. (2004) *Limitless Mind: A Guide to Remote Viewing and Transformation of Consciousness.* Novato, CA: New World Library.

Targ, R. and Puthoff, H. E. (2005) *Mind-Reach: Scientists Look at Psychic Abilities.* Charlottesville, VA: Hampton Road.

Taussig, M. (1987) *Shamanism, Colonialism, and the Wild Man: A Study in Terror and Healing.* Chicago, IL: University of Chicago Press.

Taylor, J. B. (2006) *My Stroke of Insight: A Brain Scientist's Personal Journey.* New York: Viking.

Teilhard de Chardin, P. (1959) *The Phenomenon of Man*, trans. B. Wall. New York: HarperCollins, 2002.

Thain, M. and Hickman, M. (eds) (2000) *The Penguin Dictionary of Biology*, 10th edition. London: Penguin.

Tiller, W. A. (1997) *Science and Human Transformation: Subtle Energies, Intentionality and Consciousness.* Walnut Creek, CA: Pavior.

Turner, E. (1998) "A Visible Spirit Form in Zambia," in D. E. Young and J.-G. Goulet (eds) *Being Changed by Cross-Cultural Encounters: The Anthropology of Extraordinary Experience.* Peterborough, ONT: Broadview, 71–95.

Turner, J. S. (2007) *The Tinkerer's Accomplice: How Design Emerges from Life Itself.* Cambridge, MA: Harvard University Press.

Vitebsky, P. (1995) *The Shaman.* Boston, MA: Little, Brown.

Waddington, C. H. (1957) *The Strategy of the Genes: A Discussion of Some Aspects of Theoretical Biology.* London: Allen & Unwin.

Wallace, B. A. (2007) *Contemplative Science: Where Buddhism and Neuroscience Converge.* New York: Columbia University Press.

Walsh, R. N. (1990) *The Spirit of Shamanism.* Los Angeles, CA: Tarcher.

Warcollier, R. (1948/2001) *Mind to Mind.* Charlottesville, VA: Hampton Road.

Wasson, R. G. (1980) *The Wondrous Mushroom: Mycolatry in Mesoamerica.* New York: McGraw-Hill.

Wasson, R. G., Hofmann, A. and Ruck, C. A. P. (1978) *The Road to Eleusis: Unveiling the Secret of the Mysteries.* New York: Harcourt, Brace, Jovanovich.

Wasson, V. P. and Wasson, R. G. (1957) *Mushrooms, Russia and History.* New York: Pantheon.

Weaver, M. I. R. (1982) "An Interview with C. G. Jung," in F. Jensen (ed.) *C. G. Jung, Emma Jung, and Toni Wolff*. San Francisco, CA: Analytical Psychology Club of San Francisco, 91–5.

Weiss, P. (1939) *Principles of Development: A Text in Experimental Embryology*. New York: Holt.

Wheelwright, J. (1982) "Jung," in F. Jensen (ed.) *C. G. Jung, Emma Jung, and Toni Wolff*. San Francisco, CA: Analytical Psychology Club of San Francisco, 97–105

Whitehead, A. N. (1925) *Science and the Modern World*. New York: Free Press, 1967.

Whitehead, A. N. (1929) *Process and Reality: An Essay in Cosmology*. New York: Free Press, 1969.

Whitley, D. S. (2000) *The Art of the Shaman: Rock Art of California*. Salt Lake City, UT: University of Utah Press.

Whitney, M. and Whitney, M. (1983) *Matter of Heart*. A Michael Whitney-Mark Whitney Production, sponsored by the C. G. Jung Institute of Los Angeles.

Wilcox, J. P. (2003) *Ayahuasca: The Visionary and Healing Powers of the Vine of the Soul*. Rochester, VY: Park Street.

Wilson, C. (1984) *C. G. Jung: Lord of the Underworld*. Wellingborough, UK: Aquarian.

Wilson, C. R. (1998) "Seeing They See Not," in D. E. Young and J.-G. Goulet (eds) *Being Changed by Cross-Cultural Encounters: The Anthropology of Extraordinary Experience*. Peterborough, ONT: Broadview, 197–208.

Winkelman, M. (2000) *Shamanism: The Neural Ecology of Consciousness and Healing*. Westport, CT: Bergin & Garvey.

Winter, A. (1998) *Mesmerized: Powers of Mind in Victorian Britain*. Chicago, IL: University of Chicago Press.

Wolf, F. A. (1994) *The Dreaming Universe: A Mind-Expanding Journey into the Realm Where Psyche and Physics Meet*. New York: Simon & Schuster.

Young, A. M. (1976) *The Reflexive Universe: Evolution of Consciousness*. Cambria, CA: Anodos, 1999.

Young, D. E. and Goulet, J.-G. (eds) (1998) *Being Changed by Cross-Cultural Encounters: The Anthropology of Extraordinary Experience*. Peterborough, ONT: Broadview.

Zumstein-Preiswerk, S. (1975) *C. G. Jung's Medium: Die Geschichte der Helly Preiswerk*. Munich: Kindler.

Index

Aborigines 123, 129
"absolute knowledge" 74, 76, 81, 199
"absolute space" 60
Abu Simbel temple 2
acausality, principle of 72–73, 77
active imagination 13, 26, 35, 46, 56–57,
    118, 194, 203, 205; in tandem 14, 71,
    205
Agrippa von Nettesheim 80
aliens 118, 201; abduction by 37, 40, 55,
    213; visions/encounters with 38, 39
altered states of consciousness (ASCs):
    and the ability to see ectoplasm
    123–124; archetypal states cultivated
    through ritual 194; and the brain 1–2
    see also brain and neurology; cosmic
    unity in mystical states 206; cultivation
    by ANS tuning 19, 30, 52, 194, 205;
    drug-induced 32–50; ecstatic 16, 52,
    204; ego and 24–27; hallucinogenic,
    ayahuasca 32–50; Jung on the mastery
    of 11–14; mastery techniques 13–14,
    24–31, 32–50, 51–61; monophasic
    attitude to 17; psychedelic see
    psychedelic states; role in telepathy
    108–109; roles in life and therapy
    201–209; shamanic see shamanism/
    shamans; synchronicity and 74;
    trance see trance; transformative/unitive
    states 14, 58, 63, 113, 194, 202–203,
    205
AM (amplitude modulation) waves 153
Amaringo, Pablo 35, 40, 46, 50
amoeba, psychoid processes 75–76, 150,
    152–153
ancient man of wisdom/Great Man 14, 71,
    203, 205
anima 17

anima mundi 177–178
"animal magnetism" 16, 88, 89–90
animals: ayahuasca and the mammalian
    psyche 40–45; and the "fourth drive" of
    intoxication 42–43
ANS *see* autonomic nervous system
Arbib, Michael 109
archetypes 19, 193; archetypal images 19;
    archetypal structure 19, 20, 21, 22, 26,
    45, 75, 110, 111, 193–194; numinosity
    of archetypal experience 63, 74, 82;
    ritual and cultivation of archetypal states
    of consciousness 194; transcendental
    psychoid nature of 82
Aristotle 151
ASCs *see* altered states of consciousness
Aspect, Alain 6–7, 199
atomism 79, 81, 144–145, 146, 161
atoms 175–176
attention training 52–53, 54–55, 56, 57–58
    see also meditation
Atwater, Lt. "Skip" 112
autocatalysis: molecular 156; simple
    155–156
auto-hypnosis 27–28
automatization 54 *see also* habituation
autonomic nervous system (ANS) 21–22,
    63, 126, 134; cultivation of ASCs
    by ANS tuning 19, 30, 52, 194, 205;
    meditation and 53, 55; shamanism
    and the tuning of 19, 52; spillover
    phenomena 52, 55
ayahuasca/ayahuasqueros 32–50, 56;
    the ayahuasca "diet" 40; cave painters
    redux 34–36; direct insight 108; DMT
    36–38; initial experiences 41–42;
    and the mammalian psyche 40–45;
    and mastery 45–50; psychoactive

principles 36–40; shadow-world of 49–50; transformation and the goal 43–45

Ball, P. 150
Barrett, Elizabeth 92
Baynes, M. 71
Bell, John Stewart 6
Bell's Non-Locality Theorum 6–7, 102, 199
Bennet, E. A. 71
Bergson, Henri 151, 152, 172–173
Bhagavad-Gita 55–56
biogenetic structuralism 24, 28–29, 30–31, 53–54
biological design 161–165
bio-micro-psychokinesis 121–122
Bleuler, Eugen 69–70, 75, 131
Blum, D. 100
Bohm, David 178–179
Boltzmann, Ludwig 181
bonding 22
border zones 64, 195–197 *see also* parapsychology; "The Border Zones of Exact Science" 65
Bouvet, Joachim 146
Braid, James 91
brain and neurology *see also* left brain; right brain: ANS *see* autonomic nervous system; brain's capacity for cultivating ASCs 1–2; communication modes and 197–199; demoting and finding networks 24–25; DMT and 37–38; electromagnetic waves 20, 53, 153; meditation and 53–54; mirror neurons 109–110; process in a neuron 153; quantum uncertainty and 209; shamanic consciousness and the bottom-to-top archetypal organization of the brain 20; trance induction 20; unitary brain states 1, 52, 109, 127, 134, 194, 202–203 *see also* transcendent function
brain/mind identity theory 63, 172; James' transmissive theory 78; Jung's position that psyche and brain are not identical 77–78
Braude, S. E. 95–96, 119, 122, 124, 129–130, 131, 139, 200, 201, 207–208
Broglie, Louis de 143
Brown, C. 116–118, 201
Browning, Robert 92
Buddhism, Great Perfection School (Dzogchen) 58–60

Carancini, Francesco 69, 126
Carroll, S. B. 185
Castenada, Carlos 18
cave painters 34–36
Cayce, Edgar 64
"chance" ideas 74
Charcot, Jean Martin 90
Chinese metaphyics 78–90, 145–146; *I Ching* 6, 79–80, 145
chromosomes 157
clairvoyance 72, 73, 89, 90, 101, 102; remote viewing: scientific pretensions 111–118
coincidentia oppositorum 45
colonies 160
communication modes 197–199; synchronistic communications 198–201, 203–205
Complex Psychology 12
complex recognition and management 13
consciousness: of "absolute space" 60; altered states *see* altered states of consciousness; of the group 208; integrative state of 20–21; mastery of shamanic states of 23–31, 32–50; meditation as a tool for a potential science of 58–61; nested hierarchy of 28; ordinary state of 47, 52, 57, 201–202; as an organismic function 87; polyphasic 12; "searching" consciousness 25–26; states and phases of 28–29; substrate 59; training *see* mastery of altered states; transformative/unitive states of 14, 58, 63, 113, 194, 202–203, 205; "warps" in our stream of 28–30, 47–49
contagion, psychic 48, 99–100
convergence zones 63
Cope, E. D. 161
core processes 166–167
cosmic visions 117–118
cosmos: cosmic unity in mystical states 206; process of the universe 176–180
countertransference 202
Crabtree, A. 88
Crookes, William 130–131
culture, monophasic 3, 9, 11, 12, 13, 17, 28, 42, 51, 57, 194

daime *see* ayahuasca/ayahuasqueros
dance 52
d'Aquili, E. G., and Newberg, A. B. 55

Darwin, Charles 149, 159, 182–183
deautomatization 54
decline effect 73
de Quincey, C. 173, 174, 175
Descartes, René 141, 172
Devereux, P. 43
Dickens, Charles 91
Didier, Alexis 88, 89–90, 97–98, 100, 102, 119, 128
Dingwall, E. J. 126
dissociation 16, 65 *see also* somnambulism
DMT (N, N-dimethyltryptamine) 36–38, 40
DNA 156, 157, 158, 164
Don Alejandro 48
Don Emilio 49, 50
Don Luis 48–49
Don Manuel Córdoba 48, 50, 56, 64
Dossey, L. 121–122
dreams/dreaming 1, 194; lucid dreaming 25; and the mastery of altered states 13
Driesch, Hans 75
drumming 18
Dusek, V. 144–147
Dzogchen (Great Perfection School) 58–60

ecology, interactive 182–183
ecstatic cults 17
ecstatic states 16, 52, 204
ectoplasm 64, 122–125, 127–128, 130, 132, 206–208
ego: actively imagining 56–57; and becoming "egoless" 55–57; identification with 52; meditation and the dethroning of 54–55; role of conscious ego in mastery of altered states 24–25; transcendental 26–27, 30, 56–57, 101, 203
Einstein, Albert 6, 84, 143, 148
Eisenbud, Jule 135, 136, 137
electromagnetic field 84, 143, 153, 179
electromagnetic transmissions 186
electromagnetic waves 20, 53, 153
electron clouds 175–176
Elgin, Duane 140–141
Elgonyi tribe 2
Eliade, M. 15–16, 21
Elkin, Peter 18
Elliotson, John 91
empathy: Jung's body-centred 203, 204; telepathy and 109

emptiness 54–55; empty substrate consciousness 59
endorphins 21–22
enstasy 59
entelechy 151–152, 153, 154, 172
epoché 26–27, 56
Esdaile, James 92
ESP *see* extrasensory perception
eukaryotes 158–159
Eva C. (medium) 124
evolution/evolutionary theory: colonies 160; emergence of adaptive cell behaviors 167–168; "evolution of dominance" 189; first single-cell organisms 157–159; Gaia theory and 180–184; Modern Synthesis 149, 161; from molecules to cells 156–157; multicellular organisms 159–161; and the need for a psychoid principle 149–170; non-living psychoid processes 155–156; primate societies 160; and the psychoid field 155–161; psychoid process and the evolution of novelty in anatomy 165–168; and the psychoid process encompassing and organism and its surround 161–165; sexual propagation 159
extrasensory perception (ESP): clairvoyance 72, 73, 89, 90, 101, 102, 111–118; decline effect 73; and Jung's understanding of the psyche 67; limbic connections and 110–111, 200, 203; and the need for ordinary consciousness 201–202; and non-ordinary states 98; in pre-literate cultures 98–99; rejection of neural explanations 77; Rhine's laboratory tests 73; scientific pretensions: remote viewing 111–118; seeing at a distance *see* seeing at a distance; telepathy *see* telepathy

Fagan, B. 27–28
Faraday, Michael 6, 84, 142, 147
fasting 52
Favret-Saada, J. 140
feeling of being stared at 102–104
Feilding, Everard 125–127, 128, 129
fibroblasts 165
fields: descriptive power of 179–180; electromagnetic 84, 143, 153, 179; explanatory value of 142–144; field theory and the holistic universe 84–85, 145, 148; the four universal fields

84(Fig.); gravity field 83, 84, 143, 145, 148, 179; morphic 184–190; psychoid field *see* psychoid field
Fischer-Schreiber, I. et al. 60
Flaherty, G. 88
Flournoy, Theodore 69
Francis of Assisi 46
Freeman, W. J. 109, 169–170
Freud, Sigmund 65
Frey-Rohn, Liliane 70
Fukurai, Tomokichi 135
Furst, Peter 18

Gaia theory 180–183; objections to 183–184
Gamow, George 100
Gauld, A. 125, 129, 199
Geley, Gustav 124–125
Gilbert, William 146–147
global warming 3 *see also* greenhouse effect
God 2; *anima mundi* 177–178
Goethe, Johann Wolfgang von 17
Goligher, Kathleen 124
Goulet, J.-G. 98
Grad, Bernard 121–122, 123–124
gravity 5, 6, 84, 143, 146; field 83, 84, 143, 145, 148, 179
Great Man/ancient man of wisdom 14, 71, 203, 205
Great Perfection School (Dzogchen) 58–60
greenhouse effect 182
Gregory, A. 132, 133, 134
Griffin, D. R. 171–172
Grob, C. S. 34
Grof, S. 33
Guédon, M. F. 99
Gurwitsch, Alexander 184

habituation 24, 54
hallucinogenic states, ayahuasca 32–50
Hannah, B. 72
Hansel, C. E. M. 95
Harner, M. 18
Hayden, B. 27
healing: Jungian psychotherapy *see* Jung's psychotherapy; struggle of shamanic healing 50; transformation and 21–22
hetero-suggestion 27–28
hierosgamos (wedding of the gods) 63
Hippocrates 80
Hobson, J. A. 25, 67
Hodgson, Richard 128

holons 188
Home, Daniel Douglas 128, 129–131
Husserl, E. 26–27, 56–57
Hutton, James 180
hypnagogic imagery 25
hypnosis 98; auto- 27–28

I Ching 6, 79–80, 145
icaros (shamanic songs) 35, 45, 47–49, 50, 58
identity: of brain and mind *see* brain/mind identity theory; identifying with the ego 52; of the meditator 55–58; the transcendental ego and changing the nature of 57
images: archetypal 19; with ayahuasca 35; hypnagogic 25; image generation 19
individualism 145
infrared light 133, 147, 207
integration: Mithen's views of 21; myth and 22; shamanism and 20–21
Intelligent Design 161
intentionality 169–170
intoxication 42–43
irrationality: Jung on the irrational 68–69; synchronicity and 68–69

jagé *see* ayahuasca/ayahuasqueros
James, W. 11, 65, 78, 98
Janet, P. 19, 192, 211n7, 215
Jordan, P. 22
Jung, C. G.: "The Border Zones of Exact Science" 65; call for a return to a polyphasic attitude 4, 9, 12, 195; childhood vision of God defecating on the Basel Cathedral 2; and Chinese metaphysics 78–80; compelling interest in altered states 2; on the irrational 68–69; on the mastery of altered states 11–14; on non-identity of psyche and brain 77–78; "psychoid" proposal *see* psychoid field; psychoid process/ principle; and the rose chafer 68, 71, 119, 205, 209; on shamanism 16–17; from spiritualism to synchronicity 69–72
Jung's psychology: the actively imagining ego 56–57; challenge to science 1–7; as "Complex Psychology" 12; conception of the psyche 65, 66, 77–78, 193–194; influence of the "French School" 65; positions supported by science 193–194; synchronicity *see* synchronicity

Jung's psychotherapy: accounts of his
mediumistic behavior during analytic
sessions 70–71; cultivation of shamanic
states in therapy 203–205; method of
doing analysis (his own account) 71

Kafatos, M. and Nadeau, R. 7, 176, 179
Kalweit, Holger 18
Kant, Immanuel 73
Kenrick, D. T. 110
Kepler, Johannes 80
Kircher, Athanasius 146
Kirsch, Hilde 70
Kirschner, M. W. and Gerhart, J. C.
165–168
knowledge: "absolute knowledge" of
the unconscious 74, 76, 81, 199;
non-ordinary knowing/knowing the
impossible 101–102 see also seeing at a
distance
Korolenko, Y. M. 180
kundalini 124

LaBarre, W. 34
Lamb, F. B. 41–42, 48, 50
Laughlin, C. D., Jr., McManus, J., and
d'Aquili, E. G. 11–12, 24–25, 26–27,
28, 29, 30, 31
learning: to master altered states see
mastery of altered states; socio-cultural
types of 28
left brain 204, 205; left-brain thinking/
rationality 3, 4, 109, 115, 116, 201, 204,
205
Leibniz, Gottfried Wilhelm 80, 84, 146
Lévi-Strauss, C. 18
levitation 126, 127, 130, 132, 134, 206
Lévy-Bruhl, Lucien 28, 81
Lewis, T. et al. 111
Lewis-Williams, D. and Pearce 25
Lex, B. 53–54
Libet, B. 198–199
limbic system 20, 63, 198, 200; limbic
communication 110–111, 200, 203
living planets 181–182 see also Gaia
theory
Lombroso, Cesare 125, 134
Long, William 103
Lotka, Alfred 180
Lovelock, J. E. 140, 180–183
lucid dreaming 25
Luna, L. E. 33, 34, 45, 46, 47, 49, 50,
99–100; and Amaringo, P. 35–36, 46

McDougall, William 190
McKenna, D. J. 33
Mack, J. E. 39–40
McManus, J. 53, 54
McMoneagle, Joe 112, 113, 115, 119, 201
magnetism 5, 84, 142–143, 145–148;
"animal magnetism" 16, 88, 89–90;
aristocratic "magnetism" 88–89;
"magnetic sleep" 88
Malinowski, Bronislaw 18
mantras 53–54
MAO see monoamine oxidase
Marcillet, Jean-Bon 89
Martineau, Harriet 92
Masters, R. E. L. and Houston, J. 38–39
mastery of altered states: ayahuasca and
32–50; ego and 24–27; finding a balance
46–47; Jung 11–14; management of
psychedelic states 38–40; preliminary
requirements 45–46; shamanism 23–31,
32–50; through meditation 51–61;
tuning the warps 47–49
matter: psychoid process as mental pole of
173–179; sentience of 171–176
Matter of Heart (film) 70
Maxwell, James Clerk 147, 189
meditation: attention training 52–53,
54–55, 56, 57–58; and the brain and
nervous system 53–54, 55; decision
to remain in the temple of 53–54;
Dzogchen (Great Perfection School)
58–60; historical roots of 52; and
the identity of the meditator 55–58;
mastering terror 54–55; mastery and
52–61; from the personal to the
transpersonal 59–61; settling down to
the bottom 59; as a tool for a potential
science of consciousness 58–61
mediumship: in France 88–90;
psychokinesis and "physical mediums"
see psychokinesis; whereabouts of
mediums 96–98
Méheust, B. 88, 89, 90, 93, 97, 100
melatonin 37
memories: in the morphic field 186–187;
transpersonal 60
Merkur, D. 12–13, 27, 47
Mesmer, Anton 88, 98
Mesmerism 88, 90–92
mestizo vegetalistas 33, 34, 45–46, 48, 64
meta-mind 106, 108, 111, 117
metaphyics: Chinese 6, 78–80, 145–146
see also I Ching; parapsychology and

141–144; of process and organism 173–177; towards a metaphysics of a the psychoid field 171–180; Western metaphysical precursors of synchronicity 80–81

Metzner, R. 41, 43, 44

micro-psychokinesis 120–122

mind-reading 104–106 *see also* telepathy

mirror neurons 109–110

Mithen, S. 21

mitochondria 152, 153, 158

Mivart, St. George 161

molecular autocatalysis 156

molecules 176; evolution to cells 156–157

monoamine oxidase (MAO) 36; MAO inhibitors 36, 37, 40

monophasic culture/society 3, 9, 11, 12, 13, 17, 28, 42, 51, 57, 194

Monroe, R. A. 113, 114–115, 118, 139

morphic fields 184–190

morphic resonance 186, 187

Mozart, Wolfgang Amadeus 17, 199

Müller-Ebeling, C. et al. 27

Murphy, M. and White, R. A. 24

Musset, Alfred de 199

Myerhoff, Barbara 18

Myers, F. W. H. 77, 127–128, 199

mystic union 55; cosmic unity in mystical states 206

myth: integration and 22; mythscape 21, 22, 30–31

Narby, J. 32–33, 36, 46, 150–151; and Huxley, F. 15, 17, 18

near-death experiences 38, 72, 112–113, 213

Neo-Darwinism 161

Neumann, E. 31

neurosis 13

neurotransmitters 37

New Age movements 3, 140

Newton, Isaac 84, 146

non-locality 84, 108, 179, 186, 199; Bell's Theorum 6–7, 102, 199; of the psyche 102, 111, 141–142, 190, 191

numinosity of archetypal experience 63, 74, 82

observation: observer and 55, 56–57; of own consciousness 46 *see also* meditation; participant 18–19

Ochorowicz, Julien 125

Odajnyk, Walter 54–55, 57

original thinking 13, 14, 26

Ørsted, Hans Christian 147

Ostrander, S. and Schroeder, L. 111–112

Osty, Eugène 133, 134, 207

out-of-body journeys 112–113, 114, 139

Palladino, Eusapia 125–129, 207

Palmer, Arnold 24

parapsychology: the challenge of 139–141; commonalities of spontaneous psychics 95–96; in the eighteenth and nineteenth centuries 87–92; ESP *see* extrasensory perception; and the holistic trend in physics 144–148; in the laboratory 73, 92–95, 120–122; mediumship *see* mediumship; Mesmerism in Victorian society 90–92; meta-analysis 94–95; and the need for a new metaphysics 141–144; out-of-body journeys 112–113, 114, 139; and the psyche's independence of the brain 77; psychic contagion 99–100; and the psychoid field 197–201 *see also* psychoid field; psychoid nature of reality *see* psychoid field; psychoid process/principle; psychokinesis *see* psychokinesis; research standards 93–94; science crossing into the border zones of 73, 92–95, 120–122, 133, 134, 141, 144–148, 195–197; telepathy *see* telepathy; thoughtography 135–137; two levels of activity 101–102

parasympathetic nervous system 20, 52, 53, 55, 126

participant observation 18–19

Particle Data Group, American Physical Society 94

Pauli, Wolfgang 66, 67, 72, 74, 77, 82, 83, 196, 213

Pavlov, I. P. 190

Peirce, Charles Sanders 173

penetration, symbolic 19, 30

Petrovich, Avvakum 17

Pike, N. 55

Pinchbeck, D. 36, 38, 46, 47

pineal gland 37, 38

planets, living 181–182 *see also* Gaia theory

Preiswerk, Helly (Jung's cousin) 4, 69

Price, Harry 132–134

Price, Pat 113–115, 201

primate societies, psychoid process 160

process: core processes 166–167; metaphyics of process and organism 173–177; psychoid *see* psychoid process/principle; and reality 173–177; of the universe 176–180

prokaryotes 158

proto-knowing 76

psyche *see also* soul: ayahuasca and the mammalian psyche 40–45; ego *see* ego; identity with brain *see* brain/mind identity theory; Jung's conception of 65, 67, 77–78, 193–194; location of 154–155; non-locality of 102, 111, 141–142, 190, 191; as a process *see* psychoid process/principle; self *see* self/ Self

psychedelic states: ayahuasca and 32–50; DMT and 37–38, 40; managing 38–40

psychic contagion 48, 99–100

psychic functioning, modes of 197–199; telepathy and 199–201

psychoid field 6, 66, 85, 87, 138, 144, 148, 196; in biology 168–170; and evolution 155–161; and Gaia 180–183; how to imagine it 187–188; metaphysics 171–180; mystical states and 206; parapsychology and 197–201; and the process of the universe 176–180; Sheldrake and images of 184–190; summary of arguments for a universal field 191–192

psychoid process/principle: and the evolution of novelty in anatomy 165–168; evolution's need of a psychoid principle 149–170; Gaia and 180–183; as matter's mental pole of process 173–179; metaphyics and 171–180; micro-PK and 121; non-living psychoid processes 155–156; process encompassing and organism and its surround 161–165; process in amoeba 75–77, 150, 152–153; process in a neuron 153; process in a zygote 153–154; process in first single-cell organisms 157–159; process in multicellular organisms 159–161; process in simple organisms 75–77, 150–154; process of the universe 176–180; as responsiveness 168–170; and sexual propagation 159; synchronistic nature of process 74–78; and the tinker/accomplice 163–165,

166, 170, 191, 196; ubiquity of process 151–152, 171–183

psychokinesis (PK) 119–138, 206–209; bio-micro-PK 121–122; and the consciousness of the group 208; ectoplasm and 64, 122–125, 127–128, 130, 132, 206–208; Home 129–131; micro-PK 120–122; Palladino 125–129; and the psychic's state of mind 126–127, 128, 134, 137–138, 208–209; Schneider 131–134; Serios 134–137

psychosexual energy 124, 126

puberty ceremonies 27–28

Pueblo people 2

Puységur, Armand-Marie-Jacques de Chastenet, Marquis de 88–89

quantum mechanics 5–7, 70, 82, 143; field theory, the holistic universe and 84–85; non-locality principle 6–7, 84, 102, 179; quantum uncertainty and the brain 209

Race, Victor 88

Radin, D. 93–95, 96, 100, 120, 199

Redfield, Arthur 180

red light 132, 133; infrared light 133, 207

Reichel-Dolmatoff, G. 18, 35, 99

relegation 24 *see also* habituation

remote viewing 111–118 *see also* seeing at a distance

repetition 24–25

Rhine, J. B. 67, 73, 121

rhythm 52, 110

Ricci, Matteo 146

Richet, Charles 124, 125, 128, 208, 213

right brain 117, 204, 205; right-brain attention 116

Riley, Mel 112, 201

Ripinsky-Naxon, M. 22

Ritter, Johann Wilhelm 147

ritual 21; cultivation of archetypal states of consciousness through 194; healing 22; puberty ceremonies 27–28; shamanic control through 30, 52 *see also* shamanism/shamans

Rizzolatti, Giacomo 109

RNA 156, 158

Rose, R. 98–99, 123, 128–129

samādhi 59

śamatha (quiescence) 59–60

Samorini, G. 42–43

San people 23, 27–28
Sarles, H. B. 110
Schilling, Friedrich 147
Schnabel, J. 112, 140–141
Schneider, Rudi 70, 97–98, 128, 131–134, 207
Schneider, Willy 131
Schneiter, Vater 132
Schrenck-Notzing, Albert von, Baron 124, 132
Schrödinger's wave equation 84
science: biogenetic structuralism *see* biogenetic structuralism; crossing into the border zones 73, 92–95, 120–122, 133, 134, 141, 144–148, 195–197 *see also* parapsychology; evolutionary theory *see* evolution/evolutionary theory; Jung's challenge to 1–7; Jung's positions supported by 193–194; and the lack of hypotheses in parapsychology 141; meditation as a tool for a potential science of consciousness 58–61; neuroscience *see* brain and neurology; parapsychology and scientific testing 73, 92–95, 120–122, 133, 134, 141 *see also* parapsychology; parapsychology and the holistic trend in physics 144–148; prejudice and 131, 140; scientific pretensions: remote viewing 111–118; synchronicity and scientific safeguards 73
séances 89–90, 122–123, 126–128, 130–133, 134
seeing at a distance 101–118; clairvoyance 72, 73, 89, 90, 101, 102, 111–118; cosmic visions 117–118; favorable circumstances 114–115; remote viewing: scientific pretensions 111–118; separating signal from noise 115–117; Stanford Research Institute (SRI) 113–115; telepathy *see* telepathy
self/Self 63; subliminal self 199
sensory deprivation 52
Serios, Ted 134–137, 207
serotonin 37; syndrome 40
sexual propagation 159
shadow 17
shamanism/shamans 3, 195; ayahuasca use 32, 45–50 *see also* ayahuasca/ ayahuasqueros; biogenetic structuralism and the stages of acquiring shamanic mastery 30–31; compared with meditation 52, 53 *see also* meditation;

dismemberment and recreation 16, 20; Eliade 15–16; growing understanding 18–19; healing, transformation and 21–22, 202–205; how shamanism works 19–22; *icaros* (songs) 35, 45, 47–49, 50, 58; and integration 20–21; Jung 16–17; learning to steer a trance state 27–30; mastery of shamanic states of consciousness 23–31, 32–50; misunderstandings 17; nature of shamanism 15–22; ritual 30, 52; San people 23, 27–28; shamanic journey 21, 202; shamanic journeys 16; shamanic paintings 34–36; struggle of shamanic healing 50; therapy and shamanic states 202–205; trance induction 20; transcending social boundaries 33; tuning of the ANS 19, 52
Shamdasani, S. 97
Shanon, B. 34–35, 40–41, 42, 43, 44–45, 47, 108
Sheldrake, R. 87, 93, 94, 99, 102–104, 173, 184–188, 189–190, 214
siddhis 50
Siegel, D. J. 110
Siegel, R. K. 33, 35, 42–43
Sinclair, (Mary) Craig, née Kimbrough 104–106, 201
Sinclair, Upton 104–106
single-cell organisms, first 157–159
sleep deprivation 52
Smith, J. M. and Szathmáry, E. 155–160
Society for Psychical Research (SPR) 67, 70, 97, 127–129
society, monophasic 3, 9, 11, 12, 13, 17, 28, 42, 51, 57, 194
somnambulism 65, 69, 90, 97 *see also* dissociation
soul 141, 171–172 *see also* psyche; independence of space and time 77; Jung on 77; report of seeing a woman lose her soul 108
Speman, Hans 184
Spiegelman, J. M. 70
spirit guides 17, 30, 131
spirit/shadow-world of ayahuasca 49–50
spiritualism 16, 17, 65, 67, 69, 86 *see also* mediumship; séances
SPR *see* Society for Psychical Research
Spruce, Richard 33
Stanford Research Institute (SRI) 113–115, 121
Stevenson, Robert Louis 199

Strassman, R. 36, 37, 38–40, 44, 212
substrate consciousness 59
Suess, Eduard 180
Swann, Ingo 113, 115–117, 121, 123–124
Swedenborg, Emmanuel 6, 73, 78, 81
symbolic penetration 19, 30
sympathetic nervous system 20, 52, 53, 55
synchronicity 5–7, 67–85; and the "absolute knowledge" of the unconscious 74, 76, 81, 199; altered states and 74; and Chinese metaphysics 78–80; as a cosmic principle 81–83; field theory, the holistic universe and 84–85; and the irrational 68–69; Jung 68–83; micro-PK and 121; narrower and holistic meanings of 82; principle of acausality 72–73, 77; Rhine and scientific safeguards 73; synchronistic communications 198–201, 203–205; synchronistic field 108; synchronistic function 198–201; synchronistic nature of "psychoid" process 74–78; thoughtography and 136–137; Western metaphysical precursors 80–81

Taoism 79–80, 178
Tao Te Ching 80
Targ, R. 114, 115; and Puthoff, H. E. 113–114, 121, 200
Taussig, M. 43–44
Taylor, J. B. 204
Teilhard de Chardin, Pierre 173
teleology 76, 163–164, 183, 191
telepathy 72, 102–111; causal and synchronistic elements in 108–111; feeling of being stared at 102–104; how to mind-read 105–106; limbic communication and 110–111, 200, 203; mental radio 104–105; mirror neurons and 109–110; role of altered states 108–109; and the three modes of psychic functioning 199–201; toward a mind-to-mind theory (Warcollier) 106–108
termites and their mounds 162–164
terror, mastery of 54–55
the transpersonal 59–61; transpersonal memories 60
the unconscious: searching for and finding unconscious networks 25; synchronicity and the "absolute knowledge" of 74, 76, 81, 199

thinking: left-brain thinking/rationality 3, 4, 109, 115, 116, 201, 204, 205; original 13, 14, 26; primitive 28; theory-based 28; unconscious 203
thoughtography 135–137
Tibetan Buddhism (Dzogchen) 58–60
trance: learning to steer a trance state 27–30; and n/um energy 23–24; during a séance 126–128, 131; shamanic induction of 20, 23–24 see also shamanism/shamans
transcendent function 14, 63, 194
transcendental ego 26–27, 30, 56–57, 101, 203
transcendental psychoid nature of archetypes 82
transference 205
transformation, psychological: as a life-and-death matter 51–52; shamanic healing and 21–22, 202–205; through mastery of altered states see mastery of altered states; transformative/unitive states of consciousness 14, 58, 63, 113, 194, 202–203, 205
transmissive theory (James) 78
tunnel experience 35
Turner, E. 18–19, 64, 119–120, 121, 123
Turner, J. S. 161–165, 170

unlearning 109
Upanishads 28, 59, 178
Upper Paleolithic cave painters 34–36

Vedas 52
vegetalistas 33, 34, 45–46, 48, 64
Vernadsky, Vladimir 180
Villavicencio, Ecuadorian civil servant 33
Vitesbsky, P. 23

Waddington, C. H. 185, 187
Wagner, Richard 91
Wakley, Thomas 91
Wallace, B. A. 58–60
Warcollier, R. 106–108, 214
warps of consciousness 28–30, 47–49
Wasson, R. G. 18
Wasson, V. P. and Wasson, R. G. 16, 34
Weaver, M. I. R. 70–71, 205
Weiss, Paul 184
Wheelwright, J. 70–71, 204–205
Whitehead, A. N. 7, 152–153, 154, 155, 173–175, 177–178
Whitley, D. S. 27